The News o

C000179506

CYRIL BAINBRIDGE
and
ROY STOCKDILL

THE NEWS OF THE WORLD STORY

150 Years of the World's
Bestselling Newspaper

HarperCollins*Publishers*

HarperCollins*Publishers*
77–85 Fulham Palace Road,
Hammersmith, London W6 8JB

A Paperback Original 1993
1 3 5 7 9 8 6 4 2

A catalogue record for this book
is available from the British Library

ISBN 0 586 21748 7

Set in Meridien

Printed in Great Britain by
HarperCollinsManufacturing Glasgow

'All human life is there'

News of the World advertising slogan

'The *News of the World* is a human document representing the daily life of the average man – not neglecting the more serious problems, but also touching on the lighter forms of life, bringing humour, brightness and humanity into everyone's existence'

Sir Emsley Carr

'The person who has no interest in the *News of the World* has no interest in life'

Reginald Cudlipp, editor 1953–9

About the Authors

After working on newspapers in his native Yorkshire, Cyril Bainbridge moved to Fleet Street where he worked for the Press Association news agency and then spent twenty-six years on the staff of *The Times*, where he held a number of senior editorial appointments.

He was a member of the Press Council for ten years and is a past president and fellow of the Institute of Journalists.

His other publications include *Brass Triumphant*, a social history of the brass band movement, a guide to North Yorkshire and North Humberside and *One Hundred Years of Journalism*, a history of the profession.

Roy Stockdill, too, is a Yorkshireman and joined his local evening newspaper, the *Halifax Courier*, from grammar school at 16. After a thorough apprenticeship in journalism, he worked on newspapers in Leicester, Coventry and Watford before moving to Fleet Street in 1965 to join the former *Sunday Citizen*. On the closure of that paper in 1967, he joined the *News of the World*, where he has remained for the last twenty-six years.

After ten years as a reporter, during which he covered numerous foreign assignments, he became a features executive. Since 1985, he has been series editor, in charge of the newspaper's book serializations.

Contents

Acknowledgements

I am grateful to Sir Edward Pickering for his interest and encouragement when I first suggested writing a history of the *News of the World*, and to Stuart Kuttner, the paper's managing editor, for smoothing several paths once the project got under way.

During my research I have talked to many former editors and members and former members of the staff of the paper, to all of whom I must extend my thanks for willingly devoting much time to answering my questions and recounting their experiences.

Particular mention needs to be made of the invaluable help I have received from Melanie Aspey and Eamon Dyas of the News International archives section, as well as Judith Dunn, the paper's librarian, and members of her staff, especially Dave Webb. Don Beland, former picture library manager, was also of great help in the picture research.

Finally, I am indebted to Henry Douglas, former legal manager, who read the draft manuscript and made a number of helpful suggestions.

Cyril Bainbridge

Thanks to all my colleagues, past and present, for their marvellous stories and anecdotes. Special thanks to former *News of the World* stalwarts Peter Earle, George McIntosh, Tina Dalgleish, Roger Hall and Ron Bacchus for their memories; not forgetting Rosalie Shann, Ray Chapman and Fiona Macdonald Hull, who virtually wrote their complete memoirs for me!

Thanks are also due to Melanie Aspey and Eamon Dyas in

the *News of the World* archives section for their painstaking digging and helpful suggestions.

Finally, my gratitude to Stanley, Carlos and the long-suffering staff of The Printer's Pie, Fleet Street, for their cheerful service and good-humoured tolerance towards me over so many years (and because they asked to be mentioned in this book!)

Roy Stockdill

Introduction

The *News of the World* is 150 years old. Since it was launched, it has occupied a unique place in the history of British journalism. It has remained unassailable as the Sunday newspaper with the largest circulation in the world – at one time reaching a peak of over eight million copies which, taking into account that on average each copy is read by at least three people, gave it a phenomenal readership of more than 24 million per issue.

At different times it has been criticized, patronized and complimented: 'Sordid'; 'inexpressibly vulgar'; 'squalid recorder of squalid crime'; 'panderer to the lowest human instincts'; 'an uncommonly good newspaper'; 'a British institution'; 'the legal profession's trade paper'; 'as British as roast beef and Yorkshire pudding'– these are among the epithets which, according to taste, have been applied to the *News of the World*.

John Browne Bell, who launched it in 1843 in the days of cheap newspapers resulting from the repeal of newspaper taxes (the so-called 'taxes on knowledge'), was a visionary. At a time when newspaper circulations were numbered in mere thousands, he unblushingly advertised his new paper as being a 'World Wonder' and providing 'News for the million'. It did eventually achieve that goal, although not in his lifetime or that of his family. Such huge circulations were of the future. Although at times a successful concern under the Bells, its greatest prosperity has been in this century rather than the last, when its progress under John Browne Bell and his successors was retarded through lack of sufficient working capital and indecision by its owners.

The paper began to move from poverty to prosperity after a Welsh newspaper owner, Henry Lascelles Carr, took it over in

1891 and installed his 24-year-old nephew as editor. It proved to be an inspired appointment: he subsequently became Sir Emsley Carr and occupied the editor's chair for a remarkable fifty years.

The new owner's solicitor George (later Lord) Riddell, who took shares in the paper in lieu of payment for his legal fees during the take-over negotiations, developed a deeper interest in newspapers than he had in the law. He abandoned his legal practice in favour of involvement in the management of the *News of the World*, firstly as company secretary and later as chairman, becoming a Titan of the press world.

Riddell and Emsley Carr made a formidable and legendary Fleet Street team: between them they revitalized and expanded the paper, taking the circulation from an unprofitably meagre 30,000 to a record-breaking 4,500,000 by 1941.

Its massive circulation was partly ascribed to its predilection for salacious detail in court reporting. But there was more to the scenario than that. Despite its penchant for scandalous court stories and crime scoops, maintaining and expanding Browne's original formula of strong, sensational crime interest, it also developed a reputation as, in the words of R.D. Blumenfeld, the respected editor of the *Daily Express*, 'an uncommonly good newspaper'.

It gained an envious record of journalistic scoops: it was first to announce the relief of Mafeking in 1900 and set off a round of riotous rejoicing that continued for a week; it was first to announce the death of Edward VII in 1910; and four years later a special Sunday evening edition gave first news of the assassination of Archduke Ferdinand of Austria at Sarajevo, to mention but a few of its many early successes.

Over the years it built up a remarkable circle of editorial contributors, ranging from Winston Churchill to Edgar Wallace and including archbishops and other prominent political and public figures.

In an era of strict Sunday observance the *News of the World* set patterns for mass-circulation newspaper distribution that became the envy of and an example to every other national newspaper; it pioneered competitions and circulation boosting schemes, such as free insurance for its readers, which were widely copied; and it provided much appreciated social services – locating lost relatives, tracing recipients of bequests and giving advice in its 'agony aunts' columns.

Crime scoops have always had a special place in the paper's history: it has always had the finest intelligence service and crime specialists of any newspaper. Police have sought its help in their pursuit of criminals, while it has often been the first choice of murderers and other villains when they have sought to confess their misdeeds. While crime and some of the saucier recreations of British society continue to play an important part in its coverage, the nation's obsession with television and the personalities it has created have provided a fresh injection of lifeblood that has kept the *News of the World* at the front in the competitive readership stakes.

In 1968 the *News of the World* provided the foundation on which the Australian entrepreneur Rupert Murdoch was to build his British newspaper empire when he reached a deal with Sir William Carr in order to frustrate a takeover offer by Robert Maxwell, then also seeking a foothold in Fleet Street proprietorship. Murdoch was soon in sole control.

It exploited the market in sensational memoirs; the publication of some – notably those of the film star Diana Dors and Christine Keeler of the Profumo affair – earned it strong censure.

Despite critics of its style and content, its readers have in the main remained remarkably loyal. It is an enigma which its detractors and media commentators find difficult of solution: why, in an intensely competitive industry in which fortunes fluctuate through the fickle fancies of newspaper readers, it has retained its popularity and maintained its record readership.

Newspapers can only succeed by producing a product that people want to read. Few, if any, newspapers can escape some form of criticism from time to time. Whatever allegations may be made about its presentation and sensational approach to scandal, misconduct or disclosure, the fact that under successive proprietors the *News of the World* has consistently remained the top-selling Sunday newspaper must reflect the satisfaction of its readers: that it has given, and continues to give, them what they want and, as it celebrates its 150th anniversary, is still living up to its early promise that 'all human life is there'.

ONE

Founding Fathers

We have neither prejudice to forego nor passions to con-
ciliate. Our motto is TRUTH. Our practice is THE FEAR-
LESS ADVOCACY OF TRUTH.

So, with an extravagantly bold emphasis, wrote John Browne
Bell in the first issue of the *News of the World* on 1 October
1843. Browne proved himself to be a man of considerable
vision and bravado. In a period after the reduction of newspaper duty in 1836, when newspapers were launched at a
whim and as quickly disappeared into oblivion, and when
those that survived achieved circulations, if they were lucky,
of 20,000 at the most, Bell boldly and unblushingly predicted
that his new paper would contain 'news for the million' –
although that milestone was not to be achieved until the early
1900s when the paper had passed from his family's ownership
and newspapers generally were beginning to reap the benefits
of Education Acts which, as the century approached its close,
were slowly creating a more literate community thirsting for
knowledge.

Bell was no newcomer to the newspaper scene. His father,
John Bell, was an enterprising and imaginative publisher who
was the true creator of the British Sunday press with his *Bell's
Weekly Messenger*, launched in 1796. His personal life, like his
newspaper career, had its ups and downs. His abilities as a
publisher were matched by his desire to lead life to the full.
Leigh Hunt, the poet and essayist, wrote that Bell Senior had
'as great a taste for neat wines and ankles as for pretty books'.
He was, said Hunt, a remarkable person, 'A plain man with a
red face and a nose exaggerated by intemperance, yet there

was something not unpleasing in his countenance, especially when he spoke.'

His *Weekly Messenger* was backed by a distinguished list of names, including the Prince of Wales, the Dukes of York and Clarence, and numerous successful City merchants. But its main source of success was Bell's energies and typographical skills and his nose for news.

Within the Bell family there was considerable strife and his son, John Browne Bell, who had inherited some of his father's newspaper genius but was disinherited financially by his father, launched out on his own, producing a number of papers. They included *Bell's New Weekly Messenger*, a rival and replica of his father's journal, which he launched in January 1832, a year after his father's death, and *The Planet*, another Sunday paper which survived for 310 issues between 1837 and 1844.

Bell Senior was a pioneer of cheap publishing but, not content to serve merely the book market, he had turned to newspapers and periodicals. His *Weekly Messenger* became noted for its country politics and its reports of country markets.

John Browne Bell, when he decided to launch the *News of the World*, also set his sights mainly in this direction. His other two newspapers, the *New Weekly Messenger* and *The Planet*, were ultimately merged with his new paper – *The Planet* in 1844 and the *Messenger* after his death – largely because there was insufficient time and printing capacity to produce them all simultaneously.

One effect of the reduced duties, the so-called 'taxes on knowledge', was that it allowed newspapers to be sold more cheaply. The *News of the World* was launched at three pence, with a daring but firm promise that its price would not be increased.

Difficulties quickly arose with the London retail news vendors – the 'trade' as they were known – who saw the proposed low prices, to say nothing of the possible mergers, as likely to diminish their profits. They pledged to resist by all lawful means what they regarded as these attempts to reduce their livelihoods, and a deputation was sent to meet Bell to try and persuade him to increase the price of his papers so that, in return for a guarantee to 'push' the sales of the new paper, they would receive a profit of a penny on each sale.

Bell was brief and emphatic with the deputation, according to contemporary accounts. 'Gentlemen, I brought out a paper on which the trade had 1½d profit. What have you done for it?', he demanded. 'You have pushed it – but you have pushed it out of existence. I have made up my mind and I shall adhere to the plans I have laid down.'

The 'trade' was less well organized at this time than it subsequently became, but it was nevertheless a brave move by Bell to stand up to them so firmly. He concentrated instead on the provincial sales, circulating the 'country' trade by offering copies of the paper direct on receipt of cheque or order. The name of every agent was printed at the foot of the contents bill to directly identify them with the undertaking. The policy worked, and within only a few weeks provincial news sellers were joining in the effort so enthusiastically that the new paper quickly achieved unparalleled sales of 200,000 copies.

The paper was initially printed and published from rather cramped premises at 30 Holywell Street, off the Strand. It was a bow-fronted, three-storey building in an area then noted for second-hand book shops and vendors of pornographic publications. The street was demolished in 1901 to make way for the building of Aldwych.

Posters announcing the new paper brazenly declared that it would provide 'News for the Million' and would be 'The Novelty of Nations and the Wonder of the World – the cheapest, largest and best newspaper'.

By the standards of the time, the first issue was a handsome paper. The front page carried a declaration of intent on its aspirations: to give the poorer classes of society a paper that would suit their means and the middle and richer classes a journal which from its immense circulation should command their attention.

The over-generous use of capital letters to declaim its FEAR-LESS ADVOCACY OF TRUTH spilled over to an introductory editorial inside the paper.

We present to the Public a Novelty in Newspaper Litera-ture, a Weekly Journal of the Largest Size, unexampled in point of Cheapness, and which, we trust, will be pro-nounced of the highest order of merit. Our object is to establish A First Class Journal at a Price which shall place it within the reach of All Classes of Readers. Our arrange-ments have been made without regard to expense. And we encourage the hope that public opinion will pro-nounce the 'News of the World' the Best, as well as the Largest and Cheapest of all the newspapers that are published.

Although claiming to abstain from elaborate introductory remarks, the article went on to boast that

the contents of the Broad Sheet now in the hands of the readers will manifest our determination to avail ourselves of every means of making the 'News of the World' most useful as a Political Guardian and Guide, and most inter-esting as a Newspaper to the General Reader. It is only by a very extensive circulation that the Proprietors can be compensated for the outlay of a Large Capital in this Novel and Original undertaking; but they are confident that Public Patronage will keep pace with desert, and that the numerous attractions – the intrinsic merits, as well as the extraordinary Cheapness – will be duly appreciated: and that, in point of Circulation, this Paper will soon stand first among the most Popular, as no pains will be spared to establish its character as First among the Best of the Weekly Journals.

The numerous attractions included reports of police court cases, foreign telegrams and news reports from Ireland, Scot-land, Wales and England on pages two and three, together with an account of the Lord Mayor of London's dinner. There were, on page four, answers to correspondents, chiefly on legal matters – this an early portent of future services to readers – and two leading articles, and the latest news about riots in Wales. The fifth page contained miscellaneous matter, including theatre and fashion notes, while page six carried literary and arts notices, and page seven law and police news. The final page contained agricultural and other market news.

A dozen or so years after its launch, the *News of the World*'s success meant it had outgrown its Holywell Street premises. The last paper to be printed there was on 10 October 1852. New machinery was installed at 19 Exeter Street, off the Strand, to which the paper moved its quarters. The two new machines, still hand fed, were nevertheless a great advance. They could produce 4,000 copies an hour; they required eight men to work each machine, four men to feed in the sheets of paper and four to take them off after printing. One side of the paper was printed on the first machine; the sheets were then fed through the second machine to print the other side, after which they were folded by hand and counted.

Most of its readers were still in the provinces, but the paper had by now achieved some influence through its political and foreign news coverage, particularly its authoritative dispatches from worldwide trouble spots, as well as its financial and sporting news.

The arrangements Bell had made with provincial news-agents ensured the paper's standing as *the* newspaper of provincial and rural England. More than that, the public clamour for it ensured Bell's victory over the 'trade' by enforcing them to satisfy the demand. It was becoming 'the paper of the classes and the masses'.

The make-up continued to follow the same pattern as the very early editions. Half the front page was devoted to small advertisements, the other half to comment and news, half a column of sports news and half a column of jokes, purloined from the pages of *Punch*, such as 'Judging from the initials of Mr Bernal Osborne, we should say he was perfectly qualified to say BO to a goose', and 'A Legal Conveyance – the Prison Van'.

The advertisements provide an interesting social commentary on the age which, judging by the number of announcements for medical publications and patent medicines, must have had more than its share of hypochondriacs. A reissue of *Dr Thomson's Dictionary of Domestic Medicine*, which could be had complete (dedicated by permission to the Earl of Carlisle) for 7s (35p) or in twelve monthly parts at 6d (2½p) each, was described as a work that should be in the possession of every family. It contained information relating to health and disease, sanitary economy and surgical emergencies. No more pills or any other medicines were required if sufferers from indigestion, constipation, diarrhoea, palpitation of the heart, flatulency, distension, acidity, heartburn, torpidity of the liver, cough, asthma, nervousness, biliousness, despondency, spleen or any other disorder for that matter, obtained and read, the 76th edition of *The Natural Regeneration of the Digestive Organs* by sending 3d in stamps. And if that failed, Parr's Life Pills, which were 'found to possess the most astonishing and invigorating properties', stood unrivalled in excellence. Deafness and noises in the head could be cured by sleeping in one of the medicated caps obtainable from Dr John Addison of 27 Villiers Street, off the Strand.

An explanation of the hirsute appearance of that generation might lie in the successful results over half a century that had proved that Rowlands' Macassar Oil was endowed with singularly nourishing powers in the growth and restoration of the Human Hair: it not only made hair beautifully soft, curly and glossy but was unfailing in stimulating the growth of whiskers, eyebrows and mustachios.

There was also a preponderance of introduction agencies. The Matrimonial Institution, founded in 1846, was established 'as a medium for the introduction of parties unknown to each other who are desirous of forming Matrimonial Alliances but

FOUNDING FATHERS 23

who cannot find partners in their own circle of acquaintances'. Under the heading 'Matrimony Made Easy: or How to Win a Lover', Mr James Pattison, of 37 Toriano Terrace, Brecknock Road, London, offered to send directions to 'enable Ladies and Gentlemen to win the devoted affection of as many of the opposite sex as their hearts may desire', while Madame Maxwell had a similar announcement for a process 'so simple, captivating and enthralling' with 'young and old, peer and peeress, as well as the peasant alike subject to its influence'. But beware, she warned, of female pretenders who state that they effect Thousands of Marriages in a Year; a discerning public must see the falsity of such a statement.

The news coverage included an entire page devoted to reports of courts, from the Court of Common Pleas and Middlesex Sessions to various police courts around London. Executions were then a morbid public entertainment. One issue in 1854 contained an account over three quarters of a column in length of an execution in front of Newgate of a man found guilty of the murder of his wife. The last hours and minutes of 'this wretched man' were described in great detail. The crowd assembled to witness the execution, it said, was unusually large, 'probably owing to the comparative fineness of the night and the long period which has elapsed since an execution in front of Newgate. Their behaviour was marked by the usual ribaldry and want of decency.'

The death of John Browne Bell at the age of 77 on 19 August 1855 brought a setback to the paper's progress, which had prospered so well under his single ownership. Now the property was divided into shares, with his eldest son, John William Bell, in the role of managing proprietor and trustee on behalf of his younger siblings. There was a wide age difference in Bell's children. His eldest son was then 41 but his two youngest children had been born to his current and younger wife when Bell was in his early seventies.

Bell's wife had run her own millinery business and had invented the Circassian Corset, described as 'a most desirable and healthy stay to those who are inclined to corpulency' – the only corset which 'displays without indelicacy the shape of the bosom to the greatest possible advantage; gives a width to the chest which is equally conducive to health and elegance of appearance'. She had died, it is believed, in childbirth, a few months before her husband.

The change in ownership and management resulting from Bell's death came at an inopportune time for the paper, which began to face increasing competition, especially when Gladstone abolished stamp duty in 1870, an action which led to cheaper papers.

John William Bell felt hampered by his family responsibilities, which inhibited him from taking the initiative in reducing the price of the paper. It was unfortunate and not without some irony that a newspaper that had pioneered cheap newspapers should, through Bell's timidity, fail to grasp the opportunity and strike out boldly at this time. But, to be fair to Bell, it was not an easy decision for him to take: he was faced with a tremendous personal conflict. While it was certain the paper would increase its circulation through a price reduction, larger premises and more capital expenditure would be required and the higher circulation might not compensate for the smaller profit per copy. He was deeply conscious of the effects of all this on his trustee responsibilities to his brothers and sisters. In his anguish he even sought the help of the Chancery Court, only to be told brusquely that, as he was the trustee, any decision had to be made at his own risk. It was a risk he did not feel able to take alone. He hesitated for too long and the opportunity was lost. Others bolder than he and without the weight of family concerns resting heavily on their shoulders saw the circulations of their papers soar while the once coveted fortunes of the *News of the World* dwindled.

On John William Bell's death in 1877 the estate was again divided. His two sons, Walter John Bell and Adolphus William

Bell, both solicitors and grandsons of the founder, took control and persuaded the other shareholders of the need for a reduction in price to one penny – this came about on 2 May 1880 – and for an influx of fresh capital.

> One penny will be the price of the best and most comprehensive newspaper in the world [they announced]. As a family journal, the 'News of the World' has obtained a pre-eminence which it will be our duty to preserve. Our object will be continually to afford entertainment as well as information uncontaminated by improprieties which so often make a weekly newspaper unacceptable in a family.

It went on to assure its readers that no objectionable advertisements would ever be inserted.

The price reduction brought about some revival in the fortunes of the paper, but the beneficiaries became increasingly concerned that they had received no dividends for some years. The Bell brothers found themselves confronted with a law suit brought by one of their cousins, the daughter of another of the founder's sons, who believed that any benefit could be derived only by selling off the property.

There seemed to the Bell brothers a distinct prospect, which they did not wish to throw away, that the paper's former fortunes could ultimately be restored. The Master of the Rolls, before whom the case was presented, ruled that the property should be valued with a view to selling. The brothers succeeded in raising the necessary £4,000 to buy out the other family interests and became co-proprietors.

New rotary printing machines were installed and for a time their confidence seemed justified by an upturn in the circulation. But it was only temporary. The price reduction alone was not sufficient to do the trick: to match their rivals and even retain the paper's position, larger papers were necessary – and this meant even more machinery and bigger premises to accommodate them. They tried to carry on but their existing plant was insufficient to meet the challenge of their rivals. Circulations continued to decline to less than 60,000 copies. The position of the paper was critical and cried out for drastic action to be taken.

TWO

Hold the Front Page

The *News of the World* quickly established a reputation for the quality of its reports from the trouble centres of the world. And in its early days there was no shortage of such events, with the Crimean War, the Indian Mutiny and the American Civil War, to mention only three.

The newspaper market was less crowded in those days and there were fewer impediments to hamper the production of special editions whenever a major story occurred or there were important happenings. Many were the occasions on which a special edition was rushed into print on a Friday, hours ahead of the normal publishing time, enabling the paper to be first on the streets with the news of some shattering event.

The printing process in the early years was slow and cumbersome, yet its laborious nature often made easier the production of a special edition. The features and pages dealing with the arts were prepared and run off early in the week, so that from Thursday onwards all efforts could be concentrated on the news pages, to which frequent changes were made. It is a sequence which has little altered over the years.

At a period when so much history was in the making, sections of the public were becoming increasingly articulate and eager for information about what was happening in other parts of the world. Many of them had a strong personal interest in some of the events, such as the Crimean War; thousands of people with relatives involved in the fighting were anxious for news of the conflict. The actual number of copies sold did not give a true indication of the circulation of the paper. All over the country a familiar pattern was emerging in which regular subscribers would ride or drive to the nearest agent who could supply a copy and, after perusing the news of the war, would read out the reports to small assemblies of people in towns and villages.

The paper, which was noted for its liberal and radical standpoint, took a stridently belligerent attitude towards the government of the day, especially in the months building up to the Crimean War. Five months before war was declared between Turkey and Russia, it was saying in a leader that it was impossible that either England or France could consent to such conditions as Russia was demanding of Turkey. It referred to the 'insidious designs craftily put forth by the Russians' and predicted that in the end the 'insolent pretensions of the Russian Autocrat will be signally defeated'. As affairs in eastern Europe got more gloomy, the paper found it painful, at such a critical moment, to believe there were serious dissensions in the British Cabinet as to the course England ought to pursue, yet such it feared was a fact.

There remained in the government confident anticipation that Nicholas of Russia would yield to strenuous diplomatic endeavours to bring about a peaceful solution, but the paper continued to have misgivings. While Paris and London still indulged in the song of peace, it said, it became obvious that the dismemberment of the Turkish empire had commenced and that 'the Russian vulture will not quit his prey unless he be driven from it by some stronger arguments than can be found in words'. By September its own doubts about a satisfactory adjustment of the differences seemed to be shared even by those who had been most sanguine in the anticipation of a peaceful solution. 'The crisis we have so long foreseen is approaching', it warned on 18 September. Nine days later war was declared between Turkey and Russia.

Britain and France still favoured the path of diplomacy and hesitated about other action. Week after week the *News of the World* criticized the government for dallying. In the issue of 1 January 1854 it declared:

War is a thing to be looked at with aversion but when it cannot be avoided with honour there should be no paltering with the danger. The enemy whose hostility is only to be overcome with the sword should be met with the sword, at once and resolutely. There would be no war if this course had been taken at the commencement of the present crisis.

Again, the following Sunday, it resumed the attack: 'The time for dallying has passed away. Already our statesmen have too long allowed themselves to "hope against hope". The path of duty now lies plainly open before them.'

It was not until the beginning of April, however, that war was declared by Britain and France and a month later the allied fleets made their first attack on Sebastopol. In July the allied commanders decided on an expedition to the Crimea and the destruction of Sebastopol, but its departure had to be delayed because of an epidemic of cholera among the troops.

Deaths among troops during wartime from disease and pestilence was not a new problem – in the Peninsular War 24,930 soldiers had died of disease compared with 8,999 who died of wounds or were killed in battle. But it proved to be an intensive problem in the Crimean War. The situation was exacerbated by military mismanagement and earlier economies which left the army ill-prepared for battle and the medical services ill-equipped to deal with the combination of casualties of war and the even greater number of victims of pestilence and disease. The conditions on the battle front and in the hospitals were equally deplorable.

What began as a war that, in Queen Victoria's words, was 'popular beyond belief' developed into a disastrous campaign which created an unprecedented demand at home for news. Apart from its other aspects, the Crimean War was journalistically significant in that it saw the introduction of war correspondents whose dispatches were to have an important effect on public opinion and government action. The best known of these was William Howard Russell of *The Times*, whose disclosure of inadequacies in the conduct of the war, the conditions and lack of supplies both military and medical, had great influence.

While most of the credit has always gone to *The Times* and its famous correspondent for exposing the terrible conditions to which the British forces were subjected and the subsequent dispatch of Florence Nightingale and her medical team to the military hospital at Scutari, other newspapers also played their part in drawing attention to the disastrous situation, including the *News of the World*, which consistently took a strongly critical line over the conduct, or lack of it, of the military leaders and the government. The official dispatches were invariably laudatory but bureaucracy was rife: Florence Nightingale became a heroine, a legend, and an inspiration to the men to whom she ministered but she had to fight frustrating administrative battles with higher authorities in her efforts to alleviate the catastrophic situation she encountered. That she was so successful in the circumstances was remarkable.

The casualties caused by epidemics of disease, such as the frequent outbreak of cholera, the *News of the World* thought, should hasten rather than retard the movement of troops. In a leader on 27 August it stated:

The motives which guide our commanders are, we confess, quite inexplicable. When we are informed that our own soldiers are dying by scores and French troops by hundreds a day from a pestilence against which it is utterly impossible for them to oppose the slightest physical resistance . . . there would be seen in that untoward circumstance the strongest imaginable motive for hurrying the departure to a healthier climate and affording them the soldiers' solace of dying (if they must die) with arms in their hands and in conflict with the enemy. More men have already been lost from a disease engendered and augmented by the inaction to which they have been condemned than would have sufficed to win a brilliant and decisive victory. Had the expedition sailed to Sebastopol a month ago it is highly possible that that redoubtable fortress would by this time have been in our possession at an infinitely less sacrifice of life than has occurred during the fatal weeks that their embarkation has been delayed.

The war between Russia and the allied powers of Britain, France, Austria and Turkey, created tremendous interest as news was relayed through the pages of the *News of the World* and other papers over the ensuing months of the battles of Alma and Inkerman and Balaklava, the Charge of the Light Brigade and the year-long siege of Sebastopol. The role of war correspondent was often a difficult one: they were not recognized by the military commanders and it was not easy to get their dispatches back to their offices in London speedily.

The progress of the war was recorded in the newspaper by a variety of different agencies. Much space was given to official dispatches from the army and naval commanders, often preceded by the covering letter from the Foreign Secretary: 'Lord Clarendon presents his compliments to the Editor of the *News of the World* and begs to enclose him a copy of a telegraphic message received this day.' Other reports were assembled from dispatches in foreign newspapers or borrowed from contemporaries; there were long dispatches from 'a highly intelligent and reliable correspondent', and other accounts in extracts from the letters of officers and soldiers.

Throughout the war the *News of the World* maintained its critical attacks on delays and dilatoriness on the part of commanders and government, and lamented the terrible catalogue of killed and wounded: 'We must weep for our loss but avenge it; and still more must take precautions against its future occurrence . . . It is the solemn duty of the living to see that the dead have not fallen in vain.' Events were to prove how misplaced was this fervent hope.

In most prosaic terms, the paper's leader writer characterized the year of 1856 as 'one of those marvellous periods of time which stand out high and rugged from the surface of history and become the landmarks of the student in after years. It may properly be regarded as presenting a bend in the ever-winding stream of time . . .'

Hardly had the celebration of peace in the Crimea concluded before the country was again engaged in hostilities: 'A British expedition has sailed against Persia, we have withdrawn our Minister from the Absolutist Court of Naples, British diplomacy is once more at work in the fatal passes of Afghanistan, and at the same time a British admiral has bombarded one of the capitals of China.'

At home the year had been marked by an unhappy and unusual number of domestic strains 'of a deep and hideous dye in the shape of huge defalcations, systematic embezzlements, colossal insolvencies and frightful crimes . . . Against this lengthened list of calamity and crime we are unable to record the accomplishment of any great work of national usefulness or improvement', the leader writer recorded despondently.

The subject of law and order at that time was exercising minds to an extent that is echoed today. The view expressed in a leading article of 25 January 1857 might find some late-twentieth-century agreement.

The more our prison system and principles of secondary punishment are investigated, the more unreasonable and unjustifiable they appear to be. We have permitted philanthropists and humanitarians to try the efficacy of the 'law of kindness', with regard to criminals . . . but now that their plans and systems have failed, and crimes have increased in number and enormity, so as to alarm the public mind, it is time to put those well-intentioned gentlemen aside and adopt other means for the correction of the evil and the protection of society.

Just over a year after the signing of a peace treaty in the Crimea, the telegraphs were buzzing again with reports of the Indian Mutiny – a revolt by the Bengal Army against the British in India which led to direct administration in place of that of the East India Company.

The *News of the World*'s reports of the mutiny were reputed to be 'the fullest and most graphic' that were published. The issue of 5 July 1857, for instance, contained over a column of comment on the front page, a leading article inside and three columns of closely printed dispatches on the news pages headed 'Massacre of the British, and Preparations for a Terrible Retribution'.

The paper's treatment of war news and other crucial events abroad made an important contribution to its success and was reflected in its mounting circulation. Much of this was due to the foresight of the first editor, Henry Drake Breun. He saw the potential in building up an efficient news reporting service and gave priority to the development of a service that would justify the paper's title.

When war broke out in May 1898 between America and Spain, resulting in the invasion of Cuba, Britain along with France and Italy declared a strict neutrality. Yet there was intense interest in London in the events that were taking place and the *News of the World* made special arrangements with its own correspondents to ensure it received the latest news of operations at all points in the war. 'Special editions will be published immediately on receipt of any telegram containing accounts of engagements, bombardments or any other item of immediate importance. The *News of the World* war service will be unrivalled for its excellence and promptitude', it promised.

The outbreak of hostilities was spread over six columns on the front page, with another page of war news inside. That weekend four special war editions were printed keeping readers updated with events. A week later the paper's special arrangements resulted in a scoop: the fourth war extra edition carried the first news of the great naval battle in Manila Bay in which the American Pacific Squadron attacked and almost totally destroyed the Spanish Fleet. No other newspaper printed news of the engagement until the next day.

Only the death of William Ewart Gladstone on 19 May knocked the distant war off the front page. The former Liberal

Prime Minister's death was recorded with much solemnity: his obituary occupied an entire page, with black bordering between each column.

Early in its existence the *News of the World* had established a reputation for its reporting of crime and court cases. It was not alone in this interest in the more sordid side of life: even *The Times* indulged itself in a relish for crime at that period. 'That was a good murder you had last week,' Thomas Delane, the editor, is reported to have remarked to his deputy.

Reams of copy were produced during 1888 on the activities of Jack the Ripper – the named derived from the signature on letters and telegrams sent to the police and others – who is thought to have murdered at least six women in the Whitechapel district of East London between August and November of that year, and about whose identity there has been speculation ever since. 'Another Horrible Murder at Whitechapel' and 'Another Fiendish Murder in the East End' ran the headlines as one atrocity succeeded another, each more diabolical than the one before.

No gory detail escaped the writer's attention as interest in the crimes mounted. 'The neighbourhood is in a state of wild excitement, bordering on panic', the reporter recorded after the discovery of the fourth victim. 'The victim is again a woman of the "unfortunate" class but the circumstances are so atrocious and revolting as to render it difficult to state the facts.' The reporter managed to recover himself sufficiently to provide the readers with a detailed account of the poor woman's injuries and disembowelment. 'The spectacle was altogether sickening', he wrote. 'One would have to go to the wilds of Hungary or search the records of French lower peasant life before a more sickening and revolting tragedy could be told.'

The crimes drew attention to the plight and poverty of the neighbourhood. The coroner at the inquest on one of the victims commented: 'The glimpses of life in the dens – the common lodging houses – which the evidence has disclosed is sufficient to make us feel that there is much in the nine-teenth-century civilization of which we have small reason to be proud.' Yet, he added, those on the jury who were constantly called together to hear the sad tale of the starvation or semi-starvation, misery, immorality and wickedness related to coroner's inquests did not need to be reminded of what life in a Spitalfield lodging house meant.

Out of the terrible crimes which had alarmed as well as affrighted society, said a leading article, there had arisen a demand for a better order of habitations for the poor in the lowest scale of poverty. 'People of affluence appear with excellent wishes but few come forward with their money', it added sourly.

The practice of offering rewards for the discovery of criminals had been discontinued by the government some years earlier and despite pleas at the time of the Ripper murders, including one from a vigilance committee which was set up in the Whitechapel area, the Home Secretary declined to depart from the rule. The foreman of the jury at the inquest on one of the later victims took the view that had a reward been offered by the government after the first murder the later murders might not have occurred: he offered to give £25 himself towards any reward. Subsequently the Lord Mayor of London offered £500 which was largely increased by private subscribers.

The official view was that offers of rewards tended to produce more harm than good. That was not an opinion shared by the *News of the World* which has often put up rewards – and still does – with useful effect.

There has often been misplaced criticism of the attitude of the *News of the World* towards crime and court reporting. The extent of its reporting of the Ripper murders was not extraordinary when it is considered that *The Times* devoted six leading articles to discussion of the Ripper murders and its report of his final victim was about 5,000 words in length and contained all the lurid detail; and other quality papers, notably the *Daily Telegraph*, have never missed an opportunity to report in every detail – and still do whenever opportunity arises – the more salacious court cases.

The activities of the Ripper provided a rich dessert for *News of the World* readers but the regular and unique flavour of the main course is evident from old handbills and a random selection from the paper's files of its contents. An 'Atrocious Murder on the Plaistow Marshes' was a major story in November 1864, while lesser incidents included the 'frightful' death of a boy, a child found dead on a doorstep, and a death from chewing tobacco, together with the usual fare of breach of promise of marriage actions.

Breach of promise actions were continuing to interest readers twenty years later, along with the customary round-up of courts, inquests and accidents and the report of an awful discovery in Drury Lane – 'A child found pickled in a jar'. Another issue recorded the murder of a warder at Manchester, a case of murder and suicide at Colchester and a murder in the Canonbury area of London, all reported extensively at the tops of columns on the main news page, while below were other murders and the story of a fatal glove fight in Nottingham. The foundations of the paper's interest and appeal had been solidly laid.

THREE

A Wizard From Wales

A new phase in the history of the *News of the World* began in 1891. The Bell brothers had business dealings with and were indebted to a Cardiff family firm of paper-makers, a director of which was Thomas Owen, Member of Parliament for Launceston, who was also associated with the *Western Mail*, the Welsh morning newspaper published in Cardiff. He mentioned the Bells' financial predicament to one of his business friends, Henry Lascelles Carr, co-proprietor of the *Western Mail*, who expressed interest in mounting a rescue operation for the ailing Sunday paper.

Carr had built up a high reputation as both a journalist and a newspaper manager. He was born at Knottingley, near Pontefract in Yorkshire in 1841, the son of a Wesleyan minister, and originally intended to enter the ministry too but was lured into journalism by the success of some articles he had written for various journals during his training. These were seen by the editor and proprietor of one of the leading provincial newspapers, the *Liverpool Post*, who persuaded the young Carr to join the paper's staff. His work there came to the notice of the Marquess of Bute, who put Carr in charge of the newsroom when the *Western Mail* was launched in 1869.

The foundation of the *Western Mail* was a by-product of the general election of the previous year, during which Conservative campaigners felt hampered because they had no powerful press support. Its birth was due less to the third Marquess of Bute personally than to his lawyer, L.V. Shirley, a Cardiff solicitor and fanatical Tory. The Marquess was ostensibly the proprietor but Shirley was the man who wielded power and political influence on behalf of Lord Bute, who, whilst lending his name, played little part in political campaigning.

Carr was a brilliant and eccentric newspaperman, who built up the *Western Mail* from its first home in a dilapidated old salt store to a powerful Conservative newspaper that was respected even by the fiercest radicals, who initially hated all that it stood for. The paper not only supported the Tories in a hotbed of Liberalism, it was on the side of the detested coal-owners and supported the established Church in a land of Non-conformism.

But Carr was also a man who hated injustice and fought it, regardless of politics. He championed the right of working men to organize in order to improve their conditions and hit out at 'scandalous conditions in the mining valleys'. An angry Tory called him 'the biggest radical in Wales', but Carr saw no reason why Conservatives shouldn't stand for fair play for the workers.

He advocated public parks, town bands and military displays for the people's entertainment and also campaigned vigorously against the Sunday Closing Act, declaring that those who ranted against drunkenness should do something to brighten the lives of those who did hard, dirty and back-aching work. Needless to say, the strict, chapel-going fraternity were shocked.

Carr was also an inventor, as well as a great journalist. He made one of the earliest bicycles with his own hands, which was the wonder of Cardiff until it collapsed under him one day. He designed a unique gun with a jointed stock, because his theory was that rifles were designed on the wrong principle, since the straight stock ignored the fact that the human arm was crooked and out of angle with the eye. Another of his inventions, an incubator for hatching eggs, was less than successful, as he became so excited when the first chick was born that he left the door open and allowed all the other eggs to go cold.

Awakened by burglars one night, he fired a gun out of the window to attract the attention of a policeman who, he informed the officer, was paid 30s a week to deal with that sort of situation. And when fire destroyed the *Western Mail* offices in 1893, he still managed to bring the paper out by hiring a printing press in nearby Newport and a steam traction engine to drive it. The engine was too big to get into the pressroom, so Carr had a hole knocked in the outside wall and a belt passed through. It worked – and he brought out the paper with the account of the *Western Mail*'s own fire as the splash story.

Eight years after its launch, Shirley arranged for its sale to Carr who, with a number of local businessmen, raised the money to take it over. Carr became co-proprietor as well as editor. Under the new ownership the paper continued to espouse the causes that the Bute family had championed. The paper several times found itself in legal trouble over libel actions: indeed, Carr made a study of the law of libel in regard to newspapers and lectured on the subject. One of the cases in which he was involved was to become of historic interest: the judge hearing it established the rule of law that it was not possible to libel a dead person.

Thomas Owen had been one of the *Western Mail* backers and, on hearing of the troubles of the *News of the World*, he introduced Carr to the Bell brothers and arrangements were made to form a company to take over the paper from them. The agreed price for the premises, machinery and goodwill was £25,500. Carr's nephew, Emsley Carr, who had joined him on the *Western Mail*, was transferred to London to edit the paper, and the Welsh paper's London solicitor, George Riddell, oversaw the legal side of creating the new company to manage the paper.

The new company took over control in May. Initially there was little change in the appearance of the paper. Only the imprint gives a clue to the actual time of the change: the editions of 17 May 1891 were the last to carry the imprint 'Printed and published by Walter John Bell'. The previous day the directors of the new company had met to peruse and confirm the purchase agreement. The following week the paper's imprint read 'Printed and published for the proprietors by Robert Pearce Humphris'.

It was quickly realized that drastic measures were needed to revive and re-establish the paper, and it would have to be increased in size if it were to successfully compete with its rivals, which had already forestalled it. Over the succeeding weeks changes were gradually introduced: the columns were lengthened and an extra one added; presentation was brighter; line drawings were used to illustrate some of the news stories; extracts from the latest novels were serialized and given more prominence; and special offers were later introduced, such as the Great Book Scheme, launched at the beginning of 1898 to cater for 'the great and increasing demand for good class books', by which readers who forwarded six coupons cut out from six copies of the current issue were sent 'a beautifully bound volume'. It proved such a success – in six weeks 3,000 books were distributed – that the number of coupons entitling readers to a book had to be increased from six to thirteen.

With the *Western Mail* and his other Welsh interests, Lascelles Carr had much to do in Cardiff, but he entered into the efforts to resuscitate the new acquisition with his characteristic energy and gusto. He became chairman of the new company and it was he who took the ultimate decision on all matters of principle, but he was happy to delegate matters of detail to a carefully selected team of associates and executives in whom he had the utmost confidence.

Besides Riddell, his lawyer, and Emsley Carr, his nephew, Carr strengthened the team by dispatching his cashier at Cardiff, Edgar Fifoot, to take charge of the general business management of the London paper.

Under the new management the paper was given a financial transfusion: new machinery was bought so that the much-needed increase in size could be effected, although belatedly. Fresh features were introduced and the paper's news services, both general and commercial, were expanded and built up into one of the finest in Fleet Street.

In this expansion much attention was given to sports coverage, which was to become one of the main planks in the paper's reputation. To their eternal credit, the Bell brothers had had the foresight to realize the potential of good sports reporting. One of the most popular and successful of their actions had been the engagement in 1881 of W. J. Innes, whose contributions appeared under the pseudonym of 'Pegasus' and became an important circulation booster.

Better machinery and larger premises were urgently required to deal with the new pace of activity, and Carr gathered some of his influential friends around him to raise the necessary additional finance.

The new team in charge of the paper was described as a happy family party: most of them had been friends or colleagues for many years. Likewise the readers: many were now elderly people who had read the *News of the World* all their lives and their children continued the habit when they married and left home. Handbills advertised it as 'The Best Family Newspaper'.

Circulation and revenue from advertising began to pick up and a fresh move was necessary, this time to premises in Whitefriars Street in March 1892. Here priority was given to the vast mechanical operation. The editor and his staff occupied an attic room: the only room to be carpeted was that of Edgar Fifoot, by now general manager.

Although much money had been spent in revitalizing the paper and this policy was showing the first signs of paying off, they were still lean years financially. There were occasions when the directors and managers had to have a whip round among themselves to pay pressing bills, even salaries. Sometimes creditors were offered shares in lieu of cash when it came to settling accounts; although at the time it might have appeared a risky deal, those who accepted were wise, for the shares over the years were to multiply many times over their original cash value.

The expansion in machinery and staff enabled larger papers and more editions to be produced. Greater prominence was given to the paper's own correspondents abroad – a weekly letter from Paris was given a full column of space, and the oddly named Spinnaker Boom wrote an early gossip column called Pitch and Toss.

In those days, reporters were still allowed to witness executions and in their detailed accounts of the hangings they would gravely discuss the victim's weight, the length of the drop and the subject's last words on the scaffold.

The principal method of getting news to the office from outside London was by carrier pigeon and one issue proudly told the readers how this was achieved:

When a reporter desires to use the pigeons, he leaves word the night before to the person in charge of them. When they are to fly far or on any particular business, it is better that they should only be lightly fed in the morning. The pigeons, two or four, as may be required, are caught in the morning and placed in a comfortable wicker or tin basket, like a luncheon basket with compartments. The reporter, when he leaves the office, carries the basket with him.

He writes his report very legibly and compactly so as to put as much on a page of 'flimsy' as it will possibly hold. Then he rolls the 'flimsy' neatly up and attaches it to the leg of the bird by means of an elastic band. The pigeon being released makes straight for home. Arriving at the newspaper office, it alights on the edge of the dovecot. To go through the usual circular-headed opening it pushes before it a couple of light wires and these, falling after it, close the aperture.

However, the bird is not yet into the cot. It has only gone the length of the trap. This trap, two feet square or so, has a flooring fixed upon an electric spring. The weight of the bird pressing down the spring releases the electric current, which rings a bell in the subeditor's room. The bird thus heralds its own arrival.

Extra revenue was sought by sorties into book publishing, including the launch of the annual *News of the World Almanac*. A handsomely produced *Portfolio of Photographs* of famous cities, scenes and paintings, compiled by John L. Stoddard, a distinguished lecturer and traveller, was issued in 1894 and within six months had produced a profit of £1,208. In 1902 a history of the Boer War, told in a hundred cartoons, was produced. Other ventures, however, were less financially successful. A publication entitled *Famous Footballers and Athletes* made a heavy loss, which was later recouped by the more profitable *Famous Cricketers and Cricket Grounds*.

Lascelles Carr had a profound impact on the *News of the World* at a crucial period in its development in the 1890s but his chairmanship of the company was to be relatively short-lived. After the death of his wife in 1900 his own health declined and he was persuaded to live in a warmer climate: he left for France, where he remarried. There he continued to receive encouraging reports of the continuing improvement in the fortunes of the paper he had saved. He was a short, squat man whose health deteriorated when he declined to take advice and give up smoking and drinking and keep to a strict diet. Life on those terms was not, he said, worthwhile. He continued to indulge himself and died in 1902 at the early age of sixty-one.

His brother-in-law Charles Jackson, a wealthy barrister, who had became a director two years after the takeover, succeeded to the chairmanship on Carr's death.

Carr not only rescued the *News of the World* from its plight, but in doing so he created a dynasty that was to rule over its fortunes for eighty years. The involvement of the Jackson side of the family was, however, to have significant repercussions later.

FOUR

Riddell: The Public Figure

George Allardice Riddell was an enigmatic and secretive man, eccentric, ruthlessly ambitious – and one of the two main props in the success of the *News of the World* under the new regime. His own life and career contained all the elements sought after in the exciting and dramatic series of life stories his paper regularly published.

He attempted to surround his private life and upbringing with secrecy. Though there was nothing in his background of which he need be ashamed, he showed some reticence and sensitivity over details of his relatively humble but perfectly respectable upbringing. He had Scottish ancestors and encouraged the belief that he was himself a Scot, though he was born and brought up in southeast London. He retained a trace of cockney accent and, when he had achieved fame and fortune, he would sometimes disappear to take private lessons in elocution from a tutor at the Guildhall School of Music and Drama, then housed in John Carpenter Street, a short distance from the newspaper office. His father, whom he later described on official forms as 'gentleman', was a photographer who died when George was only two, after which his mother moved back to care for her ageing parents in return for a home for herself and child.

An uncle, David William Allardice, from whom Riddell derived his middle name, took an interest in the boy's education and future career. Allardice was a wealthy merchant, the brother-in-law of George's dead father. He and his wife had a daughter called Annie and when the young George visited the Allardices at their home in Cheshire, he and his cousin came to know each other very well.

Riddell and his mother were very much the poor relations and even at an early age George was well aware of it – possibly a clue as to why in later life he was so secretive about his upbringing. During a long walk with his girl cousin, he declared: 'I'll be a millionaire one day and I'll show them.' His words were prophetic indeed, for Riddell was to rise to become a peer of the realm, a confidant to the highest in the land, chairman of the world's largest circulation newspaper and a millionaire twice over.

His uncle David got him a job as an office boy in his solicitor's London office, only a length of lawyer's tape from Gray's Inn, and undertook to pay for his articles. George studied hard and was articled by the time he was 18, then passed the Law Society's final examination with First Class Honours at 23.

An early story about Riddell told how he stood on King's Cross station with enough money in his pocket to buy a bun or a newspaper, but not both. He opted for the newspaper, in order to search the jobs column, and went hungry.

Such was his driving ambition, that in the very same year he qualified as a solicitor he and two other young lawyers took over the practice, with Riddell as the senior partner. There was a mystery about how the takeover was achieved. Riddell said he went into the office and discovered the previous senior partner had died, so he had to assume control. But records show the solicitor in question did not die until many years later in retirement.

Riddell was helped financially by £300 capital from the parents of a young woman called Grace Edith Williams, who lived near his mother's home in North London. Riddell was attracted to Grace and made her his wife in December 1888. They moved into his mother's house, keeping the best furniture, and the widowed Mrs Riddell went off to rooms in Kilburn. Riddell was what today would be called a workaholic and took just an hour off from work for the wedding. There was no honeymoon – Riddell said he couldn't afford one.

He drove his staff ruthlessly and his terrified clerks trembled when he shouted their names. One or two drew Dutch courage with a quick trip to the pub next door to the office. This enraged Riddell so much that he eventually bought the pub, saying that if they were going to waste the good money he paid them on beer, he might as well get it back!

He laid the foundations of his wealth by buying property. Every weekend he would hire a hansom cab and scour the streets of London, especially buying up corner sites because they offered the best opportunities for development. He could always sell them to department stores. A valued client was Sir Oswald Stoll, founder of a great theatre chain.

Sometimes, there were sitting tenants who had to be removed from the properties he acquired. It didn't bother Riddell. The law afforded tenants scant protection in those days and his policy was to harass them if they didn't go quietly. 'I can't afford mercy,' he said.

Nor did Riddell ever tip the cab drivers he hired. 'No one ever tips me,' he observed. Years after he had become a very rich man, he would take a hansom to his office but wouldn't hand the cabby the money through the roof. Instead, he would climb down and place the precise fare on top of the wheel, so that the driver had to climb down and get it. If the cabby cursed him, Riddell would treat him to a mouthful of ripe retorts. When one angry cab driver threatened to sue him for slander, he responded: 'You bloody fool. What do you know of the law? You can't distinguish between slander and mere vulgar abuse.'

Once, one of Riddell's clerks was facing imprisonment for debt. When he told his employer of his problems, Riddell growled: 'It's a good job you've told me now. You can bloody well write out these notes while you're inside.' However, the clerk was valuable to him, so he paid the man's debts and deducted the money in instalments from his wages.

An occasional caller at Riddell's office was his mother. She arrived once a month, a dignified little figure dressed in black. Usually he was too busy to see her but a clerk would return from the inner sanctum and solemnly hand her a golden sovereign, which she placed in a waist pocket beneath her flowing skirt. Then she would depart with a sad smile and barely a word spoken.

Riddell's marriage to Grace was doomed to end after five years, probably due to his neglect of her whilst he was spending all his time working. He told people she had taken to drink and that when she'd been brought home by the police after being found drunk in the street, he had walked out on her. It may have been true but, whatever the reason, Riddell hardly ever mentioned her again in later years. When he'd become a power in the land, none of the literature about him ever referred to her.

Grace took him to court and he was ordered to return to her but he ignored the ruling. He gave her an allowance of £300 a year which was never varied, though she made occasional calls at his office and, like his mother, was dispatched with a sovereign. On 29 October 1900 the estranged pair were granted a divorce after seven years apart. Just three days later, Riddell married his cousin Annie, the girl he had enjoyed long walks with so many years before and to whom he had confided his intention to become a millionaire. She was a ward sister at St Thomas's Hospital.

Again, Riddell went to his office before and after the ceremony, though he had mellowed sufficiently enough to entertain his staff to dinner in the evening. Grace remarried to a customs officer and when she died in 1929 she left just £35. Her first husband was by then a double millionaire.

Riddell and his second wife had few interests in common but she was a woman of taste and financial independence who was content to pursue her own projects whilst her husband continued to devote most of his time to business and his goal of amassing a fortune. They continued this largely independent relationship for most of their married life.

Annie was a generous hostess and when the couple acquired and elegantly furnished a house at 20, Queen Anne's Gate, Westminster it eventually became a regular meeting place for leading politicians and statesmen with whom Riddell had become friendly. The house had been the birthplace in 1784 of Lord Palmerston, a fact that Riddell had commemorated with one of the famous blue plaques erected by the former London County Council.

Riddell had appeared much older than his years ever since he had first acquired his own legal practice at the age of 23. He always dressed in black, a high starched collar encircling his long, thin neck. His chin was clean-shaven but he had mutton-chop whiskers and on his head he wore a hard, tall hat. Some thought he was a Methodist preacher. He was an awesome figure, with a deep, penetrating voice, and it was no wonder his clerks were terrified of him.

He seemed firmly set on a successful legal career until word reached Wales and the ears of Lascelles Carr about the decline of the *News of the World*. Until then Riddell's main contact with newspapers had been through his lawyer's role as London representative of the *Western Mail*'s Cardiff solicitors.

Lascelles Carr naturally sought Riddell's help and advice in raising finance and dealing with the legal matters associated with the new company that was to take over the *News of the World*. The work involved in the purchase was considerable and when Riddell presented his account, so strapped was finance that he was offered and agreed to take 120 of the £10 shares in lieu of his legal fees. As for other members of the small staff and suppliers of equipment in the early days of the new company to whom similar offers were made, it was in retrospect a wise choice.

Riddell became exhilarated by the novelty of newspapers and his new shareholding encouraged him to take a greater personal interest in the company and, once the early problems had been sorted out, the newspaper that was then its main asset. The Bells had also received shares in the new company but Riddell, with his new-found enthusiasm, was unhappy with the way Walter John Bell, who had been appointed general manager, was running the company's affairs. He determined to exert more influence, even control, and before the end of the first year Bell had gone, Riddell had become company secretary and the young Edgar Fifoot transferred from the *Western Mail*. The three men at the top were then all aged under thirty.

Bell continued as a director until 1894 when, having sold shares to Charles Jackson, he ceased to be entitled to a seat on the board. He received a pension of £2 a week, which was increased to £3 at the time of the death in 1919 of his brother Adolphus, whose widow was awarded a pension of £1 a week. When she died in 1922 her daughter, Miss A. Bell, was given a payment of 10s and W.J. Bell got another 10s. The direct link with the Bells ended with the death of W.J. Bell in 1926.

Riddell's additional interest in the *News of the World*, coupled with the continuing work of his legal practice, began to take a toll on his health and, after a period in a nursing home, he came reluctantly to the conclusion that he must choose between his two careers. He opted for a new life in newspapers and around 1906 withdrew further active participation in his legal practice. Being an obsessively careful man, however, he continued, as a precaution, to renew his practice certificate.

His association with Cardiff and the Carrs brought him into contact with David Lloyd George and a friendship soon developed with the young Welsh politician which was to prove beneficial to both men as they advanced in their respective spheres. Although dissimilar in character and qualities, they had some things in common which helped enhance the friendship. Both were of similar age and upbringing; each had been left fatherless at an early age, with an uncle providing for their education and encouraging them in a career; both had been struggling young solicitors whose future success was achieved in a different sphere. Riddell had no family and his interest in his work and making money left little time or inclination for close marital ties; Lloyd George, on the other hand, although married with a family, indulged in marital infidelity.

The Riddell—Lloyd George relationship was, on the whole, probably of greater benefit to the newspaperman than it was to the politician, as Riddell became a press baron alongside Northcliffe, Burnham and Beaverbrook as a result of the alliance. The friendship prospered and deepened in the second decade of the twentieth century. Although he was fascinated by politics and political personalities, Riddell never became a professional politician himself. He spent much of his time hobnobbing with the leading politicians and statesmen of the time. But he was an observer of the political scene rather than an active participant: a recorder of the conversations, attitudes and actions of his political friends which he committed to his diary with disciplined regularity.

Large parts of the diaries were published in the early 1930s, a fascinating and detailed record of the comment and discussions in the privacy of the smoke-filled rooms in which politicians and statesmen plotted their manoeuvres and to which Riddell had access through the many friendships which blossomed from his original association with Lloyd George and his increasingly authoritative voice in Fleet Street. The diaries, said The Times, had no rival as contemporary records of vivid interest and no slight historical value.

Riddell's own dining room was often the venue for quiet, unobtrusive discussions among leading politicians of the day: whether it be there, or Downing Street, or the golf course at Walton Heath in Surrey, which Riddell bought through the News of the World and where, nearby, he generously provided Lloyd George with the gift of a house, Riddell was invariably present, offering words of encouragement and joining in discussion of often momentous significance, the detail of which he would at the earliest opportunity write up in his diaries.

Not that there was any suggestion of ulterior motive behind his activities. Riddell was a man of wide interests who was fascinated by people, especially those in high places, and it was a natural instinct, once he had reached some prominence himself, for him to want to be at the centre of things. While he was well placed to make journalistic capital out of his friendships and his presence at the centre of events, if he had so desired, he did not use that advantageous position to do anything that would bring discredit on himself or his newspaper. He was, however, able to provide advice and authenticity to the paper's political notes, which gained in authority as a result.

There were two particular areas in which Riddell was able to perform a public service, apart from expressing a point of view in an influential ear or two: during the miners' strike in 1912 and liaising between the world leaders and the press during the peace conferences at the end of the First World War.

Riddell had considerable knowledge of miners and their conditions, gained through his Welsh connections, and he enjoyed the respect of several of the miners' union leaders. The strike, for a change, saw him in the role of an active participant in the events rather than an observer of them. Through his special knowledge and trust he was able to act as a go-between and provided the then Prime Minister, Asquith, and Lloyd George with much practical help in settling the stoppage and formulating the Miners' Minimum Wage Act. His advice was sought on subsequent occasions whenever there was similar trouble in the offing.

In those days when there was less Whitehall bureaucracy and security shrouding public figures, personal relationships thrived more actively. Riddell had the entrée to Downing Street's residences, firstly to No. 11 when Lloyd George was Chancellor of the Exchequer, and later, when he became Prime Minister, to No. 10. There was nothing unusual in Riddell arriving unannounced, to seek a few moments' conversation with Lloyd George, even though he may have been holding a conference with officials or ministerial colleagues. Such freedom of access and participation earned Riddell the epithet, which he undoubtedly enjoyed, of being 'the extra member of the Cabinet'.

It is not difficult to imagine the headlines that the gift of a house to a government minister would provoke in today's newspapers. But that is exactly what Riddell did for Lloyd George. There was more sensation about the blowing up of the house by the Suffragettes during its construction in 1913 than there was about the actual gift. The house was handed over in May 1916. 'In acknowledging the deed he wrote me a most charming letter – a delightful souvenir of our friendship', Riddell recorded.

Nor can one conceive of a contemporary Chancellor divulging some of the contents of his Budget speech, yet Riddell confided to his diary:

> After lunch Lloyd George opened the box containing Budget papers and read us a remarkable set of figures as to the progress of taxation and population, which he said he intended to use in his speech. We discussed the effect of a general rise in wages of five shillings per week per worker.

There were other, more personal ways in which Riddell proved himself valuable to Lloyd George, apart, that is, from providing him with a house. In 1913 there occurred the great Marconi scandal which threatened to destroy the careers of Lloyd George and other Liberal leaders. They had bought shares in the American Marconi Company at a time when the Post Office was discussing a contract with the British Marconi Company.

The implications were obvious but Lloyd George's confidence in Riddell was such that the Chancellor asked him to sound out the Conservative Opposition behind the scenes. Riddell was able to report back that Bonar Law, the Tory leader, took the view that there was some imprudence but no corruption. 'The two concerns were separate. There could be no accusation of anything beyond indiscretion,' Riddell wrote. As a result, Lloyd George and his colleagues were able to ride out an inquiry by a Commons committee and win a vote of confidence.

In the same year, 1913, a police raid on a brothel in Piccadilly caused some excitement when papers were found suggesting that some very important people were clients. Riddell squashed speculation by writing: 'The rumours are a pack of lies but they have engendered much resentment and bad feeling.' Some important people were indebted to him.

As a result, they sought his company, believing that to have his ear was also to have the ear of Lloyd George. Invitations to golfing parties at Walton Heath, where the Prince of Wales and Churchill were among the visitors, became much prized.

Riddell was in a unique position. He was neither political colleague nor potential competitor and was, therefore, always trusted: his circumspection was unquestionable. There were occasions when public figures made use of him. He records a long conversation on 29 March 1914 with Sir John French, the Army Commander-in-Chief in France, then being criticized for his indecision, 'who said he would like me to state in the *News of the World* tomorrow that his resignation would not be withdrawn and to give his version of recent events'. French had told him: 'There is no paper so widely read in the Army and by doing this you will be performing a national service.'

Riddell had, by 1914, become a respected figure among other Fleet Street proprietors, and through his activities in their trade association, the Newspaper Proprietors' Association (later the Newspaper Publishers' Association) he had become, at the outbreak of war, a member of the official committee set up to establish liaison between government and press. He became a dominating influence on this committee.

There were three main sources of war news: the formal and brief daily communiqués, the Commander-in-Chief's dispatches and 'Eyewitness' reports actually written by an official observer at General Headquarters. Lord Kitchener, the War Minister, neither understood the press and its importance to the nation nor wished to have any dealings with it. Newspaper correspondents attempted to get as near as possible to the front lines to pick up whatever news they could but they were given few facilities and their reports were subjected to severe censorship. There was, therefore, much liaison work to be done. On one occasion Riddell, with remarkable patience, sat outside Kitchener's office for a whole day seeking an opportunity to raise some of the press's problems with the Army commander.

In 1916 Lloyd George, then Minister of Munitions, had

become dissatisfied with Asquith, the Prime Minister, over the conduct of the war. At this time Riddell was in almost daily contact with Lloyd George, joining him either for breakfast or dinner. The politician was so disenchanted he was contemplating resignation, which would have enabled him to voice his criticisms. But he held back and in July of that year he was offered the post of Secretary for War. He discussed with Riddell and others whether he should accept or carry out his threat to resign and possibly bring down the government in doing so. Eventually he decided to accept, but the new post only increased his frustration until there was a final breach with Asquith. Lloyd George then headed a coalition government for the remainder of the war and until its collapse in 1922.

Riddell performed another public service for his friend in 1917 when he joined fellow newspaper proprietors, Lords Burnham and Beaverbrook, on a committee appointed to investigate the shortcomings of British wartime propaganda. 'The whole thing is in an unholy mess', he wrote. 'The waste and overlapping are scandalous. This after three years of war.'

Sometimes Riddell's bizarre sense of humour got the better of him. Once, invited to No. 10 to give his views on the paper shortage, he produced a large parcel wrapped in layer upon layer. 'This, gentlemen,' he said, 'is an article typical of many being sold to ladies in shops every day. Is the paper necessary?'

He slowly unpeeled the parcel until he could barely see over the top of the pile of wrapping in front of him. Then he held aloft its contents – a corset.

There was a shocked silence, broken by Lloyd George's loud laughter. Slapping Riddell heartily on the back, he declared: 'That's the first time I've seen a corset in the Cabinet Room.' Those who were familiar with Lloyd George's intimate relationship with his secretary and mistress Frances Stevenson – later to become his second wife – begged leave to doubt it.

Close though they were at this period, the two men did not always see eye to eye. A rail strike in 1919 was an example. Lloyd George thought the men had acted badly in suddenly and prematurely breaking off negotiations, and claimed the country was against them, yet Riddell had some sympathy with them.

At the beginning of October that year, while the strike was at its peak, newspaper printers for the first time objected to printing articles of which they disapproved, attacking the railmen. Their action caused consternation among editors and proprietors, who firmly stuck to their guns. 'I have preserved a very even keel in this strike business in the *News of the World*', Riddell reported. 'I believe that the men have a good case and that the movement is a legitimate effort to obtain justice in the matter of wages. Lloyd George with all his powers does not understand or sympathize with working men.'

In spite of occasional differences, however, Riddell was ever generous towards his friend. A fortnight after writing the above entry he was giving Lloyd George a cheque for £2,750 with which to purchase a motor car.

Through his wartime liaison activities on behalf of the press, it was logical that, in November 1918, Riddell should be appointed by the London and provincial newspapers to represent them by acting as the official link between the Peace Conference and the British press. In that capacity he attended sixteen conferences – three in Paris, three in London, four hosted by Sir Philip Sassoon at his Kent home at Lympne, and others at San Remo, Boulogne, Brussels, Spa, Lucerne and Cannes. He also attended a disarmament conference in Washington.

He and Lloyd George were not always in agreement over aspects of the peace discussions. Riddell was a doughty supporter of press freedom and often criticized some of the frustrating and restrictive arrangements for press coverage of the meetings. During the talks among the Western leaders it was Riddell who acted as press spokesman and it was largely due to his insistence that Lloyd George eventually agreed to the press being allowed to witness the handing over of the peace terms to the Germans. He was also responsible for the issue of the press passes for the signing of the Treaty of Versailles on 28 June 1919. One was issued to Elinor Glyn, the romantic novelist, who was enabled to describe the historic occasion for readers of the *News of the World*, to which she was a contributor at the time. It took place in the Hall of Mirrors at the Palace of Versailles, and Glyn, one of only two women present, had to stand on a precarious perch for some time beforehand. She had anticipated that the occasion would be one of triumph and thanksgiving but as it proceeded a sense of foreboding and emptiness overcame her. She described how her earlier excitement changed as the delegates, including the Germans, advanced in turn to the table to append their signatures. 'As I stood there upon the tottering bench, feeling that I must take care to be able to keep my balance, a sadness fell upon me . . . It seemed as if the peace of the world must be as insecure as my own footing on the bench had been', she wrote prophetically.

Away from Versailles, Glyn was to be found in the equally elaborate setting of the Ritz Hotel in Paris where, from her corner table in the restaurant, where Riddell often joined her for dinner, the writer watched the parade of personalities gathered in the French capital. Riddell's often cynical remarks she found sharply refreshing. He had a curious trick, she later recalled, of seeming not to hear or be interested in what was being said to him and then suddenly referring to it again an hour – or sometimes days – later.

All the participants in the round of peace talks were sworn to secrecy but some were less observant of the pact than others. Britain kept strictly to the bargain but newspapers would naturally seek out information wherever it was available. As much of it was misleading, this arrangement proved unsatisfactory.

Riddell's role as a buffer between bureaucrats revealing a minimum of information and pressmen clamouring for the maximum was not an easy task. He told Lloyd George emphatically that more authentic information must be made available, otherwise there would be all kinds of lying rumours circulating. The public, he pleaded, no doubt meaning the press, were sick and tired of secrecy that was only half secrecy.

His insistent pleas met with success during talks in Brussels in July 1920 when he was authorized for the first time to give the news correspondents full and accurate accounts of the proceedings twice a day. He obtained some of his own information direct from Lloyd George and supplemented this with details from deputed officials who were attending the talks. His briefings were also attended by American correspondents. His success changed the atmosphere of the conference, though it meant he bore the heavy responsibility, through the journalists, of communicating what was happening in the talks to 200 million people around the world.

Riddell had been knighted in 1909. His wartime and post-war labours on behalf of the press were rewarded by his promotion to the peerage in 1920. He first heard of this honour when he was handed a letter on his arrival on a visit to Lloyd George's home at Criccieth. In a letter of acknowledgement he told Lloyd George that 'our friendship has been one of the joys of my life and many of my happiest hours have been spent with you'. Appropriately his coat of arms bore an ancient printing press with two printers of the time of Caxton as supporters, and a carrier pigeon holding an open scroll in its beak as crest.

The two friends, however, became increasingly autocratic: Lloyd George became tetchy with those who disagreed with him, while Riddell's social advancement brought on attacks of self-importance. It was perhaps inevitable that two such strong forces would eventually draw apart. Had not Lloyd George on more than one occasion remarked to Riddell, apropos some of his coalition government colleagues, that 'There are no friendships at the top'?

Riddell increasingly disliked Lloyd George's anti-French and anti-Turk stance and his acceptance of an invitation from Arthur Balfour, the Conservative Foreign Secretary in the coalition, to accompany him to the Washington disarmament conference to perform his press liaison duties again did not enamour him to Lloyd George, who was swept from office in the general election of 1922. Lloyd George's political career began its decline and their friendship cooled off: Riddell, in his own quest for power, sought friendship with those still in positions of power.

One who saw a great deal of Riddell throughout the years of his friendship with Lloyd George was Frances Stevenson, the politician's secretary, mistress and, later, his wife. 'He is no partisan, seeing only one side of the fence and content that the other should be debarred from him except as a trespasser,' she said. 'He likes to roam on both sides taking a keen and intense interest in what is happening in every direction. Not the smallest detail escapes his attention, for he is essentially and amazingly inquisitive and acquisitive. His curiosity is remarkable and his outstanding characteristic. He has a natural aptitude for acquiring news; he thinks in paragraphs. He never forgets a face and his brain is a store of information, a faithful and accurate register of the fruits of his inquisitive mind. . . . It is very difficult to mention a person or a subject of which Lord Riddell is not able to give you a complete encyclopedic account.'

Some years after the deaths of both Riddell and her husband, Lady Lloyd George reassessed her opinion of Riddell with a more acerbic account of him. She then recalled him as a rather coarse man. 'Lord Riddell was kind to me personally and did not go too far but I heard many stories of his odd manners. He liked telling risqué stories . . . He did everything he could to ingratiate himself into Lloyd George's household and would tip the servants handsomely. But I heard from others he could be tough, hard and cruel when he wished to be. He never gave anyone credit for high ideals or altruistic motives. He always saw the worst side of a man, never the best.'

Riddell was undoubtedly acquisitive in terms of amassing a fortune through which he was able to exert influence rather than indulgence, since he was a man of simple tastes, often rather shabbily dressed in clothes that hung loosely on his spare frame. He was a man of contradictory characteristics: mean on one hand and generous on another; he overawed many of his staff by his coolness, yet he could invoke pity and sympathy and admiration of his achievements; he was rich in both wealth and power, yet he lacked grace and distinction. Contemporaries claimed, however, that he mellowed a little in later years, exhibiting a geniality which endeared him to his staff who reverentially dubbed him 'The Chief' or 'The Old Man'.

FIVE

Riddell: The Newspaperman

George Riddell's first priorities were on the commercial side of the newspaper operation which, with his customary mixture of skill, industry and ruthlessness, he rejuvenated.

The size of the paper was increased by lengthening the columns and extending them from six to seven; new presses were installed to cater for these changes; and a vigorous advertising campaign was launched on the country's hoardings. The slogan 'Good Old *News of the World*. The Largest Sunday Paper', appeared on every available site and eventually became a national catchphrase.

But availability was the key to the paper's fresh fortunes. Every newspaperman knows that the best produced newspaper in the world is of little moment unless copies can be placed in the hands of potential readers.

At the time of the Carr takeover, Sunday observance was almost universally practised. Few shops were open and the sales of Sunday newspapers were handled by a very few agents, eager to make a little extra income and prepared to risk prosecution and local unpopularity by opening their shops on the sabbath. Many of these, however, were not entirely reliable.

Riddell set about attempting to break the ancient puritan grip on Sundays. He sought to make his newspapers more widely available by initiating a method of selling the paper through direct agents, augmenting those few in the trade who already handled Sunday newspapers. This required a totally new and efficient organization through which the local agents ordered copies direct from the newspaper. The system grew slowly at first but gradually gained momentum until, a year

or so after its introduction, he had recruited thousands of
News of the World agents throughout the country and in Scotland where Sunday newspapers had previously been virtually
unknown but were soon circulating in their thousands. A
report to the directors in May 1898 on the increase in country
sales showed that when the paper was acquired in 1891 the
number of papers sent out to direct agents in the country was
657 copies: in 1898 the total was 56,593 copies.

Travellers were appointed to systematically work towns and
villages in their search for agents: one was specifically engaged
to visit market towns in a 25-mile radius of London to give
away specimen copies of the paper and with instructions to
address crowds of people in market places 'advertising the
paper in "Cheap Jack" fashion'.

All manner of different forms of transport were called on to
handle the distribution of papers – ordinary and special trains,
motor and horse-drawn lorries, messengers on bicycles, all
took part in the operation. In one remote West Country area
situated partly up a steep hill, it was recorded that the *News of
the World* salesman, on arrival at the bottom of the hill on his
bicycle, would sound an ear-piercing call on his bugle – the
signal for the inhabitants to flock down the hill to collect their
copies of the paper.

This distribution system met with considerable opposition
but Riddell, backing it up with his advertisement hoardings to
keep the paper's title constantly before the public gaze, held
steadfastly to his policy, which was ultimately adopted by his
competitors.

In this policy of expanding retail outlets, Riddell had the
support of Charles (later Sir Charles) Jackson, who had been
brought in by his brother-in-law, Lascelles Carr, a year or so
after the new proprietors had taken over and who became
chairman of the company. He and Riddell were always around
on publishing night offering tips of half-a-crown (12½p) to
production and delivery staff to ensure punctuality, since the
newspaper trains were regularly missed: this was probably one
of the earliest, if not the earliest, example of management

bribery and worker intimidation that was later to become so widespread and disruptive in the industry. Riddell would also spend hours at the railway termini tipping porters and other staff to make certain that bundles of his newspapers caught the earliest possible train and were not left on the platform. He worked late into the night in the office overseeing the distribution of the paper among wholesalers and retailers and developing yet more outlets. He would then on Sundays drive around distributing handbills extolling the paper and attempting to persuade more shopkeepers to open on a Sunday, if only for a few hours, to sell the paper.

Financially, the paper's fortunes fluctuated in the first decade of the new ownership. The first year showed a small profit of £256, followed by losses in the next couple of years. Then a profit of £1,666 in 1894–5 was expunged by a £2,000 loss the following year, but from 1897 onwards things began to improve. In that year a first dividend of five per cent was declared, followed by one of eight per cent. At the turn of the century the dividend had reached ten per cent and by the tenth anniversary a fifteen per cent dividend was achieved.

Riddell was amenable to any scheme that might increase the sales and revenue of the *News of the World*. Circulation had reached 300,000 at the turn of the century and was continuing to make rapid advances: 400,000 was achieved in 1902, approaching 700,000 in 1903 and 800,000 the following year.

Revenue from circulation by 1904 was thirteen times that of 1891. Remarkable though the growth had been up to then, the figures were to be eclipsed in the following years: by 1908 the 800,000 circulation of four years earlier had been doubled. The paper's position had been retrieved: its circulation and influence were greater than ever.

Riddell more than anyone else – Emsley Carr, the editor, included – was, after the death of Lascelles Carr in 1902, the controlling voice and the dominating influence behind the paper's extraordinary advance. He was a strong advocate of opening out the paper, brightening up its presentation of news with larger headlines and illustrations in place of the tightly packed pages of old. The public, he said, no longer had the time to sit back and read columns of close print.

While using his undoubted flair and business acumen to project the *News of the World*, Riddell also used his connection with it to foster his own outside interests. Just as later his position with the paper enhanced his friendships with statesmen and politicians, he was encouraging extensive coverage in the paper of Britain's music halls at a time when he was buying and selling music hall sites, and he organized advertising stunts with the use of a gramophone produced by a company to which he acted as solicitor.

Riddell arrived at the office one day with the machine, then a brand-new novelty, and played it in the main hall. Then he ordered a young reporter to hire a horse and wagon and go round the streets of London, playing it loudly. He told the hapless reporter: 'I want you to get summoned and I want the instrument played in court.'

'Mine was not to reason why,' said the journalist. He duly obliged Riddell by getting himself summoned for causing an obstruction, though he had considerable difficulty initially in getting the police to take him seriously. They were far too good-natured about it and the reporter had to make a thorough nuisance of himself before they would take action.

The reporter appeared in court and was fined £1, which sum was paid by the *News of the World*. Riddell was delighted at first, then furious because the second part of his plan backfired when the magistrate refused to allow the machine to be played in the courtroom.

Harry Aldridge, a fellow director who later became chairman after Riddell's death, said: 'Make no mistake, he never did anything unless the move had been nicely calculated and usually the result benefited his pocket. He used to say: "Every man has a price."'

*   *   *

With more time on his hands after his wartime and post-war activities on behalf of the British press, Riddell put much thought and effort into planning a new printing palace, and acquiring the land on which to build it in Bouverie Street, which he was able to see in operation before his death in 1934.

Much of his time was also occupied with negotiations on behalf of newspaper and periodical proprietors and the trade unions, whose activities and influence were increasing. He had been involved in the formation of the Newspaper Proprietors' Association in 1906 and became its chairman, as he was also of the Periodical and Trade Press Proprietors' Association. In recognition of his services on its behalf, the NPA commissioned Sir William Orpen to paint his portrait. On his death he bequeathed the portrait to the National Gallery of Scotland, in an attempt to strengthen his tenuous family connections with Scotland.

It is amazing that in addition to all this business activity and the heavy social programme revealed in his diaries, Riddell also found time to fit in a myriad of other interests, including hospital charities, and he never lost touch with his original profession of the law. He carefully studied every law report and wrote papers and lectured on medico-legal problems, such as ethical and legal aspects of medical confidences, abortion and voluntary sterilization of the mentally unstable – illustrations of a rather morbid interest in sex.

Golf was his relaxation, playing on what was virtually his own personal course. On behalf of the *News of the World* company he bought as an investment the Walton Heath Golf Club and installed the legendary James Braid as professional. He had a house built close to the clubhouse. Here at Walton he entertained his political friends and many were the discussions that took place there between holes and crucial decisions of national and international consequence made. Braid was thus also a party to confidences and though he heard much he revealed nothing; Riddell was to reward him in his will for his discretion.

Golf was a sport he shared with Sir Emsley Carr, who also lived near the Walton Heath Club, and through their mutual interest the *News of the World* became a leading sponsor of golf tournaments.

Unpunctuality was one of Riddell's eccentricities. He often arrived late for his appointments except, interestingly, those involving the Newspaper Proprietors' Association, where until he succeeded he had coveted the chairmanship, then occupied by Lord Burnham. It was noticed that if for some reason Burnham was a few minutes late for the start of a meeting Riddell, then vice-chairman, would hop into the hot seat, saying 'The chairman is late. Is it your wish that I should occupy the chair?'

He was eccentric throughout his life but became increasingly so in his later years. His father had died of tuberculosis, so he invariably selected an open tourer as his car. He liked to drive or to be driven at speed. To a hapless motorist with whom he almost collided whilst driving a bishop from Walton Heath back to London, he shouted: 'If I didn't have a bloody bishop with me I would tell you what I bloody well thought of you.' He bought a police whistle which he blew frantically to clear other traffic out of the way, whilst urging his chauffeur to still greater speeds. If a horse-drawn van blocked his path, he would stand up in the back of his open car and belabour the van's back curtains and sides, cursing loudly until the driver moved off.

In his final years at the home where earlier so much entertaining and political discussion had taken place, he declined to have visitors. In the end not even his long-standing colleague Sir Emsley Carr was allowed across the threshold.

One of his contemporaries, H. H. Aldridge, who became general manager after Riddell's death and later chairman, recalled a bizarre incident when an unscrupulous trade union official who was in financial difficulties sought to borrow money via Aldridge. When he was refused for fear that, in the event of a subsequent labour dispute, he might claim he had been bought off, the union man threatened he would complain to

Riddell. Days later Riddell told Aldridge he had had a call from the official and had told him he could not help. 'Was he sober?' asked Aldridge.

'I didn't see him,' Riddell replied, 'I had an idea he might be a germ carrier, so I spoke to him through the letter-box.'

Another of Aldridge's recollections of Riddell's eccentric behaviour was when he complained of lack of air in the brand new boardroom in Bouverie Street. When Aldridge said he would open some of the windows, Riddell angrily replied: 'No, that's no use. What I want are three-foot holes cut in this ceiling and the ceilings above until we are open to the sky.' Attempting to humour him, Aldridge said he would get it done as soon as possible. 'That's no use. I want it done now. At once,' Riddell demanded.

'I left the room immediately and went for a quick drink. I needed it,' recalled an exasperated Aldridge.

Other stories of Riddell's eccentricities were legion. He went everywhere with his pockets full of handbills advertising the *News of the World*, which he left in cabs, hotels, shops, banks and railway stations. He was undoubtedly the paper's greatest publicist.

To critics of the paper, he was blunt-speaking. When playing golf with the head of a brewery, who suggested the paper's reports of court cases were responsible for increasing crime, he roared: 'We fight crime and your bloody beer causes it.'

'Bloody fool' was his favourite expression. Once, he nearly caused a strike when a new telephone operator, who didn't know his voice, asked Riddell his name. The operator took exception to being called a 'bloody fool' and complained to his union, which threatened to stop the paper unless an apology was forthcoming. Told of the complaint, Riddell protested: 'Me, rude to a telephone operator! Ridiculous! I never use the words "bloody fool".'

Riddell was obsessed with his own health and that of others. When one of his staff mentioned that his doctor had said he must take more exercise, Riddell said: 'Quite right, you must have a horse.' Though the man lived in a modest suburban home, Riddell duly sent round a horse which was tethered to the front gate.

Another time, he offered to give an employee a lift home, saying: 'You need some fresh air. Get in my car.' The employee climbed into his boss's open Rolls Royce. Riddell was wrapped up in an overcoat with a fur collar, whilst his companion shivered in a jacket. They drove for miles, with Riddell dominating the conversation, until some lights appeared in the distance. 'That's High Wycombe station,' Riddell said. 'Get out and get yourself a train.' The hapless employee happened to live on totally the opposite side of London.

In his later years, Riddell spent most of his time at Walton Heath Golf Club, where he kept small and spartan rooms and slept on a single iron bedstead. He shambled about in old suits with baggy trousers. When an American reporter wrote that Riddell couldn't possibly have visited a tailor for years, he was so amused that he enclosed the article the next time he paid his tailor's bill.

His legendary meanness grew worse, even to the extent of grumbling about his funeral arrangements. 'After death,' he said, 'there is nothing but the grave and I don't want a lot of my hard-earned money spent on my funeral. You can dump my body in a bloody ditch as far as I'm concerned.' He once announced to his fellow directors that he was taking a cut in salary and they would have to do the same, whilst the firm's pensioners would have their payments cut – he was by this time a millionaire.

Lunching with Harry Aldridge at a famous London hotel, where a splendid set meal could be had for 7s 6d, Riddell had an egg, a slice of bread and a bottle of water, whilst his companion ate all the courses and a bottle of stout. The pair had been lunching at the same hotel for years and Aldridge had always settled the bill, but on this occasion had forgotten to bring any money. Riddell reluctantly agreed to pay but exploded when he saw he had been charged 15s, plus the cost of the water and stout. The manager explained that there was no reduction in the set charge, whatever the customer ate. 'Do you mean to say that I've been paying 7s 6d for years for a bloody egg, a bloody piece of brown bread and a bloody bottle of Vichy water?' Riddell raged.

'No, my lord,' the manager replied, ''Mr Aldridge has always paid.'

Riddell never entered the hotel again.

His political friendships during the First World War had earned him the epithet of 'the extra member of the Cabinet'. Lord Beaverbrook, with the content of Riddell's paper in mind, coined a less complimentary title – the Pornographic Peer – which he disliked acutely and never forgave the Beaver for inventing it.

Riddell had succeeded to the chairmanship of the *News of the World* on the death of Sir Charles Jackson in 1923, and for the next decade concentrated his energies on the development of the newspaper, adapting his diaries and on his work for innumerable charities. He had much to occupy his interest in supervising the building of the new headquarters in Bouverie Street.

He was a man of contrasting and changing temperament. On one occasion he was furious and excised from his will the printer who, in what was an editorial matter anyway, discussed with the editor the size of a new type to be used on a particular story without involving Riddell. Yet he could be excessively courteous and considerate, as when offices in Bouverie Street were being demolished to make way for the new building he had public notices posted on the hoardings presenting his compliments and apologizing for the noise.

Money to him meant power but when age and infirmity prevented him from wielding power publicly he gave his money away to the various charities he had always supported, having made more than adequate provision for his wife and been generous to his colleagues and staff.

In 1930 Riddell had an operation for prostate trouble and

was told he must have a second operation if he was to recover. He refused: then he had statistics prepared on the results of such operations and discovered that seventy-four per cent of those operated on died. Doctors continued to warn him that if he didn't take the chance he might live for only two years. Still he refused – and lived for a further four years.

Towards the end, he retired to a hotel in Scotland in order to write his will in secret. He spent hours writing it out in longhand, thirteen foolscap pages, having carefully burned a previous will in the grate in the hotel bedroom.

However, Riddell ignored his own advice that he had once given, 'Any man who acts as his own lawyer has a fool for a client.' The will was so loosely worded that two High Court decisions were necessary. He left bequests to his newspaper colleagues, his servants, old golfing chums, including his caddies, and several charities, including the Newspaper Press Fund and the Royal Free Hospital, who each got a quarter of a million pounds. Winston Churchill, Lloyd George and Frances Stevenson each got £1,000.

Lord Riddell's estate was valued in January 1935 at £1,838,901 and resworn in 1938 at £2,208,956.

On his deathbed, he was given whisky to moisten his lips. 'What brand is it?' he whispered. Told the name of the maker, he said: 'Wrong brand. I must have some of Stevenson's.' He meant Lord Stevenson, of the famous Johnny Walker label, an acquaintance from the First World War.

During his final illness, Riddell had instructed his wife to burn all his personal and business papers and letters, with the exception of his diaries which, on his death, were deposited with the British Museum. The solicitor who carried out the instructions on her behalf did a thorough job, reporting that all his letter files, boxes and cabinets had been consigned with their contents to the flames. 'This all seemed a queer ending to the extraordinary career of a great man,' he later commented. He doubted whether, if there had been no such instructions, Lady Riddell would have done otherwise since, despite their independence, her loyalty to her husband was very sincere and she was a woman of high principles.

In some people Riddell inspired fear, in others respect for his achievements but, according to his colleague Harry Aldridge, he certainly didn't inspire affection.

Within half an hour of his death, flags flying over newspaper offices in Fleet Street were lowered to half mast – an honour which exemplified the enormous respect in which he was held by his fellow proprietors and the debt that Fleet Street owed him.

His idiosyncrasies at the end were forgiven; instances of his charm and kindliness were remembered. An obituary in *The Times* said of him:

> Versatile in ability and knowledge and shrewd in business judgement, his kindly and humorous personality won him general affection from those connected with the newspaper industry. Despite the fact that, by virtue of his office of chairman of the Newspaper Proprietors' Association, it often fell to him to conduct protracted and difficult negotiations on behalf of the proprietors with the eleven trade unions of the industry, he had no greater admirers than the men's representatives on the opposing side.

The death of Riddell, on 4 December 1934, saw the end of perhaps the most extraordinary newspaper man of his generation. He left instructions that his shares in the *News of the World* were to be sold to the highest bidder. He didn't care who that was. He instructed that there was to be no mourning, no flowers and that he was to be cremated and his ashes scattered at the eighth hole at his beloved Walton Heath, the highest point of the course.

He said there should be no memorial service. But there was, against his wishes, at the famous newspaperman's church, St Bride's in Fleet Street. The church was packed, with hundreds more outside. The famous and the humble stood shoulder to shoulder and at the last moment, Riddell's old friend Lloyd George walked in.

Lady Riddell walked out on to the eighth hole at Walton Heath one winter evening and scattered his ashes, as he had requested, in the place where he had spent his happiest hours entertaining his business and political friends. 'That,' she is reported to have said, 'is the end of him.'

SIX

Sir Emsley Carr

Emsley Carr got himself into the record books by occupying the editor's chair at the *News of the World* for an incredible fifty years. When he took over, sales of the paper were as low as 40,000: at his death in 1941 they topped 4 million.

Young Emsley Carr had been encouraged into a career in journalism by his uncle, Lascelles Carr. He had worked contentedly subediting news stories at the *Western Mail* in Cardiff, and had become that paper's parliamentary correspondent at Westminster, where he made some useful political contacts. He was one of the first group of provincial journalists to be officially admitted to record the activities of the House and served as chairman of the Press Gallery.

Once the *News of the World* deal had been settled, his uncle invited him to become editor of his newly acquired paper. The change came at a fortuitous time. Elsewhere in the newspaper world there was increasing evidence of what became known as the 'new journalism'. It had been started in America by Gordon Bennett, founder-editor of the *New York Herald*, a cheap and sensational daily paper, who threw out of the window the earlier standards of journalistic propriety.

Most papers of the mid Victorian era presented news reports in a heavy manner, as solid as the furniture that characterized the period. The assassination of a foreign monarch or president would appear under the heading of the particular country, and a major political speech might well occupy two pages of small type under a heading such as 'Mr Disraeli at the Free Trade Hall', with no cross-headings and few paragraph breaks to lighten the load.

It was inevitable that the heavy preponderance of political

news and comment in the form of such unattractive, dull and impersonal columns, would have to give way to a more inviting and attractive content and presentation in order to recruit the growing army of newspaper readers. Two men, in particular, were credited with the introduction of the 'new journalism' in Britain – W. T. Stead and T. P. O'Connor.

Stead was a social reformer, perhaps the forerunner of the modern investigative journalist. He was imprisoned during his exposures into white slave trafficking when he was editor of the *Pall Mall Gazette*, in which paper he introduced brighter presentation and new features such as interviews as we now know them with popular public figures.

O'Connor, a politician as well as a journalist, did much to popularize political journalism, pioneering the parliamentary sketch when he also worked for the *Gazette*, and introducing the gossip column when he launched his own paper, the *Star*, in 1888. The innovations went even further when Alfred Harmsworth (later Lord Northcliffe) launched the *Daily Mail* in 1896, followed by Cyril Arthur Pearson's *Daily Express* in 1900.

In the light of these advances in the daily paper sphere in the early days of Emsley Carr's editorship, it was to be expected that in reviving the *News of the World* and building up its potential circulation he too would jump aboard the improving bandwagon and rid the paper of its stodgy appearance. This he did, with Riddell's help on the commercial side of the operation.

There was some good raw material on which to work: events such as the declaration of war between America and Spain in 1898, the tragic sinking in the Channel of the passenger ship *Stella* on the Good Friday of 1899, the relief of Mafeking, the bloodthirsty activities of Jack the Ripper and the dramatic story of Dr Crippen whose attempted escape to America after murdering his wife, with his mistress, Ethel le Neve, dressed as a boy, was recorded in great detail, were only a few of the sensational stories of which full journalistic advantage was taken.

The new policy was to be first with the news and this aim

was facilitated by the relative ease with which it was then possible to bring out a special edition in advance of the normal printing time. To do so showed great editorial initiative, especially with the limited staff Carr had available: it was often a case of all hands on deck. There were no departmental demarcation lines and management staff would not infrequently assist their few editorial colleagues. Even for a normal edition some of them would report on football matches and other sporting events. Three editions of the paper were then produced each week: one on Friday, which went abroad and to distant parts of the country and certain other places which had market days on Fridays and Saturdays; a small Saturday edition aimed at places where papers could not be bought on a Sunday; and the normal Sunday edition. Printing of this started at 4.00 p.m. and continued until 6.00 a.m. the following morning. In addition to the 'specials' that were brought out from time to time from midweek onwards, a big news story occurring on a Sunday would also merit a special edition in those days when there were no agreements between papers not to print after the normal run. Cabs would be dispatched to bring in a 'scratch' staff, who would have the special edition on the streets within hours.

Later, Carr would recall with a chuckle how in the early days he was the entire literary staff of the paper, how it was set up by hand compositors, craftsmen dressed in frock coats, and how the whole edition was printed on an old press which delivered the papers unfolded and uncounted. Initially, Carr was paid £5 a week for his multifarious duties of editor, subeditor, parliamentary correspondent, leader-writer and make-up man. He added a little to this income by doubling as Press Gallery reporter at Westminster for his old paper, the *Western Mail*. At this time he shared a flat for a while with Riddell who, as a trustee of the Lascelles Carr estate, handled the business affairs of Lascelles's daughter Jenny, who later married Emsley Carr.

By 1897 Carr was badly in need of additional editorial staff and he recruited as his right-hand man Robert Berrey, also from the *Western Mail* office in Cardiff. Berrey was a man of many talents and interests. According to contemporaries, he was a prolific writer who personally produced most of the stories in the paper. 'His personalized reporting was one of the greatest contributions to the early success of the *News of the World*,' Reginald Bezzant, circulation manager at the time, later recalled. 'We could never have sold the paper as we did had the contents not been so good as they were.'

Carr edited the paper from a tiny room in the Whitefriars Street premises. It was a dark and narrow room with a single window looking on to the well of the building. Behind a screen in one corner was a small antiquated washbasin on a metal stand, with a water jug beneath it – an example of the austere and primitive facilities in the building. The dark nature of the room's furnishings did nothing to improve its sombre character, which was in contrast to the nature and personality of its occupant. Lining the walls were heavy Victorian bookcases and shelves, containing the volumes that formed the nucleus of the newspaper's library, established when the paper moved to Bouverie Street in 1932. Not surprisingly, Carr spent much of his time in the attic room occupied by the rest of the slender editorial staff.

Carr was able to spread himself when the move was made to Bouverie Street. In his more spacious quarters there he would give dinner parties on Saturday nights when the paper had been 'put to bed', at which the edition and its contents would be discussed with the small, select group of his staff who were invited, sometimes augmented by a distinguished visitor or contributor.

He also liked one of his family to be present at these dinner parties, since he desperately hoped his sons would follow him into the business. This could never have been achieved during the lifetime of Riddell, who strongly resisted the recruitment of sons of members of the staff. As they grew up, three of his sons – Walter (nicknamed Wash), Horace (known as Harry) and William, who did eventually become chairman – took it in turns to attend. There were six sons altogether: one had been killed in the First World War and two others had no interest in newspapers.

Emsley Carr was a proud family man who delighted in entertaining at weekend parties at his Walton-on-the-Hill home, when it was not unusual for twenty or more members of the family to sit down to lunch or dinner. So close-knit were they that anyone from outside who happened by invitation to penetrate such an occasion was regarded by some members of the family almost as an intruder. Those attending had much to occupy their leisure time: there were squash and tennis courts, a putting green and a cricket pitch in the grounds and the Walton Heath golf course nearby.

Like Lord Riddell, Carr became an almost fanatical golfer, having been introduced to the game by Duncan Parlane, one of the early recruits to the then small editorial staff. In turn, he and Riddell – with the help of James Braid, the professional – taught politicians such as Lloyd George and Winston Churchill to play.

That Emsley Carr was ever an optimist about the state of the newspaper industry and its problems, particularly in the troubled 1930s, is apparent from his presidential address to the annual conference of the Institute of Journalists in 1932, held appropriately in Cardiff. It took place in a year when a number of long-established papers had closed and unemployment, particularly among journalists, was rife. Saddened as he and his colleagues were at these events in the industry at large, he advised against regarding the future of newspapers with dark foreboding. Indeed, on the contrary he exhibited an amazing prescience about future developments.

'If I were asked to give a forecast of what will happen fifty years hence, I should hazard the opinion that the changes will be as radical as those which have taken place during the last generation,' he said.

He went on to demonstrate sheer clairvoyance in his view of the future: 'I can see a vast change for the better in production and material,' he said. 'I see larger and brighter papers.

And I see the introduction not only of coloured supplements, but the advancement of illustration by means of photogravure, colour and additional line and artistic work. The art of publishing will be improved by the extensive use of the aeroplane. Wireless and television will be a commonplace both for news and pictures, and speeding up in mechanical production will be followed by a further development of worldwide news.'

Another facet he dealt with was the competition of broadcasting, then in its infancy. 'It would be absurd to deny the power of broadcasting but so far as this country is concerned I do not think broadcasting will materially affect the position of the newspaper press . . . The spoken word will never replace the printed word,' he confidently predicted.

Carr was honoured by being invited to be president of the Institute of Journalists for a second year. This coincided with the greatest outbreak of competitive warfare the newspaper industry had ever faced, in which there was not only bitter personal and professional rivalry but the expenditure of vast sums of money in a hectic race for circulation. Carr firmly believed that this should have been spent on better management and production of newspapers and improving journalistic conditions rather than squandered on what he called 'this insane competition'.

On the death of Lord Riddell in 1934 Emsley Carr, who had increased his holding by buying some of the Riddell shares, added to his editorial responsibilities by becoming chairman and joint managing director (with H.H. Aldridge, who had joined the staff as a clerk in 1900 and became successively circulation manager, general manager and, later, chairman).

Carr and Riddell, although long-standing colleagues who had brought the paper to its invincible position, inevitably had their differences. Carr resented Riddell's attempts at editorial interference – after one clash Carr got up from his chair and told Riddell: 'Either I edit this paper or you do' – and his insistence that sons should not succeed fathers in the company, which was restrictive to the Carr family. Riddell had also pursued a 'liquidity' policy in the years when he had been responsible for the company's finances. He refused to invest profits and, after the payment of dividends, substantial amounts accumulated in the bank. Under Emsley Carr's chairmanship the first limited attempts at diversification were made.

Although business activities occupied more of his time and his final years were dogged by indifferent health, he never lost his grip on the editorial duties of his office. He became more of a presiding editor while his deputy, Major Percy Davies, carried out the detailed editorial work. But it was Carr's proud boast that he remained a working journalist and, as if to prove it, he wrote the leading article which appeared on the Sunday before his death on 31 July 1941.

The paper he had edited for so long printed his obituary surrounded by heavy black lines.

> Sir Emsley possessed all the human virtues and more abundantly those of kindliness, generosity and forbearance. If Sir Emsley Carr was endowed with the human virtues, he had in unrivalled measure the attributes of the outstanding journalist too. His fingers were always on the pulse of the people. He sensed what they wanted in general news, in 'features', and in serial stories. His judgement was never wrong.

One of his lifelong contemporaries later said of him: 'In the face of fierce competition we of the *News of the World* became a close-knit and very hard-working team. Emsley Carr gave us high morale. He had very strong principles and one of them was that everything about the *News of the World* was always right. Nothing we did could ever be wrong. And he made the whole staff believe that.'

Although the paper was to advance and conquer fresh peaks, his death was the end of an era for the *News of the World*. It was also the beginning of the decline of a newspaper dynasty.

SEVEN

Old Characters, New Ideas

By the turn of the century the paper was beginning to advance in both circulation and profit. The editorial changes produced a more relaxed presentation in contrast to the earlier pomposity and heaviness. 'The proprietors modernized it, not without some loss of sedateness', one commentator at the time wrote.

The scales had begun to swing in its favour by the time Lascelles Carr died in 1902. The staff at this time, though small in number, were invariably men of many talents and interests as well as journalistic expertise and enterprise. It was an era in which Fleet Street abounded in Bohemian characters, of whom the *News of the World* had its share.

Robert Berrey, the editorial man of all trades, specialized in military matters and wrote books on gallant deeds and famous battles. Berrey was noted for his journalistic versatility: he had an enviable adaptability, reporting on many subjects, including crime. On Saturdays he would present the duty inspector at Scotland Yard with a bottle of whisky, which brought in return a rich harvest of otherwise unobtainable detail. He also had an ability to work at speed. He was recognized as the busiest man in the office, working long hours – on Saturdays from noon to 10.00 a.m. the following morning.

Berrey was quickly on the scene when news reached the *News of the World* office about 8.00 p.m. on a Friday evening in December 1897 of the murder of William Terriss, the actor, at the stage door of the Adelphi Theatre in the Strand. It had been announced from the footlights that no performance would be possible that evening as Mr Terriss had met with an accident.

The news was too late for the London evening papers, but the *News of the World* that evening was able to bring out one of its special editions containing the first intimation of the famous actor's violent death. Terriss was a popular stage hero, the father of the Gaiety girl, Ellaline Terriss, and his murder caused a tremendous sensation. His assassin, an out-of-work actor who had been refused relief by a panel of the Actors' Benevolent Fund, of which Terriss had been a member, took his revenge by stabbing Terriss several times as he arrived at the theatre.

The special halfpenny edition was quickly selling in the West End briefly giving the news, followed by a fuller story written by Berrey from the scene of the attack. A third edition on the Saturday had a drawing of the accused in the dock at Bow Street court and two columns recording the actor's career. By the time the special Sunday edition was produced the story had been built up to occupy an entire page.

Berrey was described as 'the greatest scoop merchant of his day'. A later editor of the paper, Arthur G. Waters, recalled as a young reporter accompanying Berrey on a late-night murder story at Redhill, Surrey, an experience that illustrates the degree of respect and friendly cooperation he enjoyed with the police. His inquiries complete and his report sketched out, Berrey was alarmed to find the telephone lines dead when he tried to telephone his report to the office. A helpful police inspector explained that the local telephone exchange was operated by two maiden ladies from their home. Berrey and his young colleague rushed there and with difficulty managed to rouse the two ladies. 'Madam, are you aware the police station is burning down?' Berrey lied. 'We have been trying to get you on the phone for twenty minutes.'

'Heavens above,' one of them replied, and restored communications.

After doubling back to the police station, they found the inspector already phoning over the story for them. It was printed and selling on the streets by the time they got back to London.

Outside his journalistic work Berrey was described as an easy-going Bohemian character and something of a man-about-town, particularly interested in the music halls that were then enjoying much popularity. Boxing was another of his interests and at one time he promoted contests in East London where the future champion and later a popular *News of the World* contributor Jimmy Wilde fought under his auspices.

The paper itself capitalized on the popularity of family sing-songs around the piano, a by-product of the music hall era, by publishing each week a song featured on the halls. The first, which appeared at the end of January 1898, was 'Our Lodger's Such a Nice Young Man', a song that was written and composed by Fred Murray and Laurence Barclay, and sung in the music halls by Vesta Victoria. A notice announcing the new feature said:

> Music halls were never more popular than they are today and music hall ditties were never more widely sung. For this reason, we have arranged with Messrs Francis Day and Hunter to publish a series of the most popular songs of the day. The series will include both comic and senti-mental ditties, these being amongst the latest and most successful introductions of the different artistes who are singing them.

Berrey also assisted in this feature by touring the London music halls in search of likely material. The works manager at the time, William Crafter, who was also interested in concert work, would often accompany Berrey on his quest for suitable songs. Crafter, a small dapper man with a high-pitched voice, sported a long and neatly waxed moustache, typical of the period. Familiarly known as 'Little Willie' Crafter because of his small stature – his height was under five feet – he was a live-wire character whose authority, despite his diminutive size, was never breached and who was much respected by his staff.

In its early days Crafter was put in charge of the song feature; a piano was installed in one of the offices so that music hall artistes could visit the office and try out suitable songs. Marie Lloyd and George Robey were among the stars who came to the office to try out new material. None of them received a fee of more than £10 but, of course, publication of one of their songs brought invaluable publicity. A couple of performers, the Darnley Brothers, were taken on the paper's payroll and one of them, Herbert Darnley, was given the title of 'musical editor'. The advent of ragtime eventually made it necessary to invite the music publishing trade to supply material and the music section in the office was then disbanded.

As an offshoot, the company engaged for a time in sheet music publication. Darnley obtained and entered into contracts with music hall artistes and songwriters as well as other music publishers, and song albums were also published.

The half-page feature in the paper ran without interruption for almost fifty years, despite an attempt by Lord Riddell in the early 1930s to have it dropped on the grounds that few people played the piano and musical evenings were then a thing of the past. Emsley Carr, resenting this interference in editorial affairs, strongly resisted – to drop it would lose half a million circulation, he claimed – and the feature continued until 1942 when newsprint restrictions, wartime conditions and changing musical tastes no longer justified its continuation. It was one of the paper's most memorable features. Forty years after its demise older readers would recall it nostalgically, some even writing to inquire if it could be restored.

Helping Berrey after the paper's move to Whitefriars Street was Duncan Parlane, a painstaking Scot who encouraged both Riddell and Emsley Carr to take up golf. A man of fine physique who stood 6 foot 4 inches, he later became the paper's drama critic, in addition to other editorial tasks. Parlane was not dependent on his journalistic earnings: he had private means and his investments in the Canadian salmon canning industry enabled him to retire, by then a portly figure, at the age of 54.

Court reports even then formed much of the staple of the paper. Those from London courts were often illustrated by line drawings by Edward (Ned) Smythe and from 1908 onwards he was frequently accompanied on his tours of the courts by an Irish journalist, William Ryan, who wrote the text to accompany Smythe's drawings, as well as dealing with foreign news and writing leaders. Both men were invariably immaculately attired in glossy silk hats and frock coats, and made an impressive sight as they perambulated between the courts. Ryan was the most courteous of men: he would even ask the office boy 'Would you mind?' whenever he required the lad's services. In his spare time 'Paddy' Ryan also found time to write a number of historical novels.

On the management side, Edgar Fifoot, the general manager, was another rather eccentric character, ever intent on saving the company's money – he always travelled on public transport rather than take a taxi – and amassed a vast bank balance for the company, as well as for himself through taking, as a young man, shares in the company in return for a modest loan on an occasion when money was particularly tight. He occupied a tiny room on the first floor which doubled as the boardroom once a month for meetings of the directors. At the side was a boxroom occupied by the cashier. The clerks, then numbering no more than half a dozen, had a room on the ground floor. One of them was H.H. Aldridge, another who benefited from receiving shares in lieu of a loan, and who subsequently became managing director and chairman of the company. Aldridge had joined the clerical staff as a youth on Mafeking night, 1900, and, like the journalists, performed a variety of tasks from bookkeeping to publicity – and even did some editorial work, reporting football matches at Chelsea and wrestling at Olympia.

The presses, over which 'Little Willie' Crafter, another beneficiary of shares, reigned, was in the basement, and the publisher, Mr R.B. Humphris, who had worked for the Bells, had a small office in a corner of the warehouse.

To promote the paper and recruit agents to sell it, an outdoor staff was built up with offices in Cardiff, Birmingham,

Manchester, Liverpool and Newcastle, and one man covering the South of England. Riddell was keen on circulation stunts, in which both management and editorial staff took part, and although some of his more extreme ideas proved impractical, those that were realistic he pursued tenaciously.

He introduced treasure hunts in which tubes containing fifty gold sovereigns were hidden in various places and clues were given in the paper. Lucky finders also discovered with the sovereigns a note saying that if they took them to the *News of the World* office, they would receive another £50. Thousands took part but Riddell's suspicious nature led him to dislike the idea. 'It seems to me,' he muttered darkly to the reporters one day, 'that some of these sovereigns are being found before they are hidden.'

There was a Popular Barmaids Competition, which may have been responsible for the paper becoming known as the 'Barmaids' Bible'. The barmaid who got the most votes won a bicycle, which was hung in the bar, festooned with ribbons. It was said that some of the *News of the World* staffmen got to know some of the barmaids rather well.

Racing and cricket competitions were also launched and another innovation was an early form of football pools, in which winners had to forecast entrants and scores.

A limerick competition joined the weekly song as a regular feature in June 1907: readers had to exercise their skill by submitting the final punch line of the limerick. The first one read:

> A cricketing peer named Lord Hawke,
> Who hails from the county of York,
> With two of the best
> Picked the team for the 'Test'
> . . . .

There was a sixpenny (2½p) entrance fee, which raised £4,000 for distribution to the winning entries. Riddell's rule with all competitions was that they must be self-supporting.

His theories about publicity were based on a policy of constant repetition of the name of the paper, and to this end he had large enamel nameplates erected at about 15,000 sites all over the country. He had handbills printed declaiming 'The *News of the World* – best Sunday newspaper' and even went around distributing them himself.

During the first five years of the Riddell–Carr partnership the paper laid the foundations – editorially and commercially – on which it established its own particular character and interests: news coverage, crime, politics, court reports (especially divorce hearings), and sport. In its features, competitions with a strong reader participation were prominent, together with life stories and serials. It was a recipe for success that sought to amuse and reflect the interests of the ordinary men and women who made up its growing readership.

At the turn of the century revenue from circulation represented seventy-five per cent of the paper's total income. Advertising was taking up on average forty per cent of the available space in the paper. Emsley Carr thought this was too much and sought to get the paper increased in size to an eight-column width so that the amount of news could be extended and a regular ratio of advertising to news established. 'An eight-column paper would give us a fine and imposing sheet,' he successfully pleaded, 'and it will also enable us to boast of again having the largest Sunday paper in Great Britain'.

The general election of 1910 provides a good illustration of the *News of the World* policy of providing the latest news for its readers. In an age when the declaration of election results was spread over a much longer period than is now the case, the paper went to extraordinary lengths to ensure that as comprehensive a list of the results as possible was given in the election special. To record all the Saturday declarations, dozens of printing offices throughout the country were used to produce special supplements in which election figures were inserted by newsagents.

Much enterprise and ingenuity was exercised to keep the

paper forging ahead of its rivals, but often there were unforeseen difficulties. A rail strike in the summer of 1911 inconveniently flared up at short notice, creating a situation that called for quick reactions to organize the delivery of supplies. Motor transport was still in its infancy but there was no alternative to distribution of all the papers by road – a formidable task since the circulation of the *News of the World* was by now over 2 million.

All manner of different forms of transport had to be found: vans, cars, steam motor buses – even car chassis with improvised open platforms – were brought into service in a major exercise the like of which had never before been undertaken. When the odd mixture of vehicles was assembled, it stretched the length of Bouverie Street, Temple Avenue and along the Embankment in one direction and along Fleet Street to the Law Courts in the other. The mixed fleet was fully extended: the steam-driven buses, for instance, were intended only for short trips in and around London but were now forced into undertaking journeys of two or three hundred miles. In most cases they reached their destinations, although many made the return journey with considerable difficulty.

The experience provided a valuable essay in the possibilities of distribution by road transport and much that was learned on that occasion helped to smooth out difficulties when another rail strike occurred in 1919.

In its self-advertising, the company was also quick to appreciate the publicity potential of the infant film industry. Just before the outbreak of the First World War the paper serialized *The Epics of Elaine*, which had been made into a silent film starring Pearl White. The paper's publicity for the serial was screened in almost every cinema in the country for a period of weeks, just one of a number of instances in which film was used as a publicity weapon for serials that ran in the papers.

EIGHT

'An Uncommonly Good Paper'

A 'stop press' item in a special Sunday evening edition on 28 June 1914 reported the assassination at Sarajevo of the heir to the Austrian throne, Archduke Ferdinand, and his wife – the prelude to the First World War.

The subsequent hostilities brought respectability to Sunday newspapers. The events in Europe created a public thirst for news which the Sunday papers helped to quench. The *News of the World* printed special Sunday afternoon and evening bulletins containing the official communiqués. It was achieved in the early months of the war often with much difficulty since some of the wartime leaders were reluctant to disclose what was happening and news from the front line was often sparse.

Earl Kitchener, the War Minister, showed little or no regard for newspaper deadlines when it came to issuing his daily bulletin which, in any event, was invariably brief almost to the point of being evasive. Often all it said was, to coin what became a notable phrase, 'All quiet on the Western Front.'

But the public, through their newspapers, demanded to know more about events and of their relatives who were engaged in them. Kitchener even resisted attempts by Lord Riddell, on behalf of all the newspapers, to seek an interview with him to discuss the unfortunate situation and how it might be rectified. Totally frustrated by Kitchener's attitude, Riddell camped in the corridor outside his room in the War Office for an entire day. 'I'm not going to see you,' Kitchener told him when he eventually emerged.

Riddell retorted, 'We can't keep the public quiet. I can tell you, from their letters they must have news or they'll storm the government.' Kitchener appeared not to hear and brushed him aside.

Soon afterwards Kitchener drowned when his ship was sunk while on the way to Russia. Thereafter, official attitudes to the release of war news changed.

Every week the *News of the World* sent consignments of newspapers to the troops in France, a gesture that built up a reservoir of goodwill towards the paper that extended into the post-war period and laid foundations for the continuous family readership that helped it maintain its large circulation.

The ending of the earlier virtual ban on war news enabled the paper to publish war maps with arrows showing how hostilities were proceeding. One of these, illustrating how German forces were being contained, was adopted by the government and translated into several languages for widespread distribution abroad.

With a much reduced staff, production was severely strained to meet the demand when circulation increased as the war progressed. The printing plant could not be expanded, and even more problematic was the shortage of newsprint.

The proprietors had foreseen the newsprint difficulties when war was declared and reduced the size of the paper to conserve supplies. Stocks were necessarily limited because of storage problems, although emergency accommodation was found in arches and vaults under Holborn Viaduct and elsewhere. Paper manufactured by British mills was carefully controlled and imports were allowed only under licence. Newspapers became importers as well as consumers, chartering their own ships to transport paper supplies: in 1916 the *News of the World* joined with Edward Hulton and Co. Ltd in chartering the vessel *Heliopolis* to make two round trips to Newfoundland, carrying Cornish china clay on the outward voyage and returning with a cargo of newsprint. Both voyages were successfully completed, although on the second trip the ship ran aground on rocks near Fowey (eventually refloated under her own steam). This venture augmented newsprint supplies by a further 4,000 tons at a period of extreme scarcity.

Wartime conditions brought inevitable increases in materials and other costs, and the price of the paper went up in March 1918 to 1½d, the first alteration since 1880.

The paper's popularity, evidenced by the growing demand for it during the war, was due to many factors, but in large part must have been thanks to its optimism and reliability. Week after week the paper cheerfully and confidently looked forward to victory; at the same time it presented a faithful and accurate view of the wartime situation.

It consistently expressed concern for the welfare of British servicemen, both in editorial articles and in practical ways such as providing instruments and other items contributed by readers for the comfort and entertainment of the troops.

A more unusual contribution was the recruitment of thousands of pigeons for the use of the Army and Navy intelligence services. Readers responded to an appeal in the paper for the supply of birds for lofts in Britain and on the front line, and the paper's Pigeon Editor, A. H. Osman, was appointed head of the government's pigeon service, with the rank of colonel.

The paper's concern about the welfare of troops in wartime continued after the signing of the Armistice and much space was devoted to the question of war pensions and related matters. Extra staff had to be recruited to process the enormous volume of inquiries: it was estimated that over 200,000 letters were dealt with and it was not unusual to receive more than a thousand in a single delivery. In most cases it was possible to help, either by proffering advice, putting readers in touch with the appropriate agency, or passing on information they could not get for themselves. Besides answering particular inquiries, informative articles were written explaining the various provisions of the pensions regulations.

The queries often disclosed the existence of general grievances, and sometimes hardship, on which the paper made representations to the pensions or other government departments which effected reforms in administration. The volume of correspondence revealed other worries about legal and medical matters on which expert advice was obtained as well as on

national insurance and rent problems. It was the beginning of
a number of reader services which played a significant part in
the paper's popularity in future years.

The rise of Sunday journalism was becoming a striking
phenomenon of the time: the wartime interest was maintained, rivalry was rampant and this led to constant striving
to keep a step ahead. Post-war Sunday papers had to be different from their daily colleagues: their readers had more time
to peruse the contents for one thing and demanded entertaining adjuncts to the latest news in the feature areas of the
paper.

The *News of the World* had already made a reputation for its
reports of divorce hearings: the more aristocratic the participants the greater the interest of the largely working-class
readership. Such cases were reported with a mass of detail, in
line with the paper's policy of concentrating largely on court
reports. The sensational reports helped confirm working-class
views of the immorality of the upper classes.

When the Judicial Proceedings (Regulation of Reports) Act,
which restricted divorce-reporting – and which Riddell had
voted in favour of in the House of Lords – became law in 1926,
many people, particularly the *News of the World*'s competitors,
believed its inability to continue reporting such cases in detail
would bring about a decline in its circulation. But this didn't
prove to be the case. By then divorce had become less of an
upper-class luxury and was something of which the middle
classes could also take advantage, and the paper continued to
build up its reputation, as well as its circulation, with its generous weekly offering of the more salacious and quirky misdeeds
of offenders in the police courts, especially those of a sexual
nature.

Whenever its concentration on the sleazier side of life was
criticized, both Carr and Riddell would spring to defend their
policy by pointing out that they not only reported the crime
but also the punishment, indicating a strong belief in the deterrent effect on others of such reports.

While the more lurid aspects of life were aired unashamedly, the paper honestly believed that as long as the punishments for these lapses were always recorded, together with any judicial admonitions, it was exercising a preventive power. Aldridge would recall a conversation he witnessed between Riddell and a subscriber who had likened the *News of the World* to the Old Testament in as much as it recorded crime. Lord Riddell retorted that it was like the Old Testament in as much as it recorded punishment. 'That is why in certain cases upon which we have been commended by the courts the readers are educated into many things which they ought not to do,' said Aldridge.

They made no secret of the fact that their paper relied on crime, especially crime involving sex, for its popular appeal. The activities revealed in the courts were the raw material of the paper's success, and in processing it there was no pretence of any spurious glamour attaching to the actors in the drama: it was straightforward, sober reporting – a record of what was said in court, the sentence imposed by the judge and, hopefully, any denunciation of sin he might utter.

'The *News of the World* is a newspaper unlike any other', wrote one commentator on the press. 'It has built up a consistent editorial policy of reporting a wide range of subjects in a way that will appeal to the masses. It is world-famed for the liberal coverage it gives to crime cases but none of these stories is over-written or presented in a "sensationalist" manner . . .'

A glance at the headlines in earlier issues gives a strong flavour of the paper's content:

ORGANIST AND GIRL
Distinguished Musician in Grave Scandal
Charge of Giving Drugs to Lady Pupil

BARMAID'S SUICIDE
A Landlord's Startling Discovery
Severe Reflections on the Men of Reigate

BROKEN LOVE VOWS
£25 for a Jilted Nurse
'Pleasant Dreams' and Picture Postcards

SOCIETY SENSATION
An Ex-MP's Married Life
Wife's Allegations

The reports of hearings extending over several days were built up from all available sources into a comprehensive chronological account of the entire case.

Even some of its court reports contained superb descriptive writing. The graphic account of the trial of Arthur Rouse, the murderer, concludes:

> The black cap is adjusted on the head of Mr Justice Talbot, the law is spoken in a court hushed and reverent, and with the words 'May the Lord have mercy' Rouse turns and goes with rapid strides from view. From the public seats comes the cry, 'Oh Arthur, Arthur!' It is the end.

On historic national occasions, such as coronations, the descriptive writing in its reports was in the grand manner. Headlines in the 1902 Coronation issue patriotically proclaimed: THE KING IS CROWNED! LONG LIVE THE KING. A large drawing of the scene in Westminster Abbey 'sketched by our special artist' adorned the front page. The artist must have had an exhausting day: inside pages contained nine other sketches of processions and highlights of the ceremony.

Although sex-crime stories were what the paper became chiefly associated with in the public mind, there was more to the paper. Its sensational court-reporting was counterbalanced with feature articles on important topics in the fields of politics, foreign affairs and economic matters, and regular commentaries on the Westminster scene written by leading political figures of the period. It was a formula by which, as another observer of the contemporary newspaper scene recorded, the paper was 'supplying pornography on the one hand and acquiring prestige on the other'.

The editorial recipe of serious comment allied to sensational crime news continued to work successfully, although the paper had its detractors who criticized the formula. Some thought it sanctimonious and hypocritical to chronicle the sexual indiscretions of scoutmasters and curates on the one hand while attaining an aura of respectability through the more serious contributions of statesmen, archbishops and judges on the other.

The paper had its own distinctive and genteel vocabulary in its reporting which left much to the imagination and appears archaic compared with the outspokenness of later generations: couples did not indulge in sexual intercourse but 'intimacy took place'; women were 'molested' rather than raped; they were not sexually interfered with but 'their clothing was disarranged'. In accounts of investigations into sexual scandals, in the best traditions of prurient tabloid journalism, the investigative reporter, having obtained his evidence by posing as a prospective client, would at the crucial moment 'make his excuses and leave'; regular use helped to turn that expression into a national catchphrase.

Whatever its critics might say about its content, the paper's record circulation, which crept up irresistibly year after year, was a phenomenon that was constantly being placed under the searching spotlight of commentators, sociologists and psychologists attempting to explain the elements of its incredible success.

'Of all newspapers most properly described as a National Institution, the *News of the World* has an appeal which baffles analysis,' said one commentator. 'It airs the sordid unabashed but privately believes in its preventive power.' This belief was given added credence by the views of a psychologist who said she believed the detailed reporting of court cases was a deterrent to crime – the *News of the World* was 'one of the most moral newspapers in the world: it always presents the facts of the cases and – what is equally important – it tells you the punishment.'

Baffling though it might be to ascertain and explain its appeal, there was no shortage of volunteers to attempt to do so. And interest was not confined to Britain alone. It was international. The head of a public relations agency thought the paper had achieved its position because 'It is so intensely human and pursues human interest with relentless determination wherever it may be found.' He continued:

It doesn't neglect the larger events in the world of international politics and economics, but to most readers these are of infinitely less absorbing interest than the strange happenings next door. If every Sunday morning the paper has become part and parcel of the day of rest it is because it gives the public what it wants to read.

What was never criticized, but was often praised, was the quality and accuracy of its reporting. A leading judge once described the *News of the World* as his trade paper; a famous Home Office pathologist whose professional work was frequently reported in its pages wrote that 'For fine straightforward factual reporting you cannot get it better than in the *News of the World*.'

And a famous Fleet Street character, R.D. Blumenfeld, for many years the distinguished editor of the *Daily Express*, wrote in the 1930s: 'The fact is that the *News of the World* is an uncommonly good newspaper; always has been, and aside from its business management is about as perfect as any organization can be made.'

While lawyers and others praised the paper's reliable and factual reportage, particularly of crime, the paper also endeared itself to some of the criminal classes themselves, many of whom established contact with members of the editorial staff. These relationships, none of them in any way illicit, often paid dividends through tip-offs leading to an exclusive story.

On numerous occasions criminals entrusted to the *News of*

the World confessions of their misdeeds. A notorious example was that of the double murderer Dr Buck Ruxton in the 1930s.

Norman Rae, the paper's crime reporter, was sent to Moffat where, in a ravine beside the main Carlisle–Edinburgh road, the gruesome discovery had been made of the mutilated bodies of two people, believed at first to be a man and a woman, wrapped in newspapers and contained in a number of parcels. The newspapers provided a valuable clue: they included a series of pictures of bathing beauties at the Morecambe Carnival from a paper that had circulated in only a small area. Rae deliberately withdrew from the press corps and was replaced by the paper's northern reporter: he then set off for the Morecambe area where he quickly picked up local gossip about the alleged disappearance of Isobel Ruxton, the wife of a Lancaster doctor, and her maid, Mary Rogerson. At that stage no serious view was taken of their absence, since Mrs Ruxton had threatened to leave on other occasions.

The doctor and his wife were an unusual mixture for that era: he was a Parsee and she a Scot. Rae frequently talked to Ruxton and became convinced he had something to do with the gruesome finds at Moffat. His wife, Ruxton told him, had gone to visit her sister in Edinburgh and the maid had left because she was pregnant. Rae questioned forty of the doctor's patients and found he had given different versions of the reason for his wife's absence: some reported hearing arguments between them, others that the doctor had been having bonfires in his garden after her disappearance.

The discovery of a further parcel then caused the pathologists on the case to change their view: the bodies, they said, were of two women after all. Inquiries eventually led to Ruxton's arrest and he was charged with the murder of the two women. Throughout his eleven-day trial he protested his innocence, but was found guilty and sentenced to death.

Rae described Ruxton as 'a nice little chap', polite but nervous and excitable, who, in pre-Health Service days, never inquired before treating his patients as to whether they could afford to pay. Ruxton also wrote to the paper's northern reporter, J.H. Milligan, who had interviewed him on several occasions while Rae was building up his background story. 'I remember well our interview in my library', he wrote. 'Pity! the library is now no more. Only the bare walls of that spacious room now remain to bear mute testimony of my choice treasures.' Another letter to the reporter, written on the eve of his execution, shows the murderer as a devoted father. It requested the reporter to help his solicitor to do all they could for the welfare and education of his children. In it he suggested the sale 'for a fancy price of my Isobel's oil painting in life size' to raise a fund for the children's education. Ruxton described the painting as being 'the talk of the art world', but it proved to be much less valuable than he believed.

On the day he was executed, Norman Rae was outside Strangeways Prison to report the scenes when he was approached by a man who, hiding his face, handed him an envelope, saying: 'Dr Ruxton asked me to give you this.' It was addressed to the editor of the *News of the World*. Back in London, Rae handed it to the editor. Inside was a second envelope containing a slip of paper on which Ruxton had written a five-line confession: 'I killed Mrs Ruxton in a fit of temper because I thought she had been with a man. I was Mad at the time. Mary Rogerson was present at the time. I had to kill her.'

The confession was dated 14 October 1935, the day after he had been arrested. Why did he have to kill the maid? She had unfortunately returned to the house and disturbed him just as he was strangling his wife. Ruxton left his confession to be made public only after his execution because as a Parsee he could not die with a lie on his lips.

NINE

Competition and Expansion

By 1929 the paper had expanded to such an extent that yet another move was necessary. The offices at this time were scattered around Whitefriars Street and Bouverie Street. To bring all departments together a new building was planned and built in Bouverie Street on one of the most historic sites in the City of London.

In its early history the Bouverie Street area had been a monastic retreat for the barefoot Carmelite friars until the suppressions of Henry VIII. It had later become the disreputable resort of ruffians, knaves and libertines – a past that the paper's detractors might well have regarded as an apposite location from which to produce a paper which largely concentrated on recording the sleazier aspects of life.

On the site of the new building 700 years earlier had stood the Priory of Our Lady of Mount Carmel and during the excavations of 1929 the vaulted crypt of the rebuilt late fourteenth-century priory church was discovered. This archaeological gem was preserved beneath the new building. (In the 1980s when the paper moved to Wapping and the 1929 building was demolished, the crypt was hoisted by crane in its entirety and replaced beneath the new office block on the site, where it can be seen by appointment.)

The finest battery of printing presses the world had ever seen was constructed by Messrs R. W. Crabtree and Sons Ltd to print 'The world's greatest and most favourite Sunday newspaper.' The sixty-six units were capable of producing 1,250,000 copies per hour. There was a patriotic pride in the new set-up: only British steel was used in the construction of the building and the plant was entirely British – 'The presses bear all the characteristics of the skill of the British engineer, who has not his equal in the world', shouted the publicity blurbs.

The total cost of the new building and its machinery was £614,726. Riddell's 'Buy British' example had a significant effect on the printing engineering industry. Up to then British manufacturers of printing machinery had found great difficulty in persuading newspaper proprietors that they could produce a rotary printing press equal, if not better than, imported models. Even generous offers to supply presses without any charge and remove them if they were found unsatisfactory were eschewed. Riddell's confidence in the British manufacturers changed the situation dramatically and Crabtree's in particular found themselves the recipients of large orders from other newspapers in this country and abroad and had to enlarge their works in order to cope.

A suitably handsome booklet, with gilt bordering and decorated with gold ribbon, was produced to mark the opening of what it described as 'this Palace of Printing'. The paper's publicists, ever anxious to back up their claims with facts, made the most of this occasion. The floor area, they pointed out, totalled nearly five acres, of which one acre in the basement was occupied by the printing machinery alone, and to meet their insatiable appetite the whole of the first floor would be devoted to the storage of newsprint. The ground floor contained the publicity and dispatch departments, the second housed editorial, advertising, administrative and commercial departments, as well as linotype and composing rooms, and the top floor accommodated a new automatic telephone exchange and left spare room for future expansion.

Lord Birkenhead – formerly F.E. Smith, the flamboyant politician and former Lord Chancellor – contributed a foreword to the booklet in which he shared some of his musings on the benefits of Sunday journalism, the rise of which he described as 'one of the most striking phenomena of our times': tremendous changes had taken place in the contents, size and presentation of Sunday newspapers.

Sunday editors covered a much larger field than their daily colleagues, he wrote.

> They know that a very large proportion of our people spends Sunday perusing not merely the news but such entertaining adjuncts as gossip, political articles, crosswords, sporting forecasts, reviews of books and plays, and the more romantic biographical details of celebrities and notorieties. Where the readers of daily newspapers have barely time to nibble a blade of these pastures, the Sabbatarian reader may browse at will. And what lush meadows are spread before his slippered feet.

He urged improved quality rather than quantity in the contents of Sunday newspapers, suggesting that articles that were closely argued and provoked the reader to sustained thought were certain to find a better prepared audience at weekends than on working days.

'It is this factor', he wrote, 'that seems to me to offer positive proof that the future of Sunday newspapers is the brightest light on the horizon of the journalistic world.'

In the post-war period, competition between newspapers became ever more intensive, culminating in the 1930s in rivalry that reached ruinous proportions, with highly competitive free gift schemes to lure potential readers into taking out a regular subscription.

Newspaper economics in the 1930s were affected by two significant factors: the high cost of competition was one, the other was the increasing cost of newsprint, which was of particular concern to the *News of the World* with its massive circulation. It was the market leader among Sunday newspapers. It was unlike other newspapers. Its consistent editorial policy of reporting in a style that appealed to the masses, linked to the liberal coverage it devoted to scandalous and criminal activities, had consolidated its position. It built on this reputation, expanding its own ideas of public duty and service by offering rewards for the apprehension of criminals and increasing the services it offered to the community.

The advice and information it passed on to its readers was always totally reliable. Allied to this was its independent editorial viewpoint, its recruitment of leading personalities to contribute features, its serialization of memoirs and its sponsorship and unsurpassed coverage of sporting events. Nevertheless, its position as leader in its field did not allow room for any complacency.

It had pioneered the offer of free insurance to readers and this became an acceptable form of newspaper competition during the 1920s. The insurance companies did not object to the competition this innovation generated: indeed, many of them derived profitable business from examining and arbitrating on claims on behalf of newspapers.

Less acceptable though was the increasing practice of canvassing for readers. In 1933 it was estimated there were 5,000 canvassers plodding through towns and villages of Britain knocking on doors in search of new subscribers to the papers they represented, often by discrediting their rivals and playing on sympathy, especially of women who answered their calls, with pleas of personal poverty and sorrow.

Julius Elias (later Lord Southwood), then owner of the *Sunday People*, the main rival to the *News of the World*, combined both operations by stealthily engaging teams of canvassers to knock on doors in areas well away from London, seeking to persuade readers to change their allegiance in return for the offer of free insurance cover and other inducements.

Canvassing was a practice the *News of the World* did not favour, according to Reginald Bezzant, circulation manager at the time, but they were forced to join in when the progress of their rival was observed. Bezzant noted that the *News of the World* started canvassing in 1928 and continued, with varying degrees of management enthusiasm, until 1939. He reckoned to have spent in that period £940,000 on canvassing alone. 'At times I had as many as a hundred teams of canvassers out in the field, each team consisting of ten men and a supervisor,' he recalled. 'Sometimes the number of teams fell to as low as twenty, according to the mood of the management.'

Elias's free insurance undoubtedly boosted the circulation of *The People* and in turn helped finance his losses on the *Daily Herald*, but it was never enough to catch up with the *News of the World*, especially when a fresh rival emerged in a rejuvenated *Sunday Pictorial*.

What the management of the *News of the World* regarded as the worst evil of all in this circulation battle was the offer of free gifts as incentives to potential readers. 'I am not opposed to any legitimate form of enterprise,' Sir Emsley Carr declared. 'But is there anyone who will admit that a free distribution of washing machines, pyjamas, pillowcases, silk stockings, fountain pens and even more elaborate gifts, such as gold wristlet watches, to capture any and every body, is consonant with the traditions of British journalism?'

Money was being squandered on these 'suicidal schemes' which should rightly have been used for the further legitimate advancement of the newspapers, which were then on the threshold of important technological developments.

The real function of journalism, Sir Emsley said, was not to encroach upon the pastures of others; not to give away what others were selling; not to increase circulation by telling hard-luck stories of poverty and degradation; but 'to present a true picture of world affairs, of news both local and general, and to present it with the highest possible standard of accuracy and attractiveness'.

From his hot seat at the time, Bezzant described these inter-war years as 'the most hectic years for newspaper circulation departments they have ever experienced – and possibly ever will experience'.

Again Lord Southwood had been responsible for initiating the practice of offering inducements and began to extend to the Sunday newspaper scene the expensively chaotic state of affairs then current among the popular daily papers.

Lord Riddell was infuriated at this development and appeared at his most ruthless in his counteraction. He

instructed Bezzant to rent two empty shops, one in Nottingham and one in Leicester, which were filled with all manner
of items from egg-whisks and saucepans to school satchels.
Any one of these gifts was distributed free to any reader of the
News of the World who presented the heading of the paper
cut out from the previous Sunday's issue. The response was
phenomenal and Riddell threatened to open other shops
elsewhere.

Riddell and Elias were formidable opponents, each unyield-
ing and defiant in their determination. But it was a costly
and suicidal course on which to embark. Riddell taunted Elias,
urging him to do better if he could. 'I'm quite ready to break
myself – after you,' he threatened. There were bitter wrangles
within the NPA. Eventually Riddell's counteraction resulted in
a truce. Discussions were immediately arranged with all the
Sunday paper proprietors and an agreement reached between
them curbing the offer of free gifts for circulation purposes.
The same unanimity did not extend to the daily papers. Their
snatching of readers from one another with the lure of gifts
continued unabated: it took the outbreak of war to stop it.

Competition among the Sundays in other ways was, however, maintained as fiercely as ever. Door to door canvassing
reached its peak just prior to the Second World War. It was
costing the News of the World £200,000 a year to combat the
attacks of its competitors who, it was estimated, were spending
nearly five times that amount in the doorstep battle for readers.
It was regarded by Emsley Carr as 'useless and extravagant
expenditure'.

Parallel with this expense was the ever-increasing cost of
newsprint, a crippling burden on newspaper finances. The size
of the News of the World's demand for newsprint – 800 tons
a week in 1938 – enabled the company to negotiate more
favourable terms than their competitors, some of whom were
forced to divert expenditure away from the costly canvassing
as a result. Newspaper control at the outbreak of war, rather
than self-regulation, finally brought an end to canvassing.

Another form of rivalry was competitions in which readers

could participate: these were approved as long as they were conducted on fair and legitimate lines. Special departments were set up to run them and think up new ideas. They provided readers, it was felt, with some relief from the cares and worries of ordinary life as well as giving them a chance of winning a substantial prize.

Bezzant was the inspiration behind several promotional gimmicks. He derived from his wife, who was one of a family of ten, the idea of sending willow-pattern trays to the mothers of ten children. Another of his schemes was to send readers celebrating their golden wedding a tray, decorated with blue birds and inscribed 'The Blue Bird of Happiness Lives at Home'. And it was Bezzant who could claim to be the first man to put advertisements on book matches. He got this idea from watching the paper's publisher, who appeared endlessly to be striking matches to relight his pipe: how many matches did he strike in a year and how many other pipe-smoking men were there like him? pondered Bezzant.

Editorially they were also highly competitive days. In 1928 the paper played a leading part in the arrest of the murderers of PC Reginald Gutteridge, who was shot and killed at Stapleford Abbots, Essex. His colleagues were frustrated in bringing the murderers to justice and the *News of the World* offered a reward of £1,000 for information leading to the conviction of the culprits. At the request of the police the reward was later doubled and within a couple of days Scotland Yard received the valuable information they required which led to the conviction and subsequent execution of two men who committed the crime. The information had come from an ex-convict to whom the reward was paid.

It was not only the memoirs of murderers for which the paper had become renowned: the life story of the notorious financier and entrepreneur Horatio Bottomley was one of the worthwhile autobiographies the paper published and the fields of entertainment and sport provided a rich harvest of memoirs over the years, with Gracie Fields, George Robey, Robert Donat, Gary Cooper, Ivor Novello, Clark Gable, Sam Goldwyn and Walt Disney, together with boxers Jimmy Wilde and Tommy Farr, jockey Steve Donaghue, cricketer Don Bradman, and Edgar Wallace, the thriller writer, among the scores of celebrities whose experiences were seized upon and serialized.

Two days after the outbreak of the Second World War, Sir Emsley Carr was able to report another record year for the company, with the paper's circulation above 4 million. 'If you ask me why we have achieved this position, the answer is simply because we know our business,' he boasted to the annual shareholders' meeting. 'It is run on sound lines by men who have grown up with the business and are masters of their professions.'

TEN

Churchill – C(ontributor)-in-C(hief)

The brightest light in a galaxy of star contributors in the 1930s was Winston Churchill, one of Lord Riddell's wide circle of friends, especially during the war years. Out of political office because of disagreements over Conservative policies – he had also moved from the Liberals – Churchill was in the political wilderness, with much of his time at this period occupied with journalism and other writing: he was producing articles for British and American newspapers and magazines, he was working on his biography of Marlborough, and he was writing for George Newnes, the publishing company with which Riddell was also associated.

Riddell wrote to the statesman and politician in July 1932 inquiring whether the writing of six articles retelling 'The World's Great Stories' would appeal to him. He accepted the invitation. 'It is awfully kind of you to have suggested this; I greatly appreciate it as I still have some unlet space for next year', Churchill wrote to Riddell. 'I do not want to write many articles then, as I have to get on with Marlborough, but these would be agreeable to do and I will manage to fit them in.'

Churchill in turn sought help from Eddie (later Sir Edward) Marsh, who had been his private secretary for many years. He asked Marsh to write 2,500 words on his views of each of the books selected which Churchill used as a foundation after he had reread the books himself. He paid Marsh £25 for each book on which he assisted.

Churchill had been taken ill in Switzerland and on his return in September 1932 he had to remain in bed: he spent much of the enforced rest working on the articles. When he received proofs of the first few, he was unhappy about their presentation. 'Are you really wise in using this fine diamond type for articles for which you have paid such a high fee [Churchill had suggested £2,000 for the English serial rights] and for advertising for which you will no doubt have heavy charges?' he asked Riddell. 'Surely it would be worth printing them a little better. I can hardly read them as they stand.'

However the articles may have looked in type, there was no doubt about the quality of their content. When Churchill delivered the first few articles, Riddell and Carr liked them so much that the original commission was extended to twelve pieces.

Churchill's authorship came in for much praise. Apart from his articles in the newspaper, after his books on Marlborough and the Great War appeared Riddell wrote complimenting him – a letter which has a prescient quality about it in the light of subsequent events.

Marlborough is a monument of industry and literary skill – the author at his best [Riddell wrote]. The *Great War* is doing well and should bring you in some shekels. I am reading it for the second time with much pleasure and profit. From the horrible state of affairs it looks as if someone in the near future will have the task of writing the history of the Second World War – that is, if any inhabitants of Europe are left to purchase the book.

Churchill's own life up to then had been adventurous and fascinating and in August 1934 Riddell was suggesting 'a new and popular story' of his life – 'the matter would have to be popular and suitable for the millions who read the *News of the World*,' he explained somewhat gratuitously.

Riddell, however, never saw the articles. He was too ill to read the proofs of them and died a few days before their publication started at the beginning of 1935.

The proofs were checked by Emsley Carr's deputy, Major Percy Davies, who sat up all one night reading the major articles in their entirety and pronounced them 'a brilliant and highly successful series'.

Churchill wrote an article on the death of King George V, which also earned him much praise. The old statesman Lord Rosebery – 'a detached and instructed critic' – had considered it to be the best written on that solemn occasion. Carr told Churchill it was gratifying to hear that Lord Rosebery had such a high opinion of the article – 'but he is only voicing the views of all Fleet Street'.

The next major series that Churchill contributed was on 'Great Men of Our Time', which appeared early in 1936, followed later in the year by a further series on 'Great Events of Our Time'.

These major serializations were not Churchill's only contributions to the paper. During the troubled times of the 1930s, Churchill in one-off articles took the opportunity to warn, through the paper's massive readership, of the dangers that were then lurking and becoming ever more threatening on the international scene, as he was doing contemporaneously in his public speeches.

He was fortunate in having the benefit of influential friends to give him help and advice, all of which gave added authenticity to the views he expressed. One who vetted scientific detail in his articles was Professor F. A. Lindemann, the physicist and future Lord Cherwell, personal adviser to Churchill when he became Prime Minister on scientific and statistical matters throughout the Second World War.

In an article in October 1937 entitled 'Vision of the Future Through the Eyes of Science', Churchill discussed the prospect of nuclear power. After reference to the revolution that coal had brought about, Churchill wrote:

Today we know that there is another source of energy a million times greater. We have not yet learned how to harness it or apply it, but it is there . . . The new fire is laid, but the particular kind of match is missing. If, and when, these sources of power become available our whole outlook will be changed. Geography and climate, which have conditioned all human history, will become our servants rather than our masters.

Emsley Carr encouraged Churchill's contributions – 'I cannot say how delighted we are to have you as our chief contributor' – and commented that, with a circulation then of over 4 million and the usual computation of three or four readers to every issue, it required no imagination to realize the enormity of the public he was addressing. For his part, Churchill had no doubts on that score either: in typical Churchillian fashion he commented: 'It is indeed a wonderful platform from which to address the stable, sagacious, good-humoured, kind-hearted central mass of the British nation and I value the opportunity of doing so.'

Long-term plans for Churchill's future contributions were discussed at one of Emsley Carr's Saturday night dinner parties at the News of the World at the end of 1937. A series of articles had already been agreed for publication in the early part of 1939 and arrangements were now laid for further series in 1940 and 1941. Churchill commented that with the addition of these arrangements he would have been working for the News of the World for eight consecutive years, adding: 'In these circumstances I shall certainly expect an invitation to the annual outing of the staff.'

Churchill's diary, however, was soon to be filled with more pressing engagements. He normally kept August and September free to write his News of the World pieces and in July 1939 he was writing to Carr expressing the hope that he would get the 1940 series in an advanced state, or at any rate 'on the stocks' before the end of September. But by that time he was back in his old job as First Lord of the Admiralty with 'not a minute to think of anything but my task'.

Three generations of the Churchill family have been contributors to the paper. Besides Winston, his son Randolph was a regular political commentator during the 1960s, and his grandson, Winston junior, has also written for it.

The fiery and unpredictable Randolph had considerable journalistic talent but his erratic nature led to frequent disputes with the editor and, after one of these, he resigned in a fit of pique.

The parting came when the editor, Stafford Somerfield, questioned the timing of a proposed visit by Churchill to America, for which the paper was paying. Churchill argued: 'You may have the power to suppress what I write but you cannot, in a free community, restrict my movements.' A tempestuous man of renowned impatience, he then exploded in typical fashion: 'Remember I am not a hack. I am an independent person and shall go where I please and write what I like.' He then stormed out, saying, 'I won't write for your bloody awful paper again.'

When John F. Kennedy was assassinated in 1963, Randolph's son, Winston junior, wrote a tribute to him in which he recalled his last meeting with the American president three months earlier. In 1967 the young Churchill wrote a series of articles for the paper on the rise of neo-Nazis in Western Germany although, according to Churchill, Stafford Somerfield had not been pleased with some of his assertions. However, he again commissioned Churchill to write three articles in May 1967 when trouble was brewing in the Middle East between Israel and Egypt. After telephoning his final article, Churchill spoke to Somerfield, pointing out that he believed war was imminent and inquiring if the editor wished him to stay in the Middle East or return home. Somerfield advised him to return home. After being back for only a few hours, Churchill heard on the radio that war had indeed broken out.

Another maverick character, although less troublesome to the editor than Randolph Churchill, was Robert Boothby, the politician and television personality, who was a political commentator for the paper for many years. During the 1930s he had been ahead of Winston Churchill in his warnings of the German threat – one of his journalistic coups had been an interview with Hitler – and the need for British rearmament.

Boothby was a prolific writer of newspaper articles of high quality: he had a fluent and lively style, wrote his articles in immaculate copperplate handwriting, and was always meticulous in meeting deadlines – all qualities that endeared him to newspaper editors.

His wisdom and great generosity were appreciated by many of his friends and their children. On Boothby's death in 1986 one of his favourite younger friends, now grown up, wrote to his widow: 'His wisdom I came better to recognize and appreciate as I grew older and read his articles (an excuse for a prurient youth to read the *News of the World*).'

ELEVEN

Red Hot News in Wartime

During the 1930s period of depression and unemployment, the *News of the World* maintained its progress. There was little enough good cheer about in those perilous times: it was Churchill who at this time said the paper provided 'amusement, diversion and instruction to the British nation in their weekend leisure'.

Having come through a decade of recession and competition, the paper now faced another period of wartime conditions, restrictions and upheaval.

In the 'phony war' period of 1938 and early 1939 the paper's resources for withstanding bomb attacks on London were surveyed and improved. Fire-fighting equipment, shelters for staff, protection from bomb blast, rescue equipment and training were all in place and ready for action by August 1939.

Emergency stand-by arrangements were made in case the London offices were bombed for printing to be undertaken at various centres throughout the country – in Reading, Luton, Uxbridge, Tunbridge Wells, Peterborough, Swindon, Worcester, Chester, Rotherham, Plymouth, Norwich and Leeds, as well as in Manchester and South London. It was assumed that if absolutely necessary each of these offices would be able to set the whole of the paper except the features page and advertisements, which would be distributed from Reading, but in practice matrices of as many pages as possible would be provided from either Reading or Manchester. Arrangements were also made for the leading article to be sent to all the stand-by offices over the news agency tapes.

Fleet Street had its introduction to incendiary bombs in 1940. There were a number of attacks in September and

December that year and others the following January and
April. But the worst raid took place on the night of 10–11
May 1941.

A contemporary account recalls the drama of that night
when, with a full moon and a low tide, London was caught
without water because the first wave of high explosive bombs
had destroyed the mains supplies.

Every fire appliance in London was called out and three
times the number could have been used . . . There was a
line of fire from Fetter Lane to Shoe Lane in the north
and from Serjeants Inn to Temple Church in the west.

The adjoining News Chronicle building had been set
ablaze by an oil bomb: our south wall was like a furnace
– even the sanitary pipes melted and fell away. To the
east, Ludgate Hill and New Bridge Street were also ablaze.
We had successfully put out a string of incendiary bombs
on our own building and extinguished fires in others. But
the News Chronicle building threatened to engulf us. We
fought it with stirrup pumps and thousands of gallons
of 'domestic water', while ready hands pushed reels of
paper and other inflammable material away from danger.
Nothing could save the News Chronicle building but
we could and did limit the fire and we saved our own
building.

Then came a minor catastrophe. The Serjeants Inn fire,
inadequately fought – there being no water available and
the few fire guards having been injured – had leaped the
narrow street to a printer and publisher's in Bouverie
Street filled with papers and periodicals. From here the
fire spread to our own stand-by buildings across the road
from the main building. A party of fire-fighters again
attacked the flames with stirrup pumps . . . The fire roared
up our area well, as in a blast furnace; the wind licked it
into our building and we had to abandon it. All that we
could possibly do was to hold the flames from spreading
still further to the next building. We succeeded in this and

so saved the fire from sweeping the whole of Bouverie Street. Just before 6.00 a.m. the all-clear sounded, the machines began to run and we printed in a red hot building – but the *News of the World* once more went out as usual.

Six hours later a major catastrophe occurred: gas mains had been shattered in Bouverie Street and Fleet Street and a series of explosions began to cause even more havoc than the bombs. The account continues:

A terrific explosion wrecked our foundry and set ablaze ground-floor offices in the north wing. Stirrup pumps were again brought into action, although they looked pitifully inadequate. They and the fire brigade, with water relayed from portable dams and the use of foam as well, got the fire under control but the gas main blazed into the sky until 2.00 a.m. the following morning when the supply was cut off. One employee was killed in the explosion and there were many narrow escapes.

Throughout the following week engineers worked in the wrecked foundry trying to get it going. The following Saturday, with debris piled all around and tarpaulins draping the wreckage and making a temporary roof, the plates for the *News of the World* were cast in the paper's own foundry and on its own equipment.

As the record proudly concludes: 'Another episode was added to Fleet Street history.'

The air raid precautions by 1942 consisted of a paid and volunteer staff of 200, all of whom had been trained in fire-fighting by the London Fire Brigade. A trailer pump had been bought and a private dam had been built to hold 75,000 gallons of water, with access to a new dam built by the Ministry of Home Security in Serjeants Inn.

Fleet Street thereafter was given a respite from enemy attack. Only one other major incident occurred, a renewed incendiary raid in the spring of 1944. The danger was ever-present, however, and the contingency plans which had been made to print the paper out of London, if necessary, had to be constantly under review. It was a result of this wartime link that led to the News of the World Organization subsequently taking over the Berrows provincial group in Worcester, which it owned until the 1980s when it was finally sold off.

As in the First World War, newsprint supplies presented a major problem. Newspaper sizes were reduced to eight and six pages on alternate Sundays to conserve stocks of newsprint, the price of which rocketed to £30 a ton, compared with £9 10s before the war.

There was a reserve of newsprint sufficient to last the paper for thirty-one weeks but half of that stock was used up at the request of the government so that imports could be reduced and valuable shipping released for the transport of war supplies. The newspapers had formed a Newsprint Supply Company among themselves to acquire newsprint and provide shipping transport and storage on behalf of all British newspapers. For a time these vessels were placed at the disposal of the government. The use of lighter quality newsprint was another device that allowed more copies to be produced and the circulation accordingly increased.

In the paper's centenary year – 1943 – circulation reached a new peak of over 5 million copies. It had been hoped that the anniversary would have been an occasion for great rejoicing but the war and Lord Woolton's food restrictions meant there could be only a modest celebration. There was a dinner for the staff and a luncheon at Claridge's attended by other newspaper proprietors and celebrities – though food rationing meant the number attending the luncheon had to be restricted to seventy-five.

Percy Davies, chairman and editor since Sir Emsley Carr's death in 1941, presided over a formidable array of press and magazine barons – Lords Rothermere, Kemsley, Southwood and Burnham, Sir Frank Newnes, Sir Ernest Benn and

Brendan Bracken, the Minister of Information. The King sent a congratulatory message and many were the tributes to 'a great national institution'. One of the speakers, Percy Cudlipp, then editor of the *Daily Herald*, whose brother Reginald was later to become editor of the *News of the World*, jokingly coined for the paper a new and undignified title – he described it as 'the Hansard of the sleazy'.

Among its old competitors. *Reynold News* praised it as 'a vigorous rival whom we greet in our mutual old age. It occupies a distinctive place in British journalism. We salute it because it is at once a national institution and an efficient newspaper.'

Despite the shortage of newsprint, the paper allowed itself the luxury of 2,000 words to blow a muted blast on its own trumpet, and other papers published greetings to their 'vigorous and virile' rival. In its leader tribute the *Daily Express* mentioned that besides the sturdy patriotism of its editorial columns, the *News of the World* also kept the interests of the fighting services in the forefront of its activities.

Typical of this was its printing for the first time in its history outside the United Kingdom. The 14th Army in the Far East was being referred to as 'the forgotten army' and the *News of the World* seized on this and arranged for copies to be printed for these units, giving them news of events at home. Matrices of the paper were flown to India and 30,000 copies were printed in Bombay and distributed to the troops – the identical paper that only five days earlier had been on sale in Britain.

Large numbers of the staff were themselves in the forces throughout the war. Some of the pre-war editorial team returned to find women reporters and subeditors helping to bring out the paper: although it did not strike them at the time, it was perhaps an omen of the future for a paper that would ultimately have at its head the first woman editor of a Fleet Street national newspaper.

TWELVE

Family Feuds and Company Conflicts

During the 1930s and 1940s the *News of the World* was subjected to an amazing web of management intrigue, family feuds between the Carrs and the Jacksons, and boardroom conflict.

After the death of Sir Charles Jackson in 1923, Lord Riddell had succeeded him as chairman and, in Jackson's will, was made a trustee to safeguard the interest of Jackson's children. Riddell had had to consider whether, in the precarious state of the paper's finances, it was in the Jacksons' best interests to have most of the family wealth tied up in the paper. He concluded that part of their shareholding should be sold and, with the approval of the other trustees and agreement of the High Court, he personally took it over. His free gift of shares in lieu of legal fees had brought him a handsome dividend: he now became the principal shareholder, with the Jackson trust second and the Carr family third.

In the next decade there was increasing conflict between Riddell and Sir Emsley Carr, which was exacerbated by Riddell's attempts at dabbling in editorial affairs.

Bertram Jones, who was to become general manager and later managing director, detected this resentment soon after Riddell brought him in as assistant manager in 1929. One of his first tasks, at the behest of Riddell, was to make detailed reports on each department, although the shrewd Jones quickly realized that the exercise was chiefly aimed at Carr's editorial empire. Jones reported that it was being run on a shoestring. 'The staff was insufficient to meet the demands of an up-to-date Sunday newspaper, particularly as at that time the Sundays were becoming seventh day papers rather than

116

summaries of the week's news,' he recalled. 'Many of the staff were ageing and there was need for younger, more energetic and vital men.' (When it had been drawn to their attention in 1928 that several employees were over 70 years of age, the directors had decided that 70 should be the maximum age for employees.)

Jones also concluded that some of the regular features had become outdated: he cited the half-page devoted to publication of a popular song. This was sacrilege to Emsley Carr and the feature continued for another decade.

Slightly less controversial was the introduction of women's features. Jones pointed out the incongruity of a situation in which the paper was spending large sums on canvassing for new readers when, apart from a fashion competition, there was little else to interest women, who formed the majority of potential readers the canvassers met on their rounds. Such features, he argued, would also bring in a new class of advertising revenue.

Carr agreed to increase women's features, but he was deeply annoyed at the report, which he regarded as a gross interference in his editorial responsibilities by the commercial wing of the business, and he never forgave Jones for his part in the exercise.

The powerful Riddell–Carr–Fifoot triumvirate which Lascelles Carr had formed when he took over the paper from the Bell family and which ruled over the paper for forty years was broken with Riddell's death in December 1934. It was further decimated by the death of Edgar Fifoot on 21 February 1939. Fifoot had remained a director after retiring as general manager in 1927. His death was a particularly sad loss for Emsley Carr who, at the next board meeting, spoke emotionally of their long business and personal relationships extending over nearly half a century. 'Night and day, year in and year out, he laboured to build up the commercial fabric of the *News of the World* with such success that he saw the newspaper grow from small beginnings to a position of unique strength in the newspaper world,' said Sir Emsley. 'It is not too much to say that he gave his life to the *News of the World*.'

On Riddell's death, Emsley Carr had succeeded to the chairmanship and, with backing from the bank, financed the purchase of Riddell shares, a quota of which he offered to the holders of Ordinary shares. This prompted the late Sir Charles Jackson's son, Professor Derek Jackson, to demand representation on the board to safeguard the interests of his side of the family. Philip (later Sir Philip) Dunn emerged as the nominee of the Jackson interest and, with the transfer to him of shares by an uncle of 'the Jackson boys', he was elected to the board. Derek Jackson was an eminent physicist whose interest in newspapers was entirely financial, although his private life was of such a bizarre nature that he often featured prominently in the gossip columns of the popular papers. In the 1930s he was engaged in pioneering research in the field of spectroscopy, working at the Clarendon Laboratory in Oxford where he became Professor of Spectroscopy. During the war he preferred the RAF to scientific war work, although he did assist in the development of radar defence.

He was a man of varied interests, including fox-hunting and racing, who found it difficult to settle down to scientific work after the war. He finally left Britain to escape crippling tax laws, and went to live first in Ireland and then in France, where he later took up his scientific work again. His views on art, literature and politics were often reactionary; his friends included Sir Oswald Mosley; he was married six times, his wives including Poppet, the daughter of the artist Augustus John, and Pamela Mitford. Although most of his income came from the *News of the World* he was never seen in the building.

Like Derek Jackson, Philip Dunn was also a controversial figure who found much in modern life not to his liking. He was the son of Sir James Dunn, a multimillionaire Canadian steel master, and had embarked on a successful business career long before he inherited substantial wealth from his father's estate in 1956. At the *News of the World* he saw the prospect of using the newspaper as a weapon with which to wield political power, and this was the incentive that led him autocratically to seize every opportunity he could to enable him to exert the power and authority he craved.

Emsley Carr, by contrast, was a more easygoing man who preferred events to flow smoothly along with a minimum of disturbance. On taking over the chairmanship he had promoted the company secretary, Leonard Wilde, who privately looked after Carr's tax and share transactions and already had a seat on the board, to be general manager. This upset the long-serving Harry Aldridge, who said he could not carry on as manager if Wilde was to become general manager. The matter was resolved by Carr offering Aldridge the position of joint managing director with himself.

Dunn was an ambitious man whose presence enlivened the former calm routine of board meetings. When he discovered that Carr and Wilde had decided to invest company money without apparently first consulting the rest of the board, Dunn threatened to reveal their 'irregularity' to shareholders unless he were appointed financial adviser as well as a director, thus tightening his grip on the company's affairs. The Carrs were a close-knit family, supportive and protective of each other, and Sir Emsley's son Harry and Dunn were reported to have almost come to blows during the meeting over Dunn's alleged threats. Dunn's intrigue over the appointment succeeded, but by that time war had been declared and Harry Carr had gone off to join the RAF. Dunn, too, went off to war, serving in the King's Royal Rifle Corps, but kept in close touch with affairs in Bouverie Street by letter and visits when on leave.

Bertram Jones's earlier brushes with Sir Emsley had so seriously strained their relations that when Wilde died in 1940, after thirty-three years with the company, Carr adamantly refused to give Jones the title of general manager. Jones later recalled: 'I remained in my old room and now all negotiations between Sir Emsley and I had to be conducted through a third party because Sir Emsley would neither see me nor talk to me. Percy [Davies], the deputy editor, and Aldridge carried messages back and forth, urging me to carry on in the hope that the matter would sort itself out in time.' Carr eventually relented: he had by then become a sick man and it was increasingly difficult to get him to sign documents and to take decisions.

A few months later his long reign was over. He died on 31 July 1941 at the age of 74.

In his will Emsley Carr expressed a wish that the board should appoint his deputy, Percy Davies, to succeed him as chairman and editor, to which they agreed, although some felt that Aldridge was better qualified so far as the chairmanship was concerned. Davies had excellent journalistic credentials: another Welshman, he was educated at Llandovery College and Aberystwyth and London Universities. His career had begun on the *South Wales Daily Post* in 1910 but was interrupted by the First World War, in which he was twice mentioned in dispatches. He had joined the *News of the World* after the war, becoming successively news editor (1921–30), night editor (1930–33) and deputy editor from 1933, when he had carried out much of the detailed work on behalf of Emsley Carr. But he lacked the strength and authority the post of chairman demanded, especially in the current circumstances of conflict and intrigue.

Carr had made another deathbed request. In a note he left for his fellow directors he recommended that his widow, Jenny, should be elected to the board on his death to join their son Harry in looking after the Carr family interests. She had discussed this with Philip Dunn at the conclusion of Emsley Carr's memorial service when it was decided she should take time to consider very carefully and profoundly the question of her election.

Lady Carr had been unaware of the existence of this memo until after her husband's death. In December 1941 she raised the matter again in a letter to Dunn, whom she asked to propose her election.

The more consideration I give the matter the more convinced I am, and so must all his fellow directors be, knowing his rectitude and honesty of purpose, that nothing but

the firm conviction that my election to the board would
be for the benefit of the great business in which you and
I represent such large interests would have induced him
to leave this advice [she wrote].

Knowing so many of my husband's thoughts and ideas
I can, without in any way intruding myself, help in the
deliberations of the board. I shall, therefore, consider it a
compliment to my husband's memory if you will propose
my election as a small acknowledgment of his recognition
of your own abilities.

It was an impassioned plea but it fell on stony hearts. Dunn
had a further meeting with Lady Carr. Davies was typically
unsure about the matter but Aldridge was adamantly against
the election of an aged lady. What appeared finally to have
resolved the matter with a rebuff was an intervention by
Bertram Jones, who pointed out that the Carr family interests
were represented by Harry Carr and if the Carrs had two seats
the Jacksons would also want two.

A terse minute records: 'Captain Dunn reported on his visit
to Lady Carr consequent upon her request that he should propose her election to the board. After full and sympathetic consideration it was unanimously resolved that the board were
unable to accede to her request.'

The Carrs were soon to suffer a further setback when Harry
Carr died in 1943 from the kidney trouble which was a family
affliction. This left that side of the family unrepresented
on the board, although the remaining brothers, Walter and
William, were both anxious to become directors.

Dunn's influence was still to be felt although he was far
away serving at GHQ, Middle East Forces. From there he
cabled to Bertram Jones: 'Resist adamantly any replacement
of Carr on board till my return, which will be immediate.'

The Carrs' requests were rejected and within months Walter
Carr had also died from the same medical condition as his
brother. William, then a major in the Army, was left to ponder

on his unfortunate situation. 'I was out on a limb. Nobody wanted me,' he later recalled.

As the war neared its end, Philip Dunn, foreseeing forth-coming wrangles, took an initiative in organizing changes at the top of the board, at the same time consolidating his own position along with that of the Jacksons. He summoned Percy Davies to an early morning breakfast meeting at Claridge's at which he openly criticized Davies's editorship: he told Davies he realized how difficult it must be to be both editor and chair-man and thought he would be a better editor if he were freed from the responsibilities of the chairmanship.

Davies, with his lack of strong character, was no match for the devious Dunn nor any use as an umpire caught between the warring factions of the two sides of the family. He had never sought to be chairman: the role had been thrust upon him, he explained. Then, with merely momentary thought, he meekly agreed to step down as chairman. Dunn immediately set about lobbying the other directors and became chairman himself.

William Carr meanwhile continued to be rebuffed in his attempts to get on the board. The other directors, all senior executives with small shareholdings of their own and support of others, saw their advantage in maintaining a situation in which they held the balance of power while the larger family shareholders played cat and mouse with each other, constantly at loggerheads.

With his rich upbringing, Dunn was a man of expensive good taste. As chairman, he took over an elegant office suite on the fourth floor of the Bouverie Street headquarters: his antique desk was said to have cost £1,000.

He then installed his own man in the editorial area. Robert Skelton, a man of military appearance and bearing, was recruited as deputy editor from the *Daily Telegraph*, where he had been night editor, but increasingly as Percy Davies's health declined he took over more of the running of the editorial operation. Skelton became acting editor and succeeded to the editorship on the death of Percy Davies in 1946.

The paper then embarked on a period of editorial extravagance such as it had never previously known. With his *Daily Telegraph* background and Dunn's backing, Skelton set up an elaborate corps of overseas staff correspondents with a corresponding increase in the amount of foreign news in the paper, new staff appointments were made at home and leading writers were invited to contribute to the leader pages on the topics he thought would most interest returning servicemen – politics, health and social welfare.

The circulation continued its advance but the other directors began to show concern at the financial implications of the scale of Dunn and Skelton's profligacy, especially as the newspaper was at that time the company's only major asset. But it was the increasing political partiality of the paper that was to become the main battleground.

It had become Dunn's practice to give leader writers the line they should take in their editorials, and the other directors strongly felt the independence of the editor and the paper's traditional impartiality were being compromised, with the paper veering towards outright Toryism.

Dunn was challenged on the political issue at a board meeting at which it was generally agreed that the paper's political stance was becoming embarrassing, especially in view of the nature of its readership and at a time of a Labour landslide. Dunn and Skelton had backed Churchill one hundred per cent in the immediate post-war General Election of 1945. Churchill himself was given a leader page to put his case for becoming the peace-time premier. There was scant mention of Labour, whose supporters among *News of the World* readers probably out-numbered Conservative voters, including as they did thousands of returning servicemen who wanted a new, fairer Britain. Attlee was put into No. 10 with an enormous majority and the paper had disastrously backed the wrong horse. But Dunn refused to abdicate what he claimed was his right to put 'the line' to the leader writers. This, too, was challenged: the paper's policy of political impartiality had been chiselled in stone many years before.

Dunn became increasingly autocratic. 'He became more and more impossible with his whims and fancies and wild extravagances,' Jones recalled. 'It became obvious to us all that he might easily send the *News of the World* crashing to disaster.'

Now sensing his own position to be under some threat, Dunn played what he regarded as a trump card. He announced that he had been talking to Derek Jackson, who had expressed a desire for a seat on the board. He attempted to drum up support for Jackson by lobbying the other directors with a series of tea parties at the Ritz Hotel and met with some support. But the plot almost backfired on him. To have two seats on the board, one for himself and one for his nominee, would unbalance the whole concern, it was pointed out. It was suggested that if Jackson were to join the board, Dunn should resign in his favour. The matter was not pursued further. William Carr meanwhile vowed to continue his fight to get on the board. With the help of his solicitor and a mutual friend he contacted Derek Jackson and discussed how they might cooperate. Carr pledged the support of his family's voting shares in favour of Dunn becoming chairman for life. It was a pledge he had no intention of ever fulfilling: he suggested it merely as an artifice to test the reaction of the other directors and as a ploy to help him achieve his aim. As anticipated their reaction was one of alarm.

Carr warned them that unless they made him a director he would back Dunn. If he did so, he argued, Dunn out of gratitude would get him appointed. His gamble paid off: he was elected and Carr then moved on to plan his next objective – the removal of Dunn and his own succession as chairman.

A conspiracy was plotted after Dunn had departed early from a directors' luncheon on 30 October 1947. In the smoky, after-lunch atmosphere of a West End restaurant, Carr casually remarked that the board did not appear to be getting on well with the chairman. In the relaxed atmosphere and the absence of Dunn they mulled over the situation and the feasibility of unseating him was discussed. Carr wisely did not seek to overplay his hand at this stage. Eventually, in return for their support in unseating Dunn, he offered the inducement of improved contracts: Aldridge additionally would become chairman for a stipulated period of five years, at the end of which Carr, as vice-chairman, would succeed him. There would be promotion for Bertram Jones to managing director. Carr argued: 'Surely you want to save the *News of the World* and at the same time end your career at the highest level?'

It was finally agreed that a letter, signed by all the directors, should be sent to Dunn asking for his resignation from the board. They all hurriedly returned to Bouverie Street where the letter was typed, signed by each director in turn and delivered to Dunn's office.

Dunn was infuriated and refused the request. A board meeting was called for the morning of 4 November. According to Bertram Jones the meeting 'was not a pleasant affair'. After some discussion, Dunn announced that he was prepared to stand down as chairman but he had no intention of resigning his directorship. This was not pressed at that moment and Aldridge was appointed.

Jones later recounted: 'Dunn got out of his chair with a flourish, congratulated Aldridge on taking over the chairmanship and then sat down at the side of the table. He said he could see no reason why from now on we should not all work happily as directors for the good of the company. I said I could not see that arrangement working out and suggested that on reflection he would see how impossible the situation would be.'

When Jones went on to point out that Dunn would no longer be able to hold his weekly editorial conference nor, as an ordinary director, continue to enjoy the luxury of his spacious office, Dunn 'flew into a rage' as he realized his power base was disintegrating. Dunn argued that Derek Jackson would never agree to his being totally removed. It was then pointed out that Jackson himself, or a representative other than Dunn, would be welcomed. After lengthy argument Dunn became reconciled to the strength of the opposition and the discussion then centred around the terms of his departure.

He eventually agreed to £50,000 compensation, free of tax, for loss of office.

The departure of his mentor left the editor he had appointed, Robert Skelton, in an exposed situation. He had been much criticized by members of the board during a comprehensive discussion of editorial policy. William Carr, supported by Aldridge, Jones and Bezzant, said he had lost confidence in Skelton as editor and a resolution was passed authorizing Aldridge, the new chairman, to negotiate terms for his departure. Skelton was paid off with a sum of £20,000 compensation, and Arthur Waters, his deputy, was appointed to succeed him.

By exercising patience and not a little intrigue, William Carr had finally triumphed.

THIRTEEN

Public Services

Services that would benefit readers were among the priorities of the newspaper and helped to develop the image of the family friend in times of need as well as a provider of entertainment to brighten what might otherwise be dull times.

An early instance of practical help came during a strike in the London docks in 1911 when, to show its concern for the welfare of strikers' families, the paper sent out vans containing tons of loaves of bread. One vanload, it was recorded, arrived at Greenhithe just as the destitute families were kneeling in prayer for food.

Not everyone considered the venture as a genuine humanitarian one and the gesture nearly ended in failure. *News of the World* contents bills had given the message: 'Look out for the free bread carts on Saturday morning.' The long line of horse-drawn vans which had been assembled was held up by police soon after it moved off. They thought there was an advertising flavour about the procession of vehicles and, in any event, processions were not allowed within the City boundaries. The organizers persuaded the authorities of the genuineness of the exercise and that difficulty was overcome by the line of vans moving off one at a time.

A more serious complication then arose for some of the vans. One of the staff who took part in the operation recalled: 'Going through Whitechapel I noticed a big crowd just ahead of us. At first I assumed they must be turning out to cheer us on our way. Imagine my surprise when suddenly there was a great shout and somebody hurled a brick at me. More howls and more stones followed. Soon there was a howling mob all around us.' The vans were rescued by police and driven

127

through the hostile crowd to a yard at the back of Plaistow police station. The wrath of the demonstrators had been aroused because the vans had been hired from a cartage company regarded as a 'blackleg' firm by the striking dockers, who were angry that the drivers were not on strike in sympathy with them. When tempers had calmed the bread was distributed in the police station yard.

The paper contained a number of features in the public service category that ran for years and brought much happiness and good fortune into many lives. Thousands of missing people, for instance, were reunited with their relatives through publication of their details in the 'Missing from Home' feature and, similarly, several million pounds in legacies were distributed to their rightful recipients through the 'Unclaimed Money' feature – 'This column may bring you a fortune', it proclaimed.

The paper was never reluctant to back and encourage what it regarded as good causes. As the number of car owners in Britain rapidly increased, the paper encouraged its readers to practise safety and courtesy on the road. It sponsored its first road safety scheme in 1928 when it launched the Knights of the Road Guild. Spotters looked out for acts of courtesy by motorists and took note of the registration number of the vehicle and the circumstances, which were published in the paper, and drivers were invited to submit their claims which, if authenticated, earned the driver a coat badge, a certificate and a cheque for a guinea. It was later felt that a car badge would be a more appropriate reward and the first blue enamelled badges were issued in 1936.

The scheme was suspended during the war years but with the immense increase in road traffic in the post-war period it became apparent that a road courtesy scheme was more urgently needed than ever. Consultations that took place with the Royal Society for the Prevention of Accidents and with road safety committees all over the country resulted in the formation of the Order of the Knights of the Road in January 1951. Its executive council, consisting of distinguished publi figures, worked closely with other organizations and police and local road safety committees, who recommended acts of bravery and courtesy for awards. The highest grade was Knight of the Road, awarded sparingly and often posthumously to people who had died as a result of their action. Then there were Companions whose record of courtesy or service to other road users was so outstanding that it merited more than ordinary membership and an Ensigns category was created for young road users under the age of 17. The guild existed until 1970.

The newspaper's interest in the annual Alamein Reunion epitomized its traditionally close relationship with the Services.

The paper organized a splendid dinner at the Dorchester Hotel in June 1946 for 150 brave holders of the Victoria Cross – what it proudly called 'The greatest assembly of valour of all time.' They ranged from old soldiers who had won the honour before the Boer War to very recent recipients from the just-ended Second World War.

Few of the VCs had ever been to the Dorchester before and some brought their wives and families, who technically hadn't been invited. But the *News of the World* didn't bat an eyelid. The then foreign editor Stafford Somerfield – later to become a distinguished editor of the paper – wrote in his memoirs:

We scrapped the table plan and the menu and said to the hotel staff: 'These chaps are heroes, give them anything they ask for. Champagne and caviar or fish and chips, it doesn't matter.'

We took the whole of an hotel in Kensington for them to stay in. I'd never gone into an hotel before and said: 'I'll take all your rooms. Yes, that's right, the lot.' Then the VCs didn't want to go home. Piper Laidlaw played the pipes as he did on the parapet at Loos in World War I and the VCs charged over the tables as the troops had charged in Flanders.

Bravery knows no class boundaries and the dinner was out-standing for its equality. Generals and privates, admirals and airmen sat together at round tables – there was no top table.

As many of the VCs were a little the worse for drink that night, Somerfield telephoned Scotland Yard to alert them to the situation. The police's response was to send a fleet of squad cars to assist the heroes back to their hotel. Imagine that happening today! Not all the VCs found the right rooms and one of them lost his false teeth down the loo. And it was a whole week later before the last to leave was finally put on a train back home.

Another group of heroes was also royally fêted at the Dorchester three years later. They were the crew of the courageous British destroyer HMS *Amethyst*, whose exploits in escaping down the Yangtze River under heavy fire from Communist Chinese guns had thrilled the nation. Also invited to the dinner were representatives from the cruiser HMS *London*, which had lost twelve men in its attempt to relieve the *Amethyst*.

Again, the *News of the World* did them proud. Guests included the First Sea Lord, Admiral Lord Fraser of North Cape, and showgirls from the famous Windmill Theatre. The admiral delighted the ordinary seamen by kissing all the Windmill girls, whose fee was a pair of silk stockings each – not easy to obtain in those days. American comedian Jack Benny, legendary for his supposed meanness, provided the cabaret for the fee of one cigar!

Since the *News of the World* had sponsored the first British Games in 1920, athletics events were always prominent among the paper's sponsorships. And when the post-war Olympics took place in London in 1948 the paper took over the Lyceum Theatre to entertain more than 1,000 athletes from all over the world, at which Lord Burghley, chairman of the Council of the British Olympic Association, paid tribute to the important part the *News of the World* played in encouraging British amateur sport.

By 1958 the paper was sponsoring over forty events in various parts of the country covering twenty different sports or other functions. They varied from the annual Alamein Reunion at the Royal Festival Hall in London to the National Town Criers' Championships in Hastings. Golf and athletics events figured prominently in the paper's sport sponsorship, reflecting the particular interests of the Carr family, but many minor sports were also represented, together with flower shows, pipe band championships and canary and cat shows.

Sponsorship and public spiritedness were often closely related, as was shown when the paper launched public appeals on behalf of the victims or the families of victims of atrocities of one sort or another. One such, which reflected the paper's close relationship with the police, occurred in 1975 when the *News of the World* launched, with its own contribution of £1,000, a fund for the widow and two daughters of a Metropolitan Police explosives officer, Roger Goad, who was killed by the explosion of a terrorist parcel bomb. Six months later the fund's total had reached nearly £23,000 and the paper's initiative brought praise from the Metropolitan Police Commissioner.

Within the pages of the paper, it was the offering of advice to readers with problems of one sort or another that was a valuable commodity. Before the First World War readers' medical queries were answered by Dr Owen Gilmore, a brother-in-law of Emsley Carr. Several hundred queries were received each week. Dr Gilmore's replies were not sent in letter form: a few lines in answer were set up by two linotype operators to help fill in their time. These replies in proof form were then pasted on a memoranda form and posted to the reader. The same practice was adopted as the scope of the queries widened, especially during and after the war, to include legal, pension and insurance inquiries, and from the replies of the various individual experts a column of correspondence was assembled and became a popular feature of the paper. Many readers cut out these columns and pasted them in a book, thus compiling a do-it-yourself reference guide to the various subjects raised.

One reader involved in a county court action in 1935 who

armed himself with information from the *News of the World* on the complicated Rent Acts was complimented by the judge, who described his knowledge as 'absolutely accurate' and joked that he seemed to know more about the subject that he himself did.

At no time was the need for advice and help more important than during wartime and in the post-war years. It was a momentous decision that the board arrived at in 1942 when a new service was introduced that was to have an influence for the next three decades and, despite the post-war development of the Welfare State in Britain, continued to fulfil a significant need.

An article in the issue of 15 March 1942 invited readers to send their individual problems to the *News of the World* where they were assured of getting sound and reliable advice from a team of experts.

The response was dramatic and the paper recruited the services of Professor John Hilton to organize the helpful advice that readers sought. Hilton was a familiar name as a distinguished broadcaster and writer; he was also professor of industrial relations at Cambridge University. Unfortunately he died in August of the following year but, as a memorial to his work, his name continued to be associated with the feature for the next thirty years. One of his close associates, Kenneth Barrett, himself a former don, was invited to take over direction of the advisory service, the nature of which was expanded with a professional staff to deal with legal, educational and medical problems. It was operated from offices at St Regis, Cambridge, and at the end of the Second World War it was decided to centralize all the paper's advice services under the bureau. It became a reader service without parallel in Fleet Street.

Barrett himself was frequently called upon to give evidence before various Royal Commissions and departmental government committees, and he and his experts were often able to influence government policy. The bureau chief was also consulted by the Law Commission, an official body to review legal practice, whose chairman, Lord Scarman, said the bureau had its finger on the public pulse.

A report on the bureau's work in 1958, by which time over 3 million people had consulted it, said:

They have received advice on every conceivable kind of problem from men of scholarship and experience and understanding. Representations have been made to every kind of public authority and voluntary body. Great concessions have been wrung for those whose circumstances are difficult or unhappy . . .

It is the policy of the bureau to neglect nothing, to take trouble over everything, to seek justice and help for the reader no matter what is the nature of his problem, to deepen the ties between the *News of the World* and its immense readership.

It was paradoxical that such a service – what the paper referred to as 'this University of Social Knowledge' – was still necessary when not only had a Welfare State been created in Britain but legal aid had been extended, a national health service come into existence, and a network of other personal and public advice and aid schemes set up. But it was precisely because there were so many agencies of help and instruction that there were inevitably gaps and administrative anomalies that the bureau experts specialized in bridging. At any rate, the problems continued to flood in by the thousand until the expensive service – it cost more than £100,000 a year to operate – was discontinued in 1974. Even then there was little diminution of demand for help: letters were continuing to arrive at the rate of 900 a week and the staff of the bureau continued to operate a fee-paying service.

There was an important spin-off from the bureau that benefited the paper's team of investigative journalists. Letters from readers who had suffered from some injustice or illegal practice were often referred by the bureau to the paper's news desk, resulting on further investigation in a news story exposé of some racket or other. This had been the justification for the considerable expenditure involved, but over the years there had been a dwindling of this editorial benefit. In 1973 the paper's legal manager, Henry R. Douglas, was asked to make a thorough investigation into its cost-effectiveness. His advice, which was accepted, was that the same sort of reader service could be given editorially at much less cost.

It would be no exaggeration to claim that the work of the bureau over the thirty years of its existence represented a significant and invaluable record of British social history. The changes in public life, in the nature of society and in personal attitudes were all reflected in the vast volume of correspondence and negotiations. Its archive was regarded as such an important record of social history that it was ultimately taken over by the University of Sussex.

The bureau was superseded by the introduction of an 'agony column' run by Unity Hall, a widely experienced journalist who was in charge of women's features.

Many of the writers whose names have appeared over the years developed perhaps a distant but nevertheless firm friendship with their readers. None more so than did Unity Hall through her agony aunt column, which was one of the most widely read of that genre in the world. Unity Hall was a tough all-round journalist, but her deeply compassionate nature was never more clearly seen than in her column.

It was here also that society's relaxation in moral standards was perhaps most discernible: subjects which had previously been taboo, such as homosexuality, masturbation, menstruation and morals generally, increasingly made their way into the paper as acceptable subjects on which worried correspondents sought to unburden themselves. While inevitably the presentation of these subjects, and others, tended to make for more erotic columns, in the capable and compassionate hands of Unity Hall they were handled in a frank, straightforward and down-to-earth manner that was helpful to other people who found themselves in circumstances similar to those whose letters were published, to say nothing of the many others to whom she wrote direct, who were indebted to her for her sound advice.

She was a most respected journalist and when her own life was threatened by a devastating stroke in September 1991 few in her profession could have been shown such affection and genuine sorrow by their readers. Her hospital room was festooned with flowers and cards and none could have had so many prayers offered or candles lit for them in churches as did Unity Hall by her friends and readers, not only in Britain but in many parts of the world. For the six months until her death while she lay desperately ill in hospital, her name continued to feature above her column, which was edited by a colleague.

Unity, who was also a prolific and successful author of books ranging from royal biographies to bestselling novels, served the *News of the World* magnificently for two decades. Her official obituary, which appeared in the paper in April 1992, concluded with the following words: 'We on this newspaper have lost a wonderful colleague. Millions of *News of the World* readers, too, have lost a true friend.'

So universally acclaimed throughout Fleet Street was Unity that another newspaper, the *Daily Mail*, paid her the supreme compliment of asking Marjorie Proops, the most famous agony aunt of them all and an old friend of Unity's, to write an obit for them. Another so-called 'quality' newspaper, which shall remain nameless, published a glowing obituary but used a photograph of someone else altogether, another Unity Hall. A former *News of the World* editor, Bernard Shrimsley, who gave the address at a memorial service in St Bride's, Fleet Street, observed that it was an irony that would have amused Unity no end.

Unity Hall's death left a void that was filled by an agony uncle – Philip Hodson, who was known for his appearances giving advice on radio and television programmes. One of his early innovations was a special section of his page devoted to teenage problems.

Parallel with this advice on emotional problems was the

medical advice prescribed by Dr Hilary Jones in the colour magazine.

Help of a more practical kind began in April 1990, when the *News of the World* launched a unique column called Captain Cash. Under the banner 'Captain Cash helps the needy and bashes the greedy', the paper introduced a new service to recession-hit Britain – giving away money to some of its hard-up readers. Every week, the generous Captain doles out financial help to deserving applicants and fends off the cheeky begging letters from others who are just trying it on.

The amounts given are usually modest, from £5 to £50 on average, and only to genuinely worthy cases whose pleas have touched the Captain's heart. Every one is thoroughly checked out before any cash is sent. The cheating scroungers get short shrift. To a girl who wrote asking for £600 to buy a wedding dress she'd fallen in love with, the Captain replied: 'You've got it wrong, it's the fella you're supposed to fall for!' And the prospective bridegroom who said it would cost him and his fiancée £5,000 to set up home, and could the Captain send something for their bottom drawer, got the reply: 'Certainly – mothballs!'

Sometimes, the stories are so moving that they start off in the Captain Cash column and move rapidly on to the main news pages. Like the story of tiny tot Sabrina Taylor, an 11-month-old baby who was so horribly scarred in a Guy Fawkes night accident that she had to wear a linen face mask because her skin was left so paper-thin that it peeled away at the slightest touch. The poor mite also lost her toes and had her left hand scorched to a stump. The *News of the World* launched an appeal to help Sabrina's unemployed parents cope with the horrendous expenses they faced and raised an incredible £50,000. Among those who weighed in with help was England soccer star Paul 'Gazza' Gascoigne, who signed a giant bottle of Scotch and a football to be raffled off for the fund.

It's always the stories of sad children that really touch people's hearts and another one was that of little 8-year-old

Tanya Donaldson, whose mum wrote to the Captain i
1992. The paper told how little Tanya was so severely l
capped that she would never grow beyond the baby sta
picture of the little tot in her mother's arms, looking like a
tiny china doll at only 22 lbs and feeding from a bottle, so
touched readers that again the money poured in.

Another Captain Cash story that became a major campaign
happened in January 1993 when the *News of the World* told
readers of a tragedy the general public knew nothing about.
The paper discovered that between eighty and a hundred
babies a year were being born in Britain without eyes, victims
of a condition called anopthalmia. The story had begun when
the Captain paid £700 for an 18-month-old toddler from
Lancashire to have a pair of blue artificial eyes fitted, thinking
it was an extremely rare case. But letters poured in from other
parents of children similarly afflicted.

The paper investigated and discovered that almost all the
letters came from rural areas and there was a possibility of a
link with pesticides. Realizing there could be a scandal as big as
the 1960s thalidomide affair, the *News of the World* demanded a
government inquiry. It also launched a fund to help children
with anopthalmia, starting with its own donation of £10,000.

The most heart-warming stories in the Captain Cash column
often involve no money at all. In February 1993 a 36-year-old
farmhand from Rochester, Kent, wrote to tell the Captain that
his 4-month-old baby sister had died twenty-eight years earlier
in Cyprus, where their dad had been serving with the RAF.
His parents had once had a photo of the child's grave but were
devastated when they lost it. Could the Captain help?

No problem. Captain Cash contacted the Ministry of Defence
who got present-day servicemen on the island to track down
the grave and take the photographs, which were placed in a
special album and rushed back to Britain and the delighted
family.

Sometimes the valiant Captain is called on to do service well
beyond the call of duty. The man behind the Captain Cash
title, Dave 'Nobby' Clark, recalls how he once managed to

get a helpless little old lady stranded for a day-and-a-half at Edinburgh airport.

The story began with a letter from the old lady's daughter, who was living in Caithness in the very far north of Scotland, near John o'Groats. Her elderly mum was in a home in Kent but the daughter had managed to obtain her a place in an old folks' home close by her family in Caithness. Unfortunately, they didn't have the money to pay for the old lady to be transported from Kent to Scotland.

Clark swung into action and arranged for British Midland Airways to fly her to Edinburgh, where she would be collected by the small Scottish airline Loganair and flown onwards to Wick, the nearest place to her family. Both airlines were delighted to agree to give the old lady a free seat on their aircraft.

On the appointed day, Clark drove from his Essex home down to the old folks' home in Kent, where he found her sitting outside the home with her suitcase. He took her to Heathrow, where she was given VIP treatment, and put her on the plane to Edinburgh. Then he drove to King's Cross railway station and dispatched her luggage, via Red Star, to its ultimate destination, and finally returned to his Essex home with the feeling of a job well done. But even the best-laid plans of mice and men, as they say . . .

Later that day, Clark decided to check that everything was OK, only to find that Edinburgh was fog-bound and there was no flight out to Wick. The old lady was stranded, had no money, no spare clothes and, being crippled with arthritis, could scarcely walk. Hurried arrangements were made to transport her to a hotel for the night and return her to the airport next morning. The next day, however, the airport was still fog-shrouded and the one daily flight to Wick was again cancelled.

Captain Cash, in the form of the gallant Clark, again leaped into action. He took a taxi to Stansted Airport in Essex and caught a flight to Edinburgh, where he found the old lady sitting lost and forlorn in the airport terminal. There was nothing to do but hire a car and drive her another 250 miles for a tearful reunion with her family. Then Clark turned round and drove back to Edinburgh. After an overnight stop, he was in the office the next day to write the story for his column.

The scroungers who try and con Captain Cash are wasting their time. Says Dave Clark: 'You can always tell them. They write in under half a dozen different names, giving various hard-luck stories, but usually it's in the same handwriting or on the same notepaper.'

The cheats would be amazed if they knew the lengths to which the Captain goes to catch them out. Clark recalls getting a letter from a couple living on an old barge in remote marshland in Kent. It was a real sob tale. The couple had had their beaten-up Ford Fiesta stolen, the husband was out of work and they couldn't get to the nearest shops which were miles away because there was no public transport. Could the Captain send them £300 to buy another second-hand car?

Clark decided to check the story out and toddled down to Kent. Sure enough, he found the barge just where the couple had said it was and it was, indeed, a remote spot with no shops for miles. There was a garage right alongside the barge and Clark decided to take a peek inside before knocking on the couple's door. There stood a Ford Fiesta looking in top-notch condition. Then, just at that moment, a bus pulled up alongside and stopped its engine. Clark engaged the driver in conversation and was informed that the bus ran by the spot regularly, every hour in fact. Needless to say, the rascally claimants didn't get a bean out of Captain Cash.

Dave Clark also tells with a chuckle the story of the Irishman whose twin daughters were both in a psychiatric home. It was a bizarre tale. One of the girls had been sexually assaulted during the 1960s at the age of 15 and had developed mental illness as a result. The other twin, being extremely close to her sister, had developed the same symptoms and both were stuck in a kind of time-warp, spending all their time listening to 1960s pop music. Sadly, their personal stereos had been stolen and they were desolate.

Captain Cash arranged for two brand-new machines to be sent to the girls' father but first telephoned the father to tell him that two Sony Walkmen were on their way and to be sure to be in to receive them. He was naturally delighted and fulsome in his thanks. Some time later, Clark was tickled to receive a message from the Irishman: 'He says the tape machines have arrived OK but he wants to know, does he still have to wait in for the workmen?'

For an earlier incumbent of the Captain Cash column, reporter Tim Spanton, there was a slightly embarrassing episode when he was dispatched to a hospital in Birmingham to take Christmas gifts to seriously ill children in the leukaemia ward. The paper decided to do the thing in style and Spanton got himself kitted out with a splendid red-and-blue Captain Cash costume in the style of the comic hero, Superman.

Says Spanton: 'I stayed at a big hotel right in the centre of Birmingham in order to have somewhere to change into the costume. Then I had to walk through the crowded foyer and out into the street to get a taxi to the hospital. I got some very strange looks. Nobody actually said anything but I noticed quite a few people edging nervously away from me!'

FOURTEEN

Crime, Confession and Punishment

Before the Legal Aid Act of 1947, which made legal aid more readily available to people of small or moderate means, including those involved in criminal cases, an accused person usually had to rely on a 'dock brief', probably a young barrister sitting hopefully in court awaiting the judge's patronage. It was not unusual, therefore, for a notorious criminal's defence to be paid for by a newspaper in return for his or her exclusive memoirs, without any actual financial benefit accruing to the accused.

Such an arrangement was made by the *News of the World* in 1949 involving one of the most gruesome murderers in criminal history: John George Haigh, the so-called 'acid bath' murderer.

Haigh was one of the most baffling criminals of the century, a son of deeply religious parents whose crime – killing his old lady victim, stealing her jewellery and disposing of her body in a bathful of acid – aroused great public interest.

He lived by his wits: he had a record of convictions for obtaining money by false pretences and with forged documents and had been in and out of prison over a period of fifteen or more years. His criminal career culminated in his killing of a 69-year-old widow living in the same London hotel whom he inveigled into accompanying him to a storeroom in Crawley, Sussex, of which he had use for what he called 'experimental purposes', on the pretext of an interest the lady had expressed in the manufacture of plastic fingernails. There, he shot her through the back of her head and, having divested her of all jewellery which he later sold to pay off debts,

141

attempted to dispose of the body by placing it in a drum containing sulphuric acid.

After his arrest, the paper was quick off the mark to seize the chance of obtaining Haigh's life story, which subsequently featured in the *News of the World*, based on an eighty-page account of his life and thoughts written in his own hand while he was in Brixton Prison awaiting trial.

After his first appearance in court it had been reported on the news agencies that he had applied for legal aid for his defence. A letter was immediately delivered to him at the remand prison in Lewes saying the *News of the World* was prepared to place the best legal advice at his disposal.

The next day Stafford Somerfield, then the paper's features editor, waiting in the White Hart Hotel in Lewes for an answer, was handed a brief telegram:

VERY PLEASED TO ACCEPT YOUR OFFER OF SOLICITORS. HAIGH.

A firm of solicitors in Horsham, Sussex, was engaged and on 12 March 1949 an agreement was drawn up whereby the paper undertook to indemnify Haigh's defence costs in return for the copyright and ownership of all manuscripts and other original material prepared by Haigh.

It marked the beginning of a fascinating relationship not only with Haigh but with his pathetic parents whose advanced age, poor health and distress at what had happened prevented them from travelling from their home in Leeds to see their son. In fact, they never saw him again. Somerfield became the go-between for Haigh and his hapless parents, visiting him on their behalf up to the eve of his execution the following August, passing messages and, finally, disposing of his few personal possessions.

In preparing the background to the Haigh memoirs, Somerfield made several visits to Leeds to interview Haigh's aged parents and maintained a regular correspondence with them as the legal process slowly advanced. After his committal, Haigh sent them a message that he was in good health and that everything possible was being done for him. 'Dear friend', his parents wrote to Somerfield, 'It is a great comfort to us to know that our son is in good health and we thank you for your personal interest and that of your paper in his welfare.'

Haigh, after his detention, had sought to escape the gallows by trying to convince prison doctors that he was insane and claimed to have committed two or more other murders and 'treated' his victims in the same way. Indeed, insanity was the basis of his defence. But that defence had been demolished by the attorney general, Sir Hartley (later Lord) Shawcross, in his cross-examination of a psychiatrist called as a defence witness, and the jury had taken only fifteen minutes of deliberation before finding Haigh guilty.

The trial judge Sir Travers Humphreys later recalled in his own memoirs, also published in the *News of the World*, that 'personally, I never had at any time during the trial the slightest doubt that the man was sane'.

After the trial in July, Somerfield wrote a sympathetic letter to Haigh's parents in which he said: 'Those of us who were acquainted with your son are now fully convinced that when he committed these deeds he could not have been responsible for them.' Haigh's parents also thought them to be out of character. 'It is a great comfort to both of us to know that you and many of your friends are convinced that George was not responsible for those deeds when he committed them. Those deeds are foreign to him naturally as we know him,' his father told Somerfield.

Haigh meanwhile had himself written to his parents enclosing a permit for them to visit him in prison. But they asked Somerfield to undertake the visit on their behalf as their age and other factors made it impossible for them to journey to London and because they believed any visit by them would cause distress to Haigh.

Prison bureaucracy initially prevented this but an appeal by the editor direct to the Home Secretary resulted in Somerfield being allowed to see Haigh on the specific understanding that the visit would be a humanitarian one to carry the parents' last messages to their son and would not be made in Somerfield's capacity as a newspaper reporter. It must have been very difficult to separate the two roles. Somerfield reported back to the parents that Haigh was glad to receive their messages, sent his love and had asked Somerfield to call and see them later on. 'Your son is in good spirits and as far as I could judge is fully prepared to meet any ordeal that might face him', he wrote, continuing:

> Is it any comfort to you to know that his bearing was such that any man, in similar circumstances, would be proud to emulate? Your son behaved towards me as a perfect gentleman and I did not find our interview a strain or difficult. He asked that I should see him again and if the authorities allow it I certainly will.

The Home Secretary saw no reason to exercise mercy in Haigh's case and the scene was set for his execution. Somerfield's final encounter with Haigh took place on the afternoon before his execution. The following day he again wrote to the pathetic parents.

> Your son said he would be writing that night but he would like you to know first-hand how he was looking and felt. I shall be pleased to do this if you so desire . . . His bearing at the end was magnificent. He showed the greatest possible courage and, I believe, was completely composed. He expressed to me the deepest appreciation of all that had been done for him and the small part that I had been able to play. We parted on the most friendly terms . . . I think it would have been his wish (if I may presume to say this on so short an acquaintance) that his passing should not cause you great suffering. This as we know is impossible but at the same time it may be some little comfort to you to know that his last thoughts were of you both and were expressed with great kindness and dignity. I believe, as I know you do, that the world did not see the real side of

poster advertising
e first issue.

NEWS FOR THE MILLION.

THE
Novelty of Nations and the Wonder of the World.
48 Large Folio Columns.

Price Only 3d.
THE SIZE OF THE TIMES.

On Saturday and Sunday, September 30, and
October 1. 1843.

WILL BE PUBLISHED
No. 1,
THE
NEWS OF THE WORLD
A Weekly Newspaper,
Containing Forty-Eight Large Folio Columns,
All the News of the Week,
Printed with a New, Distinct, and Elegant Type.

The Cheapest, Largest, and Best Newspaper.

Price Only Threepence.

Orders Received by all Dealers in Newspapers,
the Office of "THE NEWS OF THE
30, Holywell Street, Strand, London ;

Founding father: John Browne
Bell, who launched the
News of the World in 1843.

This contents bill of 1883 demonstrates the paper's early liking for crime reporting.

Right: Lord Riddell: he took shares in lieu of his legal fee – and became a millionaire.

Below: Lord Riddell's philosophy was to keep the paper's name constantly in the public eye.

Left: Sir Emsley Carr, editor for fifty years.

Below: A convoy of carts sets off with free bread for the families of striking dockers in 1911. Some of them were attacked for being 'blacklegs'.

Left: Lloyd George and Riddell at the Paris Peace Conference where Riddell supervised the arrangements for the press.

Below: Riddell's open-topped Rolls Royce awaits Lloyd George at Chequers.

Stafford Somerfield – editor of an institution 'as British as roast beef and Yorkshire pudding'.

Right: Bargains galore between the wars in the *News of the World* advertisement columns.

Britain at war: the issue of 10 September 1939.

Right: Hold the front page: telephone typists take down the journalists' stories.

Above: Last of the Carr
dynasty, Sir William Carr.

Right: Unity Hall, the paper's
much respected 'agony
aunt'.

Below: Robert Leonard Mills writes
his murder confession.

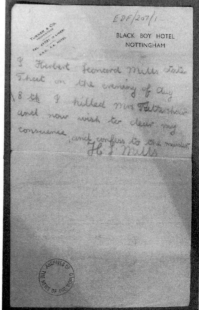

Mass murderer
John Christie,
who failed to
keep his dinner
date at the *News
of the World*.

Acid bath killer
John George Haigh.

your son. The side you knew, and of which I was permitted to catch a glimpse, was one of great charm and
natural affection. The other side can only have been
placed there by some evil force of which we are only dimly
aware and cannot understand.

A month later, when the dust of their distress had settled,
John Haigh, the murderer's father, thanked Somerfield for his
letters which, he said, had been a source of great comfort.
'May you be rewarded', he wrote. 'You will always be to us a
friend.'

At that final meeting in the condemned cell Haigh had
requested Somerfield to carry out certain last wishes, including
disposal of his possessions. To Somerfield it was 'a difficult and
unpleasant duty to carry out but I feel bound to comply with
the request'. Some of the items, including a radio and a watch,
went to his parents, his typewriter to a friend. Most macabre
of all, a green suit together with a pair of socks, a tie, a shirt and
a handkerchief went, at Haigh's request, to Madame Tussaud's
museum of waxworks. There they can still be seen dressing
the model of Haigh in the museum's Chamber of Horrors.

Haigh's legal defence cost the *News of the World* a total of
£10,600, of which over £2,250 was recouped in fees for the
syndication of his life story and the rights for reproduction of
the series of articles in book form. But the value of its exclusive
in terms of circulation was incalculable.

The memoirs of Sir Travers Humphreys, the judge who presided over Haigh's trial at Lewes Assizes, appeared in the *News
of the World* early in 1952. Stafford Somerfield had tried to sign
up the judge to write his memoirs a year earlier, recalling in
his letter that Lord Hewart, when Lord Chief Justice, had been
the last judge to contribute to the paper in 1939. Humphreys
was about to leave for a month's holiday abroad and promised
an answer on his return.

Much to Somerfield's chagrin, however, the *Sunday People*,
the main opposition paper, announced that a series called
'Cavalcade of Crime, the enthralling story of Mr Justice

Humphreys', would be appearing exclusively in their columns. 'We had looked forward with the liveliest anticipation and interest to the prospect of Your Lordship's unique reminiscences appearing in the *News of the World*', Somerfield wrote to the judge, 'and naturally we are deeply disappointed by the knowledge that we have been forestalled.'

His Lordship was also 'extremely annoyed'. He explained that he had no idea that a barrister who had earlier interviewed him was planning to publish in the *People* details of his career 'as told to himself': the judge had written to say that he strongly objected to such a description of talks they'd had. In future, said the judge rather tetchily, he would refer all newspapers and journalists to his literary agent. Meanwhile, he had decided not to write any book of memoirs so long as he remained a judge on the active list. If he decided to do so on his retirement he would let the *News of the World* know through his agent. The judge was, as one would expect, true to his word and in December 1951 agreement was reached for twelve exclusive articles on a selection of cases in which he had figured, including that of Haigh. The articles were subsequently published in book form.

Life in a newspaper office is always full of surprises: when the telephone rings in the *News of the World* office one never knows what drama is about to unfold. This is as true today as it has ever been.

Reginald Cudlipp recalls when he was editor, answering the telephone one lunchtime to a man who said he understood the *News of the World* might pay for information about the finding of bodies: he claimed to have found one in Nottingham but had not reported it to the police because he thought the *News of the World* might pay him for the news of his discovery. Becoming suspicious because the man seemed to know a great deal about the circumstances, Cudlipp got the news desk to contact the Nottingham police and get them to intercept the call while he kept the man in conversation. Suddenly the caller was interrupted by the arrival of the police at the kiosk and taken into custody. After questioning, however, he was released since apparently all he had done was to lead the police to the discovery of Mabel Tattershaw's body in an orchard off a well-known footpath in Nottingham.

Meanwhile, Cudlipp sent the paper's chief crime reporter, Norman Rae, hotfoot to Nottingham to interview the man, Herbert Leonard Mills, a 19-year-old petty opportunist with no settled way of life. Rae, a man of great experience, had lengthy interviews with Mills during which he became increasingly suspicious of his involvement. Eventually, after days of conversation during which they became friends, Rae managed to trap him. Mills had contended that no clues had been left. Rae showed him a local newspaper which reported that police had found two light hairs on Mrs Tattershaw's coat. Mills blurted out: 'They couldn't because I put my coat over her before I . . .' Rae interrupted him and asked if he realized what he was about to say. Mills replied: 'I think it is time I told you the truth.'

On a single sheet of notepaper, headed 'The Black Boy Hotel, Nottingham', he wrote: 'I, Herbert Leonard Mills, states that on the evening of August 8 I killed Mrs Tattershaw and now wish to clear my conscience, and confess to the murder.'

There followed a detailed seven-page confession, describing how the woman had got into conversation after coming to sit beside him in a cinema and invited him to see her the following day. 'I am very much interested in crime', he wrote. 'I had always considered the possibility of the perfect crime. Here was my opportunity. I have been most successful, no motive, no clues. Why, if I had not reported finding the body I should not have been connected in any manner whatsoever.'

After describing how he had strangled the woman, he wrote: 'and now, having been warned by Mr Rae of the *News of the World*, I have determined to make this statement which I realize involves a charge of murder. I now confess I murdered Mrs Tattershaw.' Rae spent an anxious night in the hotel suite with the confession under his pillow and the murderer in an adjoining room. Early next morning he delivered the confession and Mills to the local police station. Mills was subsequently found guilty and executed.

On this occasion, too, the *News of the World* paid for Mills's defence. During the trial there was a bizarre episode when the defending barrister bit the hand that was paying him by criticizing the paper for the manner in which it had obtained Mills's confession.

'The trouble with these cases was that they were invariably very ordinary people who were involved,' Cudlipp later recalled. 'Very few murderers are ever distinguished. You bought a pig in a poke. But you were doing your job of supplying the most complete reports to the public of the things they were interested in.'

Another surprise telephone call came to Norman Rae late on a Saturday night in March 1953. At the other end of the line was the ghoulish murderer John Christie. Rae had often met Christie: their first encounter had been in a Paddington police station where Christie was a special constable and he had also seen a lot of him during the inquiries and subsequent trial of his neighbour Timothy Evans, who had a flat in the same house, for the murder of his wife and baby daughter.

Some time after these early encounters, Rae had bumped into Christie near Rillington Place in Notting Hill, West London, and had gone back to Christie's house with him. Not long after this casual meeting the grisly discovery of three women's bodies in a cupboard was made by the owner of the house. Others, including that of Christie's wife, were discovered by the police. Rae's exclusive descriptive of the gruesome events, headlined MORE GRISLY SECRETS: FIRST FULL AUTHENTIC STORY had been praised as an object lesson in crime reporting.

Christie had gone on the run: now, here he was on the telephone to Rae, tired, cold and weary, and in urgent need of food. 'What would you like?' Rae inquired. 'A thick gammon rasher with two fried eggs, baked beans and some chips, some thick bread and butter and a cup of tea,' came the reply.

A rendezvous was arranged by the bushes opposite Wood

Green town hall in north London on a promise that he would not be double-crossed, and the office canteen was alerted to prepare the requested feast. Rae and a colleague drove to the arranged meeting place. Rae later recalled: 'I was picturing the thrill of it: when I'd fed Christie and let him warm through I would ring Scotland Yard and say casually: "By the way, if you want Christie I'll bring him in." We parked opposite the town hall as we had arranged, well out of any lamplight. I opened the door and we waited. Suddenly there was a rustle in the bushes and a man came forward hesitantly. Then it happened. I was too fed up even to inquire why – whether there had been a fracas at a dance or whether it was just an ordinary policeman's meet on the beat. But two policemen approached one from either side. I saw them and swore. Christie saw them and fled. Just a scurry in the bushes and he was gone. We drove on a few yards and returned when the policemen had gone but Christie never came back.'

Two days later he was arrested on the towpath at Putney, leaning on some railings, too hungry to run and too weary to care.

Later he confessed to murdering Evans's wife as well as the other victims. Rae, however, remained convinced that Christie did not murder Beryl Evans. 'Like Haigh, the acid bath murderer, he would have confessed to a hundred murders if he thought that would make him convincingly mad enough to qualify for Broadmoor instead of the gallows,' Rae argued. 'He had no conscience about murder at all. But he did not murder Beryl Evans. He may have known something about it. He may have helped Timothy Evans to get rid of her body and the child's body too. He probably did.' But Rae was convinced there were two stranglers living in the same house.

Rae, who covered around 2,000 murder cases during his career, was one of the finest crime correspondents in Fleet Street, a man with remarkable contacts among criminals, police and judiciary. Senior detectives would delay the start of a press conference – and judges their summing up – until his arrival. On one occasion when an officious court official impeded the movement of reporters from the press seats during a trial at Bristol, a note from Rae to the judge, whom he knew, pointing out their difficulties, particularly of evening paper colleagues, soon rectified the situation. After the lunch adjournment, the judge summoned the officer in charge of the court arrangements and instructed him to have the offending officer removed, remarking that, 'Journalists know how to behave in my court.'

Both Haigh and Christie, as well as more contentious individuals like Timothy Evans and Derek Bentley, who was accused of the murder of a policeman at Croydon, were all executed by Britain's chief hangman, Albert Pierrepoint, whose own memoirs appeared in the *News of the World* in 1975. Pierrepoint carried on a family tradition as hangman, succeeding his father and his uncle, and during a 25-year career, ten of them as chief executioner, he dispatched 433 men and 17 women, including Ruth Ellis, the last woman to be executed in Britain. He received a fee for each execution rather than a regular salary and it was a dispute over his remuneration, rather than repugnance at the nature of his work, that eventually brought him to give up the job in 1956, after which he kept a public house in Oldham and wrote his memoirs.

Pierrepoint was a dispassionate man who regarded his macabre occupation as a profession and approached the practice of hanging as a science, assiduously studying the technical aspects so as to ensure that the sentence was carried out as humanely as possible. But with hindsight he revised his views on his unusual career, declaring after his retirement that he did not believe that any of the hundreds of executions he had carried out had acted as a deterrent against future murder. After hanging was abolished in Britain in 1969 he campaigned against the return of capital punishment. 'In my view, capital punishment achieved nothing except revenge,' he said.

There was also a compassionate side to Pierrepoint, which emerged in correspondence with him at the time of the serialization of his memoirs. To illustrate the series, pictures had been taken of him with the young daughters of some of his friends. 'I am known to them as Uncle Albert,' he explained. 'One of the girls has been coming to our home since she was in a carrycot. She is now twelve years old and still comes to our home every week. We have no children of our own but we love having them around.'

Unbeknown to Pierrepoint at the relevant time, another of his acquaintances had been a close friend of the family of Ruth Ellis since long before 'this unfortunate tragedy'. At the time of the serialization he learnt from the acquaintance that Ruth Ellis's mother was seriously ill in hospital. 'Please be as kind to her as possible in her remaining hours,' Pierrepoint pleaded. He later wrote thanking the editor for handling the Ruth Ellis instalment 'with proper restraint'. Many items had been published about her which were untrue and unfair to her family, he said. 'Anything I have said about Ruth Ellis is correct and not in any way objectionable,' he wrote. 'When I retired rumours spread that I had done so because of the Ruth Ellis affair. I have still got the letters from the Home Office to prove this was untrue.'

Much of what was published about the way Ruth Ellis disported herself at the execution was also untrue. 'I have seen some very brave men die but none braver than any of the females I attended, including Ruth Ellis,' he added. 'She was very brave and not what some of the press have stated. I know the truth because I was there.'

Pierrepoint's own end had no drama: he died peacefully in a Southport nursing home on 10 July 1992 at the age of 87 – 'A perfect gentleman whose past never played on his conscience,' said the matron.

FIFTEEN

This Sporting Life

News of the World journalists are an inventive and imaginative lot, ever ready to steal a march on their rivals when it comes to getting a story. When you're working for the world's largest-circulation Sunday newspaper, you need that spark of initiative to stay one jump ahead. This is just as true of the enterprising bunch of fellows who produce the nation's brightest Sunday paper sports pages as it is of the news and features writers.

The paper's sports coverage has always been the envy of the rest of Fleet Street. Not only has it prided itself on having the best all-round reporting, but over the years has featured the star names of many sports among its contributors. 'Readers expect us to have the big names writing for us,' says one veteran sportswriter. The paper has rarely, if ever, let the readers down in this respect.

Typical of the way a *News of the World* sports man operates was the coup pulled off by writer Fred Burcombe, now the paper's deputy sports editor, just before the start of a Wimbledon fortnight. The sports department had been racking their brains for some time to come up with a good idea to preview the world's most famous tennis championships. Somebody came up with the notion of getting John McEnroe, then undoubtedly the top name in tennis, to write his first ever piece for a newspaper.

Easier said than done, of course, with a man like McEnroe, whose love for pressmen was known to be marginally less than his liking for opponents, linesmen and umpires. Still, nothing ventured, nothing gained, as they say. So off went fearless Fred to the Midlands, where McEnroe was playing in an exhibition for his racket sponsors.

Burcombe haunted the place for some hours but found it impossible to get McEnroe on his own, away from his entourage and other pressmen. He was 'warned off' by a PR representative and kept at arm's length. Fearing a public rebuff and having virtually given up hope, Fred tried one last desperate move to get into Mac's dressing room. He went off to spend a penny and saw that the gents' toilet had another exit into the prohibited area. Fred gulped and took the plunge. He cornered Mac. 'Do you fancy writing about Wimbledon for the *News of the World*, John?' he asked. The scourge of umpires the world over thought for a moment, then replied in a surprisingly friendly tone: 'Why not? Come and see me at Queen's Club tomorrow.' Burcome did and the outspoken views of J.P. McEnroe eventually enlivened the *News of the World*'s Wimbledon coverage for three weeks.

The fiery American was just one of scores of the world's great sporting heroes who have contributed to the paper. From cricket, great names of the past like A.C. MacLaren and Lord Tennyson – grandson of the poet – both of whom captained England, wrote for the *News of the World*, as also did one of the greatest England batsmen of all time, Walter Hammond. The memoirs of Australian batting legend Don Bradman were serialized. And it was perhaps the most famous cricketer of them all, the legendary Dr W.G. Grace, who introduced Lord Riddell and Sir Emsley Carr to the noble game of bowls, which led to the paper sponsoring an annual tournament between England, Scotland, Wales and Ireland.

By far the longest cricketing association with the paper has been that of the great Australian skipper, Richie Benaud. The then sports editor and columnist Frank Butler recruited Benaud in 1961, immediately after the spin wizard had led his Aussies to an Ashes triumph over England. Every year since then, he has put his expert knowledge of cricket, probably the most outstanding in the game, at the disposal of *News of the World* readers. Over thirty years later, he's still going strong.

His pithy comments and outstanding reporting skills have been sought by many other newspapers, who tried umpteen times to lure him away. But his loyalty to the *News of the World* never wavered. Benaud's other great passion is golf and there are those members of the present-day sports staff who maintain that the amount of money he has taken from them over the years at the game might just have influenced the great Australian!

Golf, inevitably given the paper's long connection with Walton Heath Golf Club, has always figured strongly on the paper's sports pages. The association is a long and historic one, dating back to Riddell and Sir Emsley Carr's obsession with the game, later assumed also by Sir William Carr. Riddell and Sir Emsley virtually regarded Walton Heath as their own private course which, indeed, it more or less was, since the *News of the World* owned and operated it.

Riddell and Carr's passion for golf, plus the publicity potential they could see in the game, led to the paper's sponsorship, along with the Professional Golfers' Association, of a matchplay competition with a top prize of £250, a very considerable sum in those days. Previously, the largest amount of prize money a professional golfer could hope to win was £50 in the Open championship.

The *News of the World* tournament was the forerunner of the great professional events of today. The very first of these tournaments in 1903 was won by one of the greatest players of his day, James Braid, recruited as the professional at Walton Heath the following year. Braid, from Earlsferry in Fifeshire, was a weekend golfer until he moved to London in 1893 to work for the head clubmaker, a boyhood friend, at the Army and Navy Stores.

Braid entered his first pro tournament in 1894, finishing fifth, then came to prominence the following year with an exhibition match against another leading professional, John Henry Taylor, who was to become the *News of the World*'s first golf correspondent. Braid had a string of successes in the *News of the World* tournament, managed to finish as runner-up in

1927, at the age of 57, and was still playing at Walton Heath at the age of 80.

Taylor had started as a caddie and, along with Braid and Harry Vardon, was one of the three leading professionals of the day. Between 1894 and 1914 the trio dominated the British Open championship, Vardon winning it six times and Braid and Taylor five times apiece. Such was Lord Riddell's passion for golf that he had a plaster cast of Vardon's hands grasping a club in his office.

Taylor was succeeded as golf correspondent by another of the game's all-time greats, Henry Cotton, three times British Open champion between 1934 and 1948. Cotton wrote for the *News of the World* for many years and was an extremely close personal friend of Sir William Carr. Cotton, though a golfing genius, was something of an eccentric when it came to writing about the game. His copy was always delivered handwritten, often in green ink and usually on the notepaper of whichever luxury hotel he happened to be staying in at the time. Sometimes it was the George V in Paris, the Savoy in London or the New York Biltmore.

On occasions the great man's dispatch would arrive on small, oblong sheets of thin card. Their origin was a mystery for a long time until a diligent sports subeditor eventually solved it. Cotton was not one to waste anything lightly, so, rather than use up expensive writing paper, he pressed into service the dividers from packets of Shredded Wheat.

Cotton was hardly ever seen in the office but suffered from the delusion that everybody moved in the same exalted circles as he did. He would frequently telephone and cheerfully ask the newest, youngest member of the sports department: 'Seen Bill this morning?' The 'Bill' referred to was, of course, his great chum, Sir William Carr who, as chairman of the *News of the World*, did not often lurk in the humble surroundings of the sports department.

Carr was usually to be found either in the panelled splendour of his second-floor Bouverie Street office or in the similarly panelled surroundings of the Falstaff, a now long-demolished hostelry which was in those days the office pub, just round the corner in Fleet Street. Henry Cotton never appeared in the Falstaff to buy the sports staff a drink, as far as anyone can recall, but 'Bill' Carr certainly did.

On one occasion, when a young subeditor was invited to have a drink and requested a rum and coke, the chairman snorted and said: 'Why don't you drink Scotch?' However, it didn't do the young man, who'd done his National Service in the Royal Navy, any harm in sticking to the traditional navy tipple, for he went on to work for the *News of the World* for over thirty years and is today the paper's current sports editor, Bill Bateson.

Bateson, an ebullient Arsenal supporter whose booming acclaim of his favourite team frequently rings round the paper's present-day sixth-floor offices at Wapping, leads his staff from the front. When a tabloid *News of the World* was being planned in the mid 1980s, sport appeared to have been forgotten as the dummy pages for news and features were being planned in secret over several weeks in an office far removed from the rest of the editorial department. Finally, on the weekend before the switch to tabloid, he took some blank sheets home and came back the following Tuesday with his own proposals. His vision was accepted and in 1992 the paper won a major award for the best-designed sports pages in Sunday newspapers.

The *News of the World*, through its long commitment to sponsorship of golf and other sports, has been responsible for encouraging many young people to take up sport as a professional career. Indeed, among their ranks were hidden some stars of the future. Typical was a letter received in 1979, from the winner of the Sir William Carr Trophy for an under-23s golf tournament, who wrote on behalf of all the competitors to thank the paper for its sponsorship. His name – Ian Woosnam, who went on to become one of the biggest stars in world golf in the 1980s and 1990s.

Soccer, inevitably, occupies the lion's share of the paper's sports pages during the winter months. And here, again, the *News of the World* has a long and honourable history of culling great names in the game to contribute to its pages.

Two of the greatest legends of all time in British football were among them. The great Tom Finney, one of the finest players who ever pulled on an England shirt, was a contributor for many years. And the idol of Geordieland, Newcastle's Jackie Milburn – 'Wor Jackie', as the fans called him – was a soccer columnist in the paper for over twenty years. Another top star writer in pre-Second World War days was the wizard of dribble, Alex James.

Other top soccer stars to have written for the paper include George Best, Jim Baxter in the Scottish pages and the ex-player, Fulham chairman and TV pundit Jimmy Hill. In more recent times, the tradition of having the biggest names in the game writing for the paper was maintained by England's 1990 World Cup skipper, Gary Lineker, whose exclusive views on domestic and world soccer were given a platform in the paper.

And it wasn't just the stars who made the *News of the World* the number one read on Sundays for the fans. In Reg Drury, the paper had probably the best-informed and most widely read soccer reporter in Fleet Street. The paper's chief soccer writer for more than twenty-eight years, Drury had a contacts book and reputation for accuracy and inside knowledge that was the envy of all his rivals.

When Reg finally hung up his notebook and pencil and called it a day at the end of 1992, he had been reporting football for an incredible forty-nine years, starting as a star-struck fifteen-year-old on a North London local paper, covering a match between Tottenham Hotspur and Portsmouth at White Hart Lane in February 1944. As a tribute to Reg, the *News of the World* devoted a two-page spread to his memories, including the reproduction of the original programme for his very first match, which included instructions on how to use an air-raid shelter. Reg's memories also took in another wartime match during which one of Hitler's V1 rockets cut out over the ground. Play paused for a moment, then carried on, Reg reported.

In his long career, Drury knew everyone who was anyone in soccer. He was a confidant to players and managers alike and a good friend to many younger players on the way up. And when the *News of the World* gave him a farewell dinner at the House of Commons earlier this year, the list of guests from the soccer world read like a Who's Who of the game, all there to pay tribute to one of the most respected and gentlemanly sports writers in Fleet Street.

From the world of boxing there were champions like Jimmy Wilde, Freddie Mills, Don Cockell, Archie Moore and Dai Dower, all of whom had their memoirs published in the *News of the World* or contributed to its columns. From rugby came the Welsh wizard and top BBC personality Cliff Morgan and British Lions star Vivian Jenkins.

There was tragedy, too, when the *News of the World*'s top rugby union writer, Welshman Lloyd Lewis, was killed in the Turkish Airlines DC10 crash at Orly Airport, Paris, in 1974 whilst returning from a France–England game. Lewis was hugely popular throughout the rugby world, but especially in his native Wales, and his memory is perpetuated in the Lloyd Lewis Memorial Trophy, presented every year as the Man of the Match award in the Welsh Rugby Union Cup final.

Horse racing, the so-called Sport of Kings, is another activity that has always been guaranteed strong coverage in the paper. For a while in the 1980s the *News of the World* sponsored the greatest steeplechase of them all, the Grand National, until it was taken over by its sister paper, the *Sun*. However, the *News of the World*'s interest in the turf goes back more than a hundred years.

The paper's first racing editor, W. J. Innes, writing under the pseudonym of Pegasus, was among the foremost writers of his day, not just on racing but on rowing also, in which sport he promoted championship events. But it was as a racing tipster that his career really took off in 1881, when he pulled off a remarkable double by selecting an American-owned horse called Foxhall to win both the Cesarewitch and Cambridge-shire handicaps. The horse duly obliged at long odds and Innes was said to have not only delighted his readers but made him-self a fortune as well.

He became a very familiar figure to thousands of smokers, when his photograph was reproduced, surrounded by a horse-shoe, riding whip, saddle and stirrups, on tobacco papers in which loose tobacco was sold.

Innes's tips were closely followed for over twenty years, until his death in 1903. He was succeeded as Pegasus by Martin Cobbett, who also wrote books on country life, and then by Captain Tommy Browne, a leading amateur jockey and horse-breeding expert, who wrote the racing column for thirty years.

The Pegasus pseudonym still appears every Sunday above the racing tips in the *News of the World* and is regarded by punters as one of the best-informed racing services in any newspaper. Holders of the title have almost always been men who were steeped in the ways of the turf, with the unfortunate exception of one careless and short-reigned tipster who included in his list of a dozen horses to follow during a National Hunt season two that had died, one that had been sold to Argentina, one that had been shot the week before and another that had gone to stud.

A more recent Pegasus, the jovial Stanley Agate, retired in 1987 after writing the column for twenty-seven years. His tip-ping achievements included napping the Derby winner on no fewer than twelve occasions.

A somewhat less successful flirtation by the newspaper with the turf happened in the 1950s, when someone suggested that as many of the paper's readers liked a flutter, they might also care to share in the ownership – at least by association – of a horse. Enthusiastically, the paper bought two horses and readers were invited to write in with suggested names for them.

Ten thousand replies poured in and the names Paper Boy and Misprint were finally settled on. However, despite being handed over to the expert care of racing legend Sir Gordon Richards, the champion jockey-turned-trainer, and having another top jockey of the day, Scobie Breasley, aboard them, neither horse managed to earn its oats.

It was somewhat embarrassing for the paper, as so many *News of the World* readers had their money riding on the animals that they sometimes started favourites. It was said that a hapless hack who had been deputed to write enthusiastically about the horses – and who had told the readers to back them – once considered starting his column after they had lost (yet again) with the words: 'Sometimes it is difficult to know what to write!'

But a major reason for the *News of the World*'s great influence and success amongst sports fans was always its coverage of minority sports, like snooker, angling, darts, bowls and even pigeon racing. Old-timers in the sports department still vouch for the reader fury that would descend upon their heads if, no matter what momentous, world-shattering news the rest of the paper was carrying, they left out the pigeon results!

Decades before sports like snooker and darts became top-rating television audience-pullers, the paper was enthusiastically and comprehensively covering these most popular of working men's pastimes.

In snooker, as in virtually every other sport, the paper led the way by having the greatest name in the game as its correspondent, the one-and-only Joe Davis. Davis, a gentleman if ever there was one, helped like no one else to dispel the myth that success at snooker and billiards was the sign of a misspent youth. Joe, who won no less than fifteen world snooker titles with a cue he bought at a church bazaar for 7s 6d in pre-decimal money, was the *News of the World*'s snooker and billiards writer for many years.

It was Davis who recorded the big breaks and wrote about them long before the television moguls took snooker out of the smoky halls and put the players into evening dress with bow ties and fancy waistcoats. And the tradition was carried on right into the 1980s and 1990s with another Davis, the masterly Steve, who also featured in the *News of the World*, as did his Irish rival Dennis Taylor, another world champion, and the young Scots whiz kid Stephen Hendry, who wrote a column in the Scottish editions in 1991–2.

In darts, too, the paper was in the vanguard of the game long before television discovered it. Today, the game has been elevated from the pub saloon bar and turned into big business, with major tournaments running up to the world championships. But for over sixty years the BIG one, the tournament they all wanted to win, was the *News of the World* title.

In thousands of pubs and working men's clubs throughout Britain, it was simply the only tournament that mattered and every average pub player dreamed of standing on the stage at the Alexandra Palace in London, where the grand finals were held every year, and accepting the applause of the cheering multitude who always turned up to watch.

Top professional stars like Eric Bristow, Bobby George and Mike Gregory were all title-holders in the 1980s. Yet the tournament's appeal lay in the fact that the pro's were regularly embarrassed by some unknown who had his moment of glory. For, truly, the *News of the World* darts tournament was the people's event.

It was the organizers of the tournament who pioneered the idea of a giant dartboard on stage, with coloured lights that lit up in the appropriate sector to show what score had been made, so that those at the back of the hall could keep track of the games. And one nice little touch: for years, the tournament Master of Ceremonies was the appropriately named Les TREBLE!

It's often been said that the largest participation activity in Britain is not soccer or cricket or any of the major television sports – but angling. There are several million anglers of both sexes who every weekend cheerfully go off with their rods to spend lonely hours by a river bank. And they would surely raise an outcry the length of the land if the *News of the World* were to drop one of the most popular features of its sporting pages, the 'Fish of the Week' spot.

Every Sunday, keen anglers turn avidly to the feature to read about who has been landing the big ones. And the paper awards prize rods every week to the readers who hook the star catches in their sections. Fish of the Week has been running in the paper for sixty-five years, having been started originally by a father-and-son combination. Remarkably, the junior member of the team, the late George Clifford, was still judging the contest when it celebrated its fiftieth anniversary.

But for long service there's no one to beat former world table tennis champion Johnny Leach, yet again the biggest name in his particular sport. The world champ of 1951 was signed up by the paper the following year to oversee a coaching scheme for young players at Butlin's holiday camps and has been writing about table tennis ever since. Many of the talented youngsters unearthed by Leach went on to win international honours.

Coverage of minor sports goes back to the 1920s, when Lord Riddell suddenly developed an interest in speedway racing, then very much in its infancy. From a primitive beginning at the Crystal Palace in 1928, it became one of the most popular sports in Britain before the Second World War.

Introduced from Australia, it received scant notice in this country until Riddell decided to present a belt for an annual competition amongst London dirt-track riders. Fellow *News of the World* director Harry Aldridge reckoned he'd discovered the reason for his Lordship's sudden interest in the strange new sport when he accompanied Riddell to Crystal Palace one evening and was introduced to an Australian lady rider whom Riddell announced was his niece!

Sir Emsley Carr was regarded as an authority on almost every sport and it was for services to sport, not newspapers, that his son Sir William received his knighthood. Apart from golf and racing, another of the Carr family's great passions was for athletics and in 1923 the paper ran an Olympic Games Training Scheme, designed to boost the athletic capabilities of the nation. The following year, the paper sponsored the

London to Brighton relay race, each runner being awarded a commemorative medal.

Sir Emsley Carr helped to establish one of the most prestigious events in the athletics calendar, the British Games, and the paper sponsored the games from 1925. A race, the Emsley Carr Mile, was named in his honour, which became virtually the Blue Riband of the track for successive generations of great British milers, including the world's first four-minute miler, Dr Roger Bannister, who won the event in 1951.

How appropriate it was then, that another Amateur Athletics Association champion, Doug Wilson, should become not only the athletics correspondent for many years but also the paper's advertising manager.

The *News of the World*'s passion for sponsoring major sporting events brought the paper valuable publicity over the years. But one story it perhaps could have done without was what became famous in 1956 as the affair of Nina and the Five Hats. It started off as a straightforward sporting event and turned into a diplomatic incident that hit every front news page.

The paper decided to sponsor an athletics match between Great Britain and Russia, even though the Cold War was at that time in one of its iciest stages. The Russian athletes were warmly welcomed to Britain but, unfortunately, one of the Russian women, a giant discus thrower called Nina Ponomarova, was accused of shoplifting in Oxford Street. It was alleged Miss Ponomarova had taken a fancy to four little feathered hats and a woollen beret and helped herself, without bothering to pay for them.

The trivial affair blew up into a full-scale diplomatic slanging match between Britain and Russia, with allegations and counter-allegations being hurled back and forth. Eventually, the Russian team caught the plane back to Moscow, the planned athletics match never took place and the *News of the World* was left nursing a bill for £6,000 as a result of the cancellation.

Sponsorship of numerous major sporting events, for so long a flamboyant tradition, virtually came to an end with the

arrival of Australian Rupert Murdoch, who took over the paper
in 1969. One of the earliest things the new proprietor did was
sell Walton Heath Golf Club, the spiritual home of Lord Riddell
and the Carr family. In the tough, competitive world of newspapers in the 1960s and 1970s, such things were an expensive
luxury.

SIXTEEN

Sir William Carr

No history of the *News of the World* would be complete without a pen portrait of the remarkable man who was its chairman for seventeen years from 1952 to 1969. Sir William Carr – 'Bill' as he was universally known to everybody, family, friends and staff alike – was in his way as extraordinary a character as Lord Riddell a generation before.

His full name was William Emsley Carr and he was a very proud man. Proud of his great uncle, Lascelles Carr, who'd bought the *News of the World* in 1891, and proud of his father Sir Emsley, editor for half a century, whose name he perpetuated. Carr was a shy man, a trait which he sometimes disguised with rudeness. However, such were his other qualities that if he'd abused someone it was usually forgiven and his loyalty to his friends and staff was unwavering.

He was not the natural heir to the Carr empire. He attained the *News of the World* throne through unfortunate circumstances. Of the three sons of Sir Emsley, Harry Carr was the one who was being groomed to succeed. After an apprenticeship at the *Western Mail* in Cardiff, he had been news editor at the *News of the World* under Percy Davies and was already a director, representing the Carr family interests. His sights were set first on becoming deputy editor to Davies, although by then war had broken out and he was serving in the RAF. He asked that no one else should be appointed to the post until the war had ended and he looked forward confidently to promotion then.

Harry's twin brother Walter had not worked on the paper and although he had ambitions of a directorship, he was not regarded as a serious contender. But the sudden and unexpected deaths of both Harry and Walter created a new situation.

Not only was there now no Carr on the board but the expected order of succession was upset. This was the background against which Bill Carr had set about his ultimately successful battle against his cousins, the Jacksons, and their nominees.

Until then, Carr had been regarded as a relatively junior and unimportant member of the family. To provide him with an interest, he had been given a minor post on the business side of the newspaper. His leanings were commercial rather than journalistic. He had no literary skills and could never have adapted to his distinguished father's combined role as company chairman and editor. Even so, when unusual circumstances brought about his advancement, he regarded it as no more than his birthright.

Carr's days on the fringe of the *News of the World* empire had left him with an inferiority complex but also plenty of time to pursue an active social round. He hid his basic shyness behind an outward air of bonhomie and social indulgence. He liked long, well-lubricated lunches at the Savoy Grill, which later became jokingly known in the office as the directors' 'canteen'. The table talk, helped along by a never-ending flow of drinks, would continue well into the afternoon, long after the food had been consumed, after which Carr would be driven home by his chauffeur.

He was a brilliant mathematician, at least before lunch, and could do complicated sums on the back of a cigarette packet. But no one with any sense paid much attention to his post-lunch decisions and it was usually left to the long-suffering managing director, Mark Chapman-Walker, to sort out the worst of the chairman's indiscretions.

Carr was a connoisseur of Scotch whisky and maintained his expertise by sampling at least two bottles a day. He was an inveterate gambler who won or lost thousands at the roulette table or on the turn of a single card. His favourite gambling spot was John Aspinall's Claremont Club in Grosvenor Square. Often, after playing chemin de fer for several hours, he would finish off upstairs playing backgammon with Lord Lucan.

He always did things in style, like the day he told Stafford Somerfield, who became editor of the *News of the World* in 1960, to hire a ship to take competition winners on a cruise. 'I thought he meant a boat on the river,' said Somerfield in his memoirs. 'But, no, he meant the *Queen Mary*!'

Somerfield telephoned Cunard and asked what it would cost to hire the huge liner for a weekend. They were a bit surprised but they obliged. The *News of the World* took 1,000 readers to Las Palmas for Christmas and the crew declared it the best trip ever for tips – which said something about the spending power of the paper's readers. Winners were allowed to take their families with them on the trip and one family totalled fourteen. Carr and Somerfield joined their faithful readers on the cruise and Carr insisted on meeting as many of them as possible, so the cocktail parties started at 10.30 a.m. every day. Also along for the trip was Carr's pal, snooker ace Joe Davis, whose trousers fell down on the dance floor and a thoroughly good time was had by all.

Possibly due to his drinking habits, Carr suffered severely with gout and was often in considerable pain.

He ran the *News of the World* rather like a family grocery store. He loved the prestige of being its chairman, as much for the social kudos it brought him as for the business side. He treated the staff like old family retainers. Hardly anyone ever got fired and once a year they all trooped, with wives, husbands and sweethearts, down to the palatial Carr home in Sussex, where they lined up to be greeted by Sir William and Lady Carr, played croquet and were served strawberries and champagne by flunkeys in tails.

One anecdote neatly illustrates Carr's paternalism towards his employees. Another annual function for editorial staff was picturesquely known as the Leg o'Mutton Supper. It was a strictly stag – men only – affair and invariably turned into a long, riotous evening. At one of these jolly occasions, the show business reporter, who was well in his cups, found himself in conversation with Sir William. No one knew quite what possessed him but the reporter gripped the chairman firmly by the tie and uttered the interesting question: 'Why are you so f***ing rich and I'm so f***ing poor?'

Next day, the unfortunate man arrived at the office and, with a vague recollection of what he'd done the night before, expected to be told to pick up his cards. He got into the lift and bumped straight into Carr, who merely regarded him sorrowfully, shook his head and remarked: 'Oh, the silly things we do and say at times.' And no more was ever said about it.

Another reporter, Roger Hall, who later became Carr's personal assistant, tells how he was arrested by police for obstructing the pavement outside Bow Street Magistrate's Court whilst trying to sign up for the paper somebody involved in a spying case. He was fined the petty sum of £2 but Carr took it as a slight on the paper and insisted he must appeal. The *News of the World* hired a top barrister, at a cost of many hundreds of pounds, and got Hall's conviction squashed.

Stafford Somerfield tells another delightful anecdote in his memoirs of a night at the Savoy when Carr and Mark Chapman-Walker had a heated debate about a political point which they decided only the then Prime Minister, Sir Alec Douglas-Home, could resolve. Somerfield was instructed to telephone Downing Street and make an appointment for the next day.

Next morning, the three top men from the *News of the World* were duly ushered into the Cabinet room to see Douglas-Home, who was flanked by his advisers. The problem was, none of the three could remember why they were there and when Sir Alec asked why they wanted to see him, there was a long silence. It was Chapman-Walker, a former publicity head of Tory Central Office, who spoke first. 'The situation, Prime Minister,' he said.

'Could you define that a little more closely?' Douglas-Home replied.

Somerfield, thinking on his feet despite a severe hangover, leaped in with: 'Rhodesia, sir.' Douglas-Home then proceeded to give a smooth and erudite rundown of the Rhodesian situation and sat back.

Carr finally made his contribution: 'May I suggest, Prime Minister, that you don't wear those half-moon glasses when you next appear on television. It gives you a wrong image.' Sir Alec thanked him gravely, then offered the trio refreshments. Outside in Horse Guards Parade, Carr said to Somerfield: 'Don't you ever do that to me again.'

Sir William loved motor cars and bought Rolls Royces for the Carr family and senior executives as though they were Ford Prefects. Hedda Hopper, the famous American columnist and socialite, got one in part payment for extracts from her autobiography. She had lunched with Carr and jokingly chided him over the payment she'd received, saying he'd got her story for nothing. 'Well, not quite,' he replied, aware the paper had paid her £5,000 for six extracts although such had been the reader response that the series was extended to twelve.

Next day, a Rolls was left outside her hotel, the Dorchester, and a representative of the suppliers handed her the keys. When a surprised Hedda Hopper asked why, the deliverer replied: 'When a gentleman buys a lady a Rolls we never inquire into the reasons.'

Said Hopper later: 'It was the handsomest bonus I ever received.'

Another story told with glee by *News of the World* staff concerned the time Stafford Somerfield drove his office Jaguar home late at night – in the days before the breathalyzer – and awoke next morning to find the car gone. Assuming the car had been stolen, he duly reported it to the chairman. Sir William Carr's response was: 'Go and get yourself another one.' Some little time later, Somerfield's neighbour, who had been out of the country for a while, discovered the missing Jaguar in his garage.

Roger Hall, who'd had the might of the paper behind him in his court battle, later accompanied Carr, Somerfield and 1,000 *News of the World* readers on the famous *Queen Mary* cruise. During the trip, he convinced Carr that he should become public relations officer for the News of the World group, as the company had just gone public on the stock exchange. Little did Hall, though a veteran newsman, realize what he was in for. He became, he recalled, a combined PR man and personal minder for Sir William. He was expected to be at the chairman's beck and call, day and night, and act as a messenger between him and the other directors.

Said Hall: 'He would have won any competition for the most autocratic chairman in Britain and, for many, a summons to his office was equivalent to an invitation to take a seat in the electric chair.' Hall recalled that once during a rail strike, there was a meeting of top executives to discuss alternative distribution for the paper and he was sent to fetch the man in charge of the publishing operation to see Sir William. The man concerned and his father before him had served the paper for more than eighty years combined.

When told that the chairman wanted to see him, he trembled like someone with the plague and could hardly get his jacket on. He'd never had a summons to Carr's office before and he didn't believe his father had ever had one, either. Outside the office he became trance-like and Hall virtually had to drag him through the door. When Carr asked him a question about the likely print run for the paper, the poor fellow became speechless.

'I had to take him out into the corridor and sit him on the floor before I could get the figure out of him,' recalled Hall. 'When Sir William subsequently asked me the reason for the man's odd behaviour, I decided to tell him the truth and said he was frightened to death of him. I was told that was rubbish and I should arrange for the man to see a doctor. I didn't bother.'

On another occasion, Hall found himself in an embarrassing situation when Carr phoned him at about 2.00 a.m. after getting home from Walton Heath Golf Club. After some initial difficulty in understanding what the chairman was talking about, Hall finally gathered that he had earlier that evening fired the club secretary, a retired cavalry colonel. Hall was instructed to go to the club the following day and take over until a new secretary could be found.

Hall said: 'In the morning I rang him and suggested he might like to reverse the sacking decision. He told me to come to the country for lunch. Wonder of wonders, he was drinking water and was in a much more reasonable frame of mind. He agreed he had been hasty and the golf club secretary was allowed to keep his job.'

Another of Sir William's gaffes occurred during a reception for competitors and delegates to the British Games, the big athletics meeting which the *News of the World* promoted. Guest of honour at the dinner, at the Dorchester, was the chief of police from Jamaica, which was due to host the Common-wealth Games the following year. Carr's views on race, it should be mentioned, would have raised more than a few eyebrows today.

After eating little and drinking a lot, he insisted that a match should be arranged with white athletes pitted against black ones. The Jamaican police chief didn't share his view and next day, fortunately, his executives – including athletics writer and former mile champion Doug Wilson – managed to convince him that the idea was a non-starter.

Another extraordinarily flamboyant gesture of Carr's cost the *News of the World* a great deal of money in 1967. Over a liquid discussion with his pal and rival Sir Max Aitken, chair-man of the Express Newspapers group, who were keen pro-moters of powerboat racing, Carr made a bet that he could build a boat that would win the big *Daily Express* Cowes to Torquay race.

Next day, he ordered work to go ahead. The leading power boat designer of the day was engaged and a top yard in the Isle of Wight commissioned to build the craft. Eventually the boat, looking like a man o'war and bearing the number 353, the prefix of the Fleet Street telephone exchange, was completed at a cost of £100,000. It was exhibited at the Earl's Court Boat Show and among visitors to inspect her were Princess Margaret and her then husband Tony Armstrong-Jones.

Initially, everything augured well. The boat broke the diesel record for a measured mile on the Solent and top driver Peter Twiss, then also holder of the world air speed record, was hired to drive it. Then came calamity. The ninety-miles-an-hour craft took part in the *Daily Express* race but didn't finish. And in the very next race, the boat exploded into flames off the Dorset coast and sank beneath the waves off Portland Bill, taking with it £100,000 of *News of the World* money.

Among the four-man crew who had to swim for their lives away from the wrecked boat, until picked up by a rescue vessel, was the paper's long-serving promotions manager, Ron Bacchus, an ex-naval man who'd already been sunk three times before. He said: 'We all tried to get sloshed that night but we were so shocked that the booze just wouldn't work.' An expensive venture, indeed . . . and all the result of a wager, fuelled by alcohol!

Promotions man Bacchus, who originally joined the *News of the World* as a lift boy just weeks before war broke out in 1939, gives an insight into the firm's paternalistic attitude towards its employees. He said: 'After the war I was transferred to an aircraft carrier in the Pacific and when I was demobbed in 1946, I had the chance to stay on in Australia. But all the time I'd been in the Navy the firm had paid my mother half my £2-a-week salary, so I thought I'd better do the decent thing and go home. When the paper was 100 years old, everybody got an extra week's wages but, of course, my mother got mine.'

Under Bill Carr's chairmanship, the *News of the World* went sponsorship crazy. Literally scores of events up and down the country – some big affairs but many of them minor, local tiddlers – had the paper's stamp on them.

Besides the darts, golf and athletics tournaments, the big ones included the annual El Alamein Reunion at the Royal Albert Hall, with, inevitably, the forces' sweetheart Vera Lynn an ever-present. One year, Marlene Dietrich starred, with Burt Bacharach, her musical director, conducting the band of the Welsh Guards.

The paper also sponsored beauty contests, like Miss United Kingdom, and even, for a time, Miss World. But at the same time there were the giant leek contests, flower and vegetable shows, a national town criers' championship, crown green bowls tournaments, the world pipe band championships, a rowing regatta on the Serpentine, pigeon racing, greyhound racing, small-bore rifle shooting at Bisley, old-time dancing competitions in conjunction with Butlin's and a huge Star Gala in Battersea Park, attended by a host of top show biz stars and with all the proceeds going to the Variety Club's charities. Carr thought it was all good publicity and brought in reader goodwill, though what the paper decided to sponsor often depended on who he'd had lunch with.

So that was Sir William Carr, the contradictory, autocratic chairman of the *News of the World*. According to Roger Hall, he was a man whom it was easy to dislike, particularly when he was boorish and rude after drinking two bottles of Johnny Walker Red Label. He made mistakes, especially after lunch. But he was also intensely loyal to his staff and they usually forgave him his rudeness and indiscretions.

Hall tells two stories that illustrate graphically the two sides of Carr's nature. Everybody was saddened when a young chief subeditor died in his early thirties. He was a Scot of great charisma, a great party-giver and hugely popular in the office. But he had a severe hole-in-the-heart condition and was living on borrowed time. Eventually, he died on the operating table.

Because of his medical condition, the man had been unable to obtain any life insurance. Sir William Carr sent Hall to see his widow, who had been left with one child, a 7-year-old daughter. Hall was instructed to tell the widow that Carr would pay for the girl's education out of his own private pocket until she was 17.

But even after he had left the *News of the World*, following the takeover by Rupert Murdoch, Carr's autocratic ways hadn't changed. Hall recounted running into his old boss one day at Walton Heath Golf Club, not having seen him for more than a year. Carr ordered his former 'minder' to fetch him a Scotch. Hall jokingly told him: 'Not this time, everything's changed.'

Carr stared at him hard and said: 'Nothing's changed. Get me a Scotch.'

Said Hall: 'I got the Scotch. I never saw him alive again.'

SEVENTEEN

Circulation Highs and Lows

On his election as chairman, Carr set about reorganizing the business and diversifying the company's interests, ending its sole dependence on the newspaper. The directions he took were not always successful or profitable. A number of magazines were acquired and holdings were taken in businesses like Berrows Newspapers of Worcester, a provincial newspaper group, Convoys, a warehousing and travel company, and Bemrose, a firm of colour printers on Merseyside. There were also interests in commercial television, as well as a number of smaller companies whose activities ranged from chemicals to insurance.

The only Fleet Street link was a brief one, a joint interest in the mid 1950s with Associated Newspapers in the *Daily Sketch* (later absorbed by the *Daily Mail*), which was sold back to Associated after four years. Carr's extravagant lifestyle was maintained, largely through the News of the World Organization, as the reorganized company became known. But his various new ventures were less than spectacular. The paper remained the backbone of the operation, contentedly marching on with the sort of circulation figures that proved it was giving its millions of readers just the fare they wanted.

Even in wartime, when the number of pages was severely restricted, the style and content had scarcely changed at all. The paper was as patriotic as ever. Percy Davies, then chairman and editor, had reported to the shareholders in 1943: 'Our policy has been to give priority to government announcements on such matters as food, fuel, cooking, clothing, etc., to the disadvantage of the commercial advertiser.' He was able to add, somewhat smugly: 'From the moment war was declared, we have maintained close and almost daily contact with the government departments concerned. The prestige of our paper has never stood higher in the eyes of the government.'

Communiqués and official wartime news and dispatches from correspondents were given on the front page but, unlike many other papers, the *News of the World* realized that people wanted to read other news as well. Many aspects of life were continuing much the same as they had always done. Thus, the paper continued to chronicle the courts, still a source of some of the best stories. The accounts of people's peccadilloes were much enjoyed by the troops overseas, many of whom were sent copies of the paper by their families, and served as a reminder of home.

Because papers were reduced to six or eight pages until well after the war had ended, reports were compressed and headlines squeezed so that every column contained as much as could be crammed into it. The leader page, the prestige feature of the paper, continued to be given over to an article written by a leading public figure, and the John Hilton advice column was sacrosanct.

Despite these restrictions on space, a strong team of foreign correspondents had been appointed. These included the distinguished journalist Clare Hollingworth, filing from the Far East, the flamboyant Richard Wyndham in the Middle East and Reginald Cudlipp in America. Wyndham, who had been appointed in 1943, was a man of wide-ranging talents and enjoyed a circle of distinguished and Bohemian friends. Besides being a writer, he was also an artist of some repute. His friends included the composer William Walton, poets Osbert and Sacheverell Sitwell, Constant Lambert, the conductor, and leading literary lights like Cyril Connolly and Tom Driberg, originator of the *Daily Express*'s William Hickey gossip column.

Wyndham kept a well-stocked wine cellar at his home in a converted mill and liked driving open cars with a beautiful blonde at his side. He once gave the *News of the World*'s accountants near heart failure when he bought an aeroplane on the paper and crashed it. Sadly, Wyndham met a violent death. After the war, he was sent to Palestine to report on the troubles there and got a sniper's bullet in the head when he stood up in a trench to take a photograph.

The expensive team of foreign correspondents was swept away in the aftermath of Dunn's and Skelton's departures. Reginald Cudlipp was recalled from America. Cudlipp, a tall and distinguished-looking man who might easily be mistaken for a diplomat or a judge, was one of a trio of Welsh brothers, all of whom achieved distinction in Fleet Street's top echelons. He had first been recruited to the *News of the World* as a sub-editor just before the war by Harry Carr, whose copy he had often handled when they were colleagues on the *Western Mail*.

Cudlipp recalled: 'The place in those days was really a family concern. You felt you were joining a family, that you were regarded paternalistically. They were poor payers but, on the other hand, you could reckon in those uncertain days that you would still be there in ten years' time. The annual wayzgoose at the Carr home was like an annual family gathering. The great thing about the *News of the World* was the continuity, which was maintained in spite of the upheavals of the time.'

When Cudlipp returned after five-and-a-half years in the army, it proved difficult to find him, and others like him, a satisfactory role. The continuing newsprint rationing was to restrict any expansion in the size of the paper for some time. He turned down an offer to become syndications editor, selling the paper's articles to other publications, and was made letters editor for a time. Even this though, with the bulk of the correspondence being dealt with by the John Hilton Bureau, offered little scope.

His situation was unhappy until he was sent out to America as staff correspondent. While he was there, Percy Davies died and Skelton succeeded as editor. Skelton took to Cudlipp and, over a bottle of claret at Skelton's Kent farmhouse home, confirmed his appointment for a further three years with the additional title of assistant editor. After only two months, however, Cudlipp received a cable telling him that Skelton had gone and that Arthur Waters had become editor. Waters recalled Cudlipp and made him features editor.

Waters was a long-serving member of the staff who, according to Cudlipp, had never wanted to be editor. He was a brilliant writer in the old *News of the World* idiom of the 1920s and 1930s. His style was flowery and richly descriptive and he didn't let the facts get in the way of a good story. It was Waters who had written the splendid, colourful account of the trial of the murderer Rouse, quoted in chapter 8. 'He was a great devotee of the turf,' Cudlipp remembered. 'In his book, the Grand National was as important as the Russian Revolution. He could get hold of a man like Freddie Fox, one of the great jockeys of the time – the Lester Piggott of his day – and talk to him for a couple of hours. You wouldn't see Waters for the rest of the week but suddenly he would appear with a whole page feature based on the talk.'

Waters's wife owned a pub in Covent Garden, to which he devoted virtually as much attention as he did to affairs at the *News of the World*. He had a long, lugubrious face and was niggardly with money, the firm's as well as his own. He never lunched out unless it was free, stopped the daily papers for the staff and recouped inside a year the amount of the payoffs to Dunn and Skelton.

His editorship was dogged by ill health and he appointed Cudlipp as his deputy to relieve him of much of the day-to-day responsibility for the paper. Cudlipp leap-frogged over two other assistant editors to the job, though Sir William Carr, then the chairman-elect, was believed to prefer Stafford Somerfield.

Cudlipp was in Iceland on holiday when, in 1953, Waters died. On his return, he was appointed to the editor's chair, creating a record unequalled in Fleet Street before or since, as his two brothers were also national newspaper editors – Percy, the eldest, at the *Daily Herald*, and Hugh (later Lord Cudlipp), at the *Sunday Pictorial*.

Cudlipp inherited the editorship of the *News of the World* in a period when the paper had achieved an all-time high in circulation but was soon to be facing difficulties. The circulation had peaked in June 1950, at an amazing 8,443,000. At this time, newsprint was still restricted and the paper was producing issues of only eight, or sometimes ten, pages. The signs that it would be impossible to maintain such a vast circulation were already on the wall.

Arthur Waters had believed that what sold newspapers was sex, crime, beer and sport. To an extent, he was right. But there was more to it than that in the new society that was growing up in immediate post-war Britain. Men returning from the war were producing young families and they had new interests – listening to the radio, television, gardening, hobbies and owning their own home. Car ownership was growing, too, and family outings were becoming more common. Two other groups of people were important: teenagers, who increasingly had money to spend on clothes and entertainment, and the elderly, with time on their hands to pursue leisure interests.

By the mid 1950s, the *News of the World* was still selling just over 8 million. But competition amongst newspapers had returned with a vengeance. Money was being spent on lavish sales promotions and the paper had to spend equally lavishly just to stay in the same place. Ironically, in one way the vast circulation was a handicap for, with the cost of newsprint soaring, every extra page to an issue meant a substantial financial outlay.

Editorially, new features were introduced. A popular pre-war feature had been the weekly short story, written by a well-known author. This had been suspended during the war years, a victim of the paper restrictions. It was reintroduced in 1956 and most of the leading authors of the period were contributors. Among them were writers of the calibre of Ursula Bloom, Somerset Maugham, Wolf Mankovitz, Alec Waugh, Eric Linklater, Francis Durbridge and Christopher Landon, whose novel, *Ice Cold in Alex*, was made into a hugely successful film. Another popular contributor was H. E. Bates, who wrote two country stories, 'The Cowslip Field' and 'The Poison

Ladies', for the paper in 1957. Bates was asked by the editor to 'put a little more action' into the second story and had to be chivvied along again the following year by the features editor, who was relying on a Bates contribution as the centrepiece of a new series. At the time, the author was immersed in writing *The Darling Buds of May*, which became an instant success, just as the televised version became an enormous hit of the 1990s.

The short stories were usually illustrated with drawings by Arthur Ferrier, the *News of the World*'s popular cartoonist from 1923 to 1959. Ferrier also created a leggy blonde character called Sally, whose exploits were closely followed, especially during the war when they helped keep up the forces' morale. Ferrier was also an accomplished portrait painter, particularly of beautiful women whose pictures adorned the walls of his Chelsea studio. The studio was a venue for many memorable parties, for Ferrier was an enthusiastic host, with a wide circle of friends from Fleet Street and the theatre. He was an ever-present at first nights, sketching caricatures of the stars to accompany the theatre reviews. He worked for the *News of the World* for thirty-six years and died in 1973, aged 82.

There had always been close ties between the paper and the theatrical world, especially the music halls, stemming from the weekly song feature and the serializations of the life stories of famous entertainers like Maurice Chevalier and Grace Fields. A more unusual association was that of Leslie Holmes, who was appointed publicity manager in 1947. Holmes had been a drummer in Henry Hall's orchestra before joining up with another entertainer, Leslie Sarony, to form The Two Leslies. They were a leading variety and radio act in the 1930s and throughout the Second World War. Holmes accepted the *News of the World* job because of the greater security it offered and for the next thirteen years he was part of the behind-the-scenes circulation team, travelling to motor racing and greyhound meetings, golf tournaments and the many other events promoted by the paper. He met an unfortunate end when in 1961, at the age of 59, he was found dead in bed at his Sussex home,

CIRCULATION HIGHS AND LOWS 181

having apparently taken too many sleeping pills with alcohol.

At the time the *News of the World* achieved its circulation peak, Reginald Bezzant was the circulation director whose efforts had played a major role. Twenty-five years earlier, the entire total circulation of all the Sunday papers put together had amounted to 16 million – now the *News of the World* had reached half of that figure on its own. Bezzant, a quiet, unassuming man, worked for the paper for almost half a century and earned widespread respect in Fleet Street. His 23-year unbroken chairmanship of the NPA's Sunday Circulation Managers' Committee marked the esteem in which he was held. His long period of office covered the war years, a supreme test of his patience and ingenuity. He handled the many problems with a calmness that was his hallmark.

Reg Cudlipp believed a circulation of over 8 million could not be sustained indefinitely. Whilst still deputy editor, he had submitted to the board a report explaining why the circulation must eventually fall. At that time, Sunday newspapers cost 2d for a six- or eight-page paper, so for an outlay of around 1s 6d (7½p) readers could buy every Sunday paper going.

'Each time the price went up, the editor had to write an apologia and explain the new "sweeties" it contained,' Cudlipp recalled, 'because nobody understood why newspapers were going up in price. To overcome the blow to the readers' pockets, you would have to announce some big new series. You knew that each time you went up in price, and that is something editorial people cannot do anything about, you would shave off 100,000 or more readers. In addition, on its huge circulation the *News of the World* lost 150,000 readers every year through death alone. You had to make up that number in order to stand still.'

Cudlipp also saw that far-reaching social changes were at work. He added: 'Everybody was getting a car, everybody was getting a television and people were earning more money and going abroad for holidays. The whole scene was changing and what I had forecast came to pass. It had been commonplace on a Sunday to go to the pub, have lunch and then go to bed with the *News of the World* and the wife in the afternoon. But the pattern was changing. The *News of the World* was strongest at a time when there was no rival entertainment. But the moment it had to take its place with other forms of entertainment and leisure, then it had to share the swallows.'

Similar facts of life were relayed to the shareholders in the company's 1959 annual report. Referring to the new competition from television and travel, Sir William Carr stated: 'I do not deplore these social changes. On the contrary, I find them a stimulating challenge, but it means that we in the newspaper business must be on our toes, alert to change and ready to make our papers even more attractive and in keeping with contemporary requirements.'

Editorially, Cudlipp strove to produce a varied newspaper. 'We were always suffering criticism by MPs and others that newspapers were getting salacious,' he recalled. 'We had to maintain a careful balance.'

The paper often carried adventure stories with headlines like CALL OF THE JUNGLE, THE LION MEN and WHITE WOMAN AMONG SAVAGES. A letter to the editor just before Christmas 1956 enclosed a photograph of the writer, one James Wharram, with two girls and a dog aboard a home-made catamaran. 'When you receive this,' Wharram wrote, 'we will be sailing across the Atlantic.' The craft, made from two canoes lashed together, had been built in the author's hayloft in Manchester for £200.

It was almost a year-and-a-half before the *News of the World* heard from Wharram again. He'd sought to prove that such a dangerous expedition could be undertaken without large-scale sponsorship and, with commendable patriotism, wrote: 'England was made great by people who went out into the world and accomplished exploration or development on their own initiative.' The ordeal of crossing the Atlantic eventually proved too much for the frail craft and it broke up – but not before Wharram and his companions had reached Trinidad. He described the voyage in an article headed ALONE AT SEA, ONE MAN AND TWO GIRLS, and the £1,000 he was paid by the

News of the World enabled him to build a new and larger craft in which to resume his explorations.

The list of contributors to the paper continued to read like a directory of the famous and distinguished. Robert Boothby and Aneurin Bevan were regular political commentators. Boothby once remarked: 'There is nothing to touch the *News of the World* in getting through to the masses. Churchill knew that. They never tried to censor anything I wrote – even over Suez when they disagreed with my line.'

Cudlipp also recruited the Archbishop of York, Dr Cyril Garbutt, as a frequent contributor. The archbishop appreciated the logic of Cudlipp's appeal that a congregation of 2,000 in York Minster could be transformed into an audience of nearly 20 million by writing his words of wisdom in the *News of the World*. The prospect of reaching such a vast audience acted as a tempting lure to many other celebrities also.

A national readership survey around this time provided an interesting insight into the *News of the World*'s widespread appeal. It showed the paper was read by an estimated 18 million adults aged 16 and over, or forty-eight per cent of the total population of Great Britain. Fifty-two per cent of the readers were male. The disturbing fact was that the highest proportion of readers were in the 45 to 64 age group – clearly, the paper was in need of more younger readers.

In June 1955, the paper's circulation dipped below the 8 million mark for the first time in many years. Exactly three years later, it went under 7 million. In all, in the five years from 1954 to 1959, it slumped from over 8 million to 6,432,000. It was by no means entirely Cudlipp's fault. The social factors he had warned about years earlier were as much to blame. But the board of the paper didn't see it that way and he found himself in conflict with some of his fellow directors. Shareholders were never given the background. Sir William Carr told an extraordinary general meeting that it was not in the best interests of the company that details should be given of differences between the editor and the other directors.

Cudlipp had worked long hours to try and turn the paper

around. But he wouldn't delegate work to others. He regarded himself as a working, not a socializing editor. He was constantly writing and rewriting, changing headlines, making up pages. But some of his staff found him, whilst being a man of great social charm, tyrannical in the office. Some of the fed-up journalists confided their complaints to Carr one night in the Press Club. And soon afterwards, the National Union of Journalists Chapel (office branch) held a meeting in the office at a vital production time on a Saturday to emphasize their protest.

The combination of circumstances – the conflict with the board, the unhappiness of some of the staff and the social changes to which Carr had referred in his 1959 report – brought about a change of editorship at the end of the year. Cudlipp was paid off with a cheque for £23,000, for 'purely business reasons' it was said, and went off to become an expert and consultant on Anglo–Japanese trade. He was succeeded as editor by the ebullient Stafford Somerfield.

EIGHTEEN

A New Editor, A New Decade

Stafford Somerfield had been Sir William Carr's choice as editor of the *News of the World* for some time, though not all the other directors agreed with him. The internal politics of the paper had forced him to have a lengthy wait for the editorship. The two men had much in common. Both liked a drink or three, in Carr's case Scotch and in Somerfield's champagne. They were both sociable, gregarious characters who enjoyed doing things in style. Neither were remote figures to their staff. As mentioned in earlier chapters, Carr was a benevolent chairman who would often buy drinks for even the newest and youngest members of the staff in the office pub, the Falstaff, which boasted the longest bar in Fleet Street.

Somerfield, too, often held court in the Falstaff, which was appropriate as he was something of a Falstaffian figure, portly, jovial, witty and sometimes boisterously outrageous. He had two fingers missing from his right hand, the result of a wartime encounter with a grenade. He was proud of his Devon birth and upbringing and, when elated at some success the newspaper had had, would occasionally burst into an old Devonian song. He much enjoyed the social side of being a national newspaper editor. He liked entertaining and being entertained. He and his wife, Dibbie, who was an expert on dog breeding and a leading light in the Kennel Club, frequently hosted large dinner parties for leading politicians, businessmen and sporting celebrities.

One of Somerfield's first acts when he moved into the editor's chair was to have a large oil painting of his illustrious predecessor Sir Emsley Carr, resplendent in white tie and tails, hung in his office.

As he took up editorial responsibility, Cudlipp's earlier prophesies about the dwindling circulation of the paper were proving only too correct. Somerfield's job was to stem the bleeding and give the paper a transfusion. He decided to change the style and presentation, making the paper brighter with bigger pictures and larger typefaces for headlines. Somerfield had been northern editor in Manchester before being brought back to London as deputy editor. Whilst in charge of the northern editions, he had fought for greater autonomy from London's grasp and once he became editor he allowed a freer rein to his former Manchester colleagues, who also produced the Scottish and Irish editions of the paper.

He wanted to change the content of the paper, too. The court reports had to be retained, in order to keep the older readers who'd been brought up on them. But he believed there had to be more investigative journalism – finding out the stories and scandals behind the news, a form of reporting which was then in its infancy. On his very first day in the editor's chair, he pushed the boat out for the staff in his office and told them: 'The circulation's going down the drain. We want a series of articles that will make their hair curl.'

What he came up with was the intimate memoirs of Diana Dors, the buxom, blonde film star whose off-screen love life was more colourful than any film she'd acted in. Somerfield's aim was to get the paper talked about and the series certainly achieved its target. The former Miss Fluck – the actress's real name – was paid £35,000, a staggering sum of money in 1960, for her revelations which were published over two months.

In fact, by the standards of later kiss 'n' tell stories of the 1970s, 1980s and 1990s, the memoirs were about as exciting as a bedtime cup of warm milk. But they were among the first of their genre and in 1960 it was pretty hot stuff. The series brought the *News of the World*, and Stafford Somerfield in particular, much public odium and notoriety. He was assailed for allegedly exploiting sex and was censured by the Press Council for debasing standards to a level which was 'a disgrace to British journalism'.

Somerfield was not the sort of editor to take such criticism lying down and he mounted a vigorous defence. Questioned on television by a panel of all-party MPs about what he thought the purpose of a newspaper was, he quoted one of the paper's most distinguished former writers, Sir Winston Churchill, who had once said of the *News of the World*: 'Long may it continue to educate and amuse the British race.' Somerfield added: 'I don't think I can improve on that.'

One of the questioners was Jeremy Thorpe, the Liberal MP for Barnstaple – Somerfield's birthplace – and an old friend. Attacking Somerfield for the newspaper's alleged slant towards sex, Thorpe asked whether he was proud of the Diana Dors series. Somerfield replied that he was proud of the paper as a whole and that Thorpe was being selective. (Ironically, Thorpe was himself to be the subject of a major sex scandal, which occupied acres of space in the newspapers, two decades later.)

Somerfield's defence was that the crime reports and sex in the paper were balanced by other news, contributions from major public figures like the Archbishop of Canterbury, sport, an entertainments page, women's features and competitions. And he declared that it was not the Press Council's job to exercise control over a newspaper's contents.

Later, Somerfield was again quizzed on television, this time about chequebook journalism, a new phrase in those days. Again, the Press Council were being censorious. Somerfield's attitude was simple – the *News of the World* paid for stories because that was sometimes the only way to get them. His view was that the great majority of the paper's contributors, including churchmen, politicians, businessmen and lawyers, accepted money. Basically, he saw no difference between paying a saint and a sinner – and sometimes the sinner's need was greater!

Somerfield refused to change the policy and content of the *News of the World* to appease his critics. The regular Sunday menu of low life, high politics and just about everything in between, continued. The Diana Dors series had put on thousands of extra copies and increased the circulation for the first time in many years. But an increase in the paper's cover price wiped out the gain, the sales dipped and the battle had to start all over again.

With the Diana Dors success still fresh in its mind, the newspaper looked for other revealing disclosures of film stars' lifestyles. The memoirs of another blonde bombshell, the American star Jayne Mansfield – later to die tragically in a road accident – were acquired. Then it was the turn of Brigitte Bardot. The *News of the World* had been planning to publish extracts from an unauthorized biography but word reached the French sex kitten and a deal was done whereby Miss Bardot agreed to cooperate in a series of interviews. At the last minute, however, pleading tiredness after completing a film, she attempted to pull out. Somerfield scurried to Paris and he and the paper's writer, Gerard Fairlie, retrieved the situation with armfuls of flowers. Many years later, Somerfield wrote in his memoirs that his abiding memory of Miss Bardot was the way she sat cross-legged on the floor, then stood up without effort and without using her hands or arms.

Towards the end of 1960, the *News of the World* swallowed up one of its smaller rivals, the *Empire News*, a Manchester-based newspaper with a circulation of around two million. The paper's principal circulation was in the Midlands and north of England and it was the only Sunday paper to be sold on the streets on a Saturday night. Like the *News of the World*, the *Empire News* had a reputation for getting good exclusive stories and features. One of its most notable successes was in being the first paper to reveal the existence of a third man – Kim Philby – in the Burgess and Maclean spy scandal.

It had been originally part of the Kemsley Newspapers group, acquired by Roy (later Lord) Thomson in 1959. The deal suited the *News of the World* because its northern and Irish editions were then being printed on the Manchester presses of the *News Chronicle*, which had given notice to terminate the contract. The *News of the World* bought the *Empire News* title and goodwill and Thomson agreed to print the *News of the*

World at his Withy Grove plant in Manchester.

The acquisition of the *Empire News* didn't do as much for the *News of the World*'s circulation as was hoped, however, for the two papers already had a large overlapping readership, with more than half the *Empire News* readers taking both. On the editorial side, the *News of the World* gained a popular football competition that was to run for years, Spot the Ball. Three additions to the editorial strength from the *Empire News*'s London office were reporters Peter Earle and David Roxan and sports desk man Charles Sampson.

All three were to play major roles in the paper in years to come. Sampson, one of those people of whom it was genuinely said he didn't have an enemy in the world, eventually became a highly popular and respected sports editor of the *News of the World*, succeeding to the job when the long-time incumbent Frank Butler retired. Roxan was a tireless reporter who operated diligently in a number of more serious areas of the paper's news coverage. He was at one moment in his career the labour and industrial correspondent, deputy political writer, health and medical correspondent and also covered social services.

By far the most flamboyant of the three was Peter Earle. Over the next two decades, Earle was to become one of Fleet Street's best-known eccentrics, a tall, gangling figure who frequently amused his colleagues by declaiming his views loudly to the world in general in a Dickensian style of address, invariably starting with, 'I say, my dear fellow . . .' Favoured colleagues would be addressed as 'My old china', whilst women were treated by Earle with an old-fashioned courtesy. Altogether, he was a character from another age.

One of Earle's early stories for the *News of the World* involved a 1960s version of the slave trade. One day, he was sent by the news editor, Bill Taylor, to see three gentlemen of doubtful character at the front door of the office. They were three 'spivs', as Earle described them, who claimed they were selling illegal immigrants from Pakistan to their own countrymen to work in sweatshops, back-street factories in the Midlands. Earle thought initially they were bogus.

The previous Sunday, the paper's political correspondent Noyes Thomas had written a front page 'splash' story about the illegal immigrant problem being raised in Parliament. It was decided to follow up Earle's information and he accompanied the three men on a tour of London railway stations, where they openly accosted and grabbed Pakistanis buying railway tickets to the Midlands. News editor Taylor was astonished to get a phone call from Earle from a service station on the M1, in which the reporter told him: 'This isn't a con trick after all. The cars are stuffed with Pakistanis with false passports and we're going north.' A bemused Taylor replied: 'For God's sake, be careful.'

It was the start of the most remarkable exposé of the decade so far. Earle and Noyes Thomas made a number of trips with the rogues, who were virtually kidnapping the unfortunate Pakistanis – who spoke little English – and transporting them to the Midlands, where they 'sold' them to other factory-owning Pakistanis. As they were illegal immigrants, the bewildered victims then had no choice but to place their lives in the hands of their new masters.

To emphasize the scandal, and in order to complete the necessary evidence, Earle and Thomas actually 'bought' their own illegal immigrant for a fee of £5. Inevitably, the story made a huge front page 'splash' and the paper ran a television advertisement on the Saturday night before publication, with the slogan: 'We've bought a man for £5.' Even today, Earle still recalls the many phone calls which came into the office as a result. 'You twits,' said one caller from the London area. 'You can get 'em down here for £2!'

Critics of the *News of the World* raised questions about the way the paper had got the story. But Stafford Somerfield reacted with typical sang-froid. He sent a memo to Earle and Thomas, saying: 'I don't care if we all go to prison. It's been a damned good story.'

Earle went on to become as near-legendary a character at the *News of the World* as Norman Rae a generation before. He was fond of describing himself as 'but a simple soldier of the line' and frequently declared his contempt for what he pictur-esquely called the 'bastard generals'. He meant editors, execu-tives and proprietors. However, he had one thing in common with his proprietor, Sir William Carr. Like Carr, he was a con-noisseur of a certain amber liquid, to the extent that some of his younger colleagues pondered on whether Earle was the original role model for what much later became a catchphrase in the satirical magazine *Private Eye* – 'A legend in his own lunchtime.'

There are many true stories about Peter Earle but one of the best concerned the time he was dispatched to knock on a woman's door and tackle her about a story the paper was chasing. The lady was dubious as to whether or not the eccen-tric figure before her was a genuine pressman and demanded: 'How do I know you're from the *News of the World*?'

Earle drew himself up to his full height and declared indig-nantly: 'Madam, I've just admitted it!'

Another time, he was sent to Rome to try to interview the Earl of Warwick, whose son was causing a bit of a rumpus by selling off some of the heirlooms from Warwick Castle which were supposed to belong to the nation. Earle tracked down the aristocrat to his Roman villa and introduced himself in dramatic style with an opening gambit that was pure Shake-speare. 'My Lord of Warwick, a great storm gathers against you in England!' Earle declared. The Earl, amazed to be so addressed, invited him in and gave him a full interview.

And on yet another occasion, when Earle was sent to inter-view a wanted man against whom an arrest warrant had been issued and who was living in luxury on Spain's Costa del Crooks, he opened the conversation with: 'Not to put too fine a point on it, old cock, the shit has hit the fan.'

However, notwithstanding his eccentricities, Earle had remarkable contacts among policemen and members of the criminal underground alike and his network of informants even extended into the security services. Earle, like any good reporter, preferred to keep them to himself, so some gave themselves exotic codenames. Frequently, a bemused colleague would pick up Earle's phone and find himself taking messages from someone who called himself 'Grey Wolf' or 'The Fiery Horseman'. Such a thorn in the side of the criminal fraternity was Earle that one gang involved in shootings and fraud placed a £1,000 'contract' on his head.

It was Earle who was principally responsible for breaking to an eager public what became the biggest scandal story of the decade – the Profumo Affair of 1963. Scandal in high places, especially when it has all the right ingredients – sex, spying, political intrigue, crime, passion and the law – is always a spicy dish to set before a newspaper's readers. And the Profumo story had the lot.

It blew up at a time when Harold Macmillan's government was still jumpy over two major espionage cases, the Portland spy ring and the affair of William Vassall, a homosexual Admiralty clerk who had been jailed for spying for the Russians. Two daily paper reporters had also been jailed for contempt of court for refusing to reveal their sources to an official tribunal set up to inquire into the Vassall case. So there was little love lost at the time between Fleet Street and Whitehall.

The Profumo Affair began, as so many momentous events do, in a trivial way, with a small-time crook being accused of the attempted murder by shooting of a call-girl, Christine Keeler. It was a relatively unimportant case but Peter Earle knew what lay behind it. For months he had been quietly ferreting out rumours about a high-class call girl ring for top people, organized by the West End osteopath Stephen Ward. Earle had known Ward for several years and had heard the stories about the wild parties on Lord Astor's Cliveden estate well before the rest of Fleet Street.

One day, Sir William Carr walked into Stafford Somerfield's office and told the editor: 'Make some very discreet inquiries about a scandal involving a girl and a minister.'

Somerfield replied, 'I already have,' and produced from his drawer a 3,000-word memo. Earle had been busy. Somerfield, however, had decided against publishing anything until all the details were known and the paper had secured Christine Keeler's own story. But Sir William disagreed. He felt it his duty to tell Harold Macmillan about the coming storm.

Mark Chapman-Walker, managing director of the *News of the World* and former Tory Central Office public relations director, was deputed to break the news to the Prime Minister. Chapman-Walker was also a close friend of John Profumo, the War Minister, whose name was being linked with Keeler. Chapman-Walker, when he first heard of his friend's involvement, held his head in his hands and cried: 'Oh, no, Jack!'

He went to Downing Street and told Macmillan's private secretary the story, as the Prime Minister was abroad at the time. The head of the security services was immediately alerted, then the PM's private secretary John Wyndham (later Lord Egremont) confronted Profumo, a friend, himself. The minister categorically denied any relationship with Keeler – just as he lied to the House of Commons in a statement that was to bring about his downfall and resignation from public life.

Millions of words have been written about Christine Keeler's affair with Profumo at the same time as she was sleeping with a Russian naval attaché, Eugene Ivanov; about her and her friend, Mandy Rice Davies; about Stephen Ward's suicide as his trial neared its end at the Old Bailey; and about the way the affair rocked the Macmillan government. The whole saga was made into a hit film, *Scandal*, in 1988. But there is one story that has remained untold in print to this day. Until now . . .

When the Profumo affair was breaking, the *News of the World* bought Christine Keeler's story for £23,000 and Peter Earle and Noyes Thomas were deputed to 'mind' her and keep her away from the rest of Fleet Street. They had her safely tucked up in a hideaway, when one afternoon the telephone rang. It was Stafford Somerfield. He called Earle to the phone and demanded that the reporter ask Keeler the question: 'Who else is in this? Is there any other government minister involved?'

According to Earle, he interrogated Christine Keeler to the

point of tears until she swore that there was no other minister whose name might figure in the scandal. He relayed the answer to Somerfield, who told him in a heavy, formal manner: 'I hope you are right. You have just made a very momentous pronouncement and it is down to you.' Earle replaced the phone.

What he did not find out until much later was that whilst he was speaking to Somerfield, on the editor's other line was the paper's former distinguished political writer Randolph Churchill, who was acting as a go-between between the *News of the World* and Downing Street. Keeler's categorical assurance that there were no other skeletons to emerge from the cupboard was relayed by Earle to Somerfield to Churchill, who passed it on to Macmillan's private secretary. From him, it went to the Prime Minister himself, who was facing an angry Cabinet meeting, with other ministers clamouring to know the extent of the likely damage. Thus, Earle was unwittingly at one end of a direct line to the Cabinet room at a time when matters of very high politics indeed – history in the making, in fact – were being discussed.

The serialization of Christine Keeler's story put thousands of extra copies on to the *News of the World*'s circulation. And once again the paper was pilloried for it. Somerfield was admonished from all sides, including the Press Council, for making commercial gain out of the affair. His response was simple: Christine Keeler had a right to tell her side of the story. Though not innocent, she was young and unsophisticated, compared with the other people involved, and had been exploited all her life. Anyway, what was wrong with honest, commercial ends? Somerfield argued. That was what the newspaper business was all about.

The point was well made, for the Keeler affair contributed to a record year for the *News of the World*. Sir William Carr was able to tell the shareholders that the paper, selling before the war at 2d, with a circulation of 4 million now had a circulation of 6¼ million selling at 6d. With a total readership of 17 million it was still the highest circulation in the world.

Noyes Thomas, one half of the team that produced the Keeler story, was another brilliant journalist. A former officer with the Gurkhas during the war, he had been a lieutenant colonel on Mountbatten's staff in the Far East. A nephew of the poet Alfred Noyes, after whom he was named, Thomas travelled all over the world for the paper before being appointed political correspondent. He was responsible for one of the top political scoops of the 1960s when he revealed exclusively that the Labour Prime Minister, Harold Wilson, was going to make his secretary, Marcia Williams, a life peer. No one else in Fleet Street had the story and it was vigorously denied by Wilson's press secretary, Joe Haines. Not just denied but refuted with a substantial degree of personal scorn aimed at Thomas by Haines (who subsequently became political editor of the *Daily Mirror* and wrote a sycophantic biography of his boss, Robert Maxwell).

However, Thomas had the story from a very high source in the Labour Party – and government – and was proved to be one hundred per cent correct when Wilson did, in fact, make Mrs Williams a peer, with the title of Lady Falkender.

Whilst big serializations like the Diana Dors memoirs and the Christine Keeler story were undoubtedly the icing on the cake, the bread and butter of the *News of the World* during much of the 1960s was still the reporting of court cases . . . errant vicars chasing choirboys over the church pews; women who were the victims of what was often called 'a serious offence' at the hands of men who were variously described as 'beasts', 'fiends' and 'monsters'; and colourful accounts of domestic dramas involving spouses and their respective lovers.

There were some classic headlines above some of the cases, the type that made the reader desperate to read further. Stafford Somerfield once recalled his all-time favourite *News of the World* headline was: INCIDENT IN A WATERCRESS BED. Another minor gem was: THE MONSTER STOPPED FOR PIE AND PEAS.

One day, a subeditor was handed a short piece about a workman whose pick had split open a water main, causing shoppers to be drenched. He wrote the headline: WORKMAN'S PICK CAUSES FLOOD. The chief subeditor feared a misprint and advised him to change it. The subeditor thought for a moment, then said: 'You're right. Let's change it to "tool".'

A sharp blow to the *News of the World*'s traditional content was delivered by the law in 1962, when publication of committal proceedings in magistrates' courts was severely restricted to no more than the barest details – the accused's name and address, the charge or charges, names of solicitors in the case, the magistrates' decision to commit the case to a higher court and whether or not bail was granted.

Previously, newspapers had been able to report the prosecution's case at the committal proceedings, then report the full trial when the case came before Quarter Sessions or Assizes, thus getting two bites at the same cherry. But government lawyers argued that it was unfair that the public should be able to read only one side of the case before it came to trial. The accused might not get a fair trial because potential jurors could be prejudiced by the reports, was the belief.

This was the latest in a long history of restrictions on the press's reporting of court cases, beginning in 1926 with the curtailing of what could be reported in divorce cases and continuing with curbs on juvenile court hearings and domestic proceedings. The press was almost unanimously opposed to the new law and none more so than the *News of the World*.

The paper argued that public interest in, and knowledge of, the workings of justice had to be maintained and this could only be done if the human dramas of the courts were able to be reported in full. It was unrealistic to imagine that newspapers would send reporters to sit in court merely to record a list of names, charges and decisions and many cases would end up never being reported at all. But the press lost the day and a formerly rich source of material dried up.

However, there were still the Assize courts and Quarter Sessions, with the judges and barristers in their wigs and robes and all the panoply and majesty of the law. Reporters spent much of their time covering the Assize courts, where the big, dramatic stories happened. Often, the cut and thrust of the cross-examination of witnesses and defendants by counsel would be reported almost verbatim, sometimes over a whole page if it was a really sensational case. No one ever put it on a notice board but there was an unwritten law for reporters: 'Give us every cough, spit and fart.'

A reporter assigned to cover a particular Assizes would usually find himself there for however long the court sat, sometimes a fortnight. There was an office joke for years that anyone who was out of favour would find himself stuck at Wigan Assizes for the duration. This gag arose from a throwaway line of Stafford Somerfield, who remarked one day that his acid test of a good news story was 'Will the mill girls of Wigan read it?' In fact, of course, there wasn't an Assize court at Wigan but it was a joking threat to anyone who'd blotted their copybook.

Some of the court reports were mini-masterpieces of literary composition. The *News of the World* had subeditors who could take what today would be a sordid little case of, say, indecent assault and turn it into a short story of Barbara Cartland-type proportions. By today's standards, the style was hypocritically prudish and had changed little from that of previous generations. Words like 'rape' and 'intercourse' were still not used. Instead, there were sentences like: 'It was then that he committed the offence.' The result was to leave the reader guessing as to what had actually happened to the unfortunate victim. It was titillating in a way that would be unacceptable today – but this was an age of rather less sexual explicitness.

A classic example of the genre was written by a tiny midget of a man called Eric Davies, who used to amuse his colleagues by driving an enormous motor car. He was so small that he couldn't reach the pedals and see over the steering wheel at the same time, so Davies would drive the huge car home in the early hours of the morning, after a long Saturday in the office, peering between the spokes of the steering wheel and occasionally mounting the pavement.

Davies, who was the son of the former editor Major Percy

Davies, was a master of the impossible. When it was thought that a court case was too disgusting or horrifying even for the *News of the World* to print, it would be thrown at Davies and he would be told to get on with it.

The particular case in question concerned a woman who was charged at the Old Bailey with causing grievous bodily harm to her husband. The facts were, bluntly, that the couple had quarrelled and the wife had taken her revenge by taking a carving knife and cutting off the husband's penis with it whilst he was insensible through drink. No one thought it was possible to get the story in the paper but Davies managed it without ever saying what had actually happened.

Ironically, the *Daily Telegraph* published the same story in explicit detail. But on the following Sunday, it was the *News of the World*'s account that was being animatedly discussed in every pub in the land. The story masterfully met the criteria that was always being urged on young reporters joining the paper by the older hands – and still is today, for that matter – of what constituted a good *News of the World* story. It's a formula that has remained unchanged over generations – will they be talking about it in the pub on Sunday lunchtime?

NINETEEN

The Swinging Sixties

Under Stafford Somerfield, the *News of the World* continued to make the headlines as well as print them. The newspaper was often in the forefront of controversy and not always of the most welcome kind. Still, at least the paper was maintaining Somerfield's stated intent when he'd first assumed the editor's chair of getting it talked about. Halfway through his editorship, another public storm blew up. But whereas the rows over the Diana Dors and Christine Keeler serializations had focused on purely moral issues, this time the government's law officers were involved and the affair was to have far-reaching consequences for Fleet Street generally.

It was in the December of 1965 that a horrified nation first heard of two names that were to become among the most despised in criminal history – Ian Brady and Myra Hindley, the Moors Murderers. Over coming months, the terrible story of the evil child-killers was to emerge in sickening detail. But *News of the World* staffmen in the Manchester office were already investigating reports of missing children well before the names Brady and Hindley first came before a stunned public.

It began with a casual lunchtime chat between reporter Jack Nott and northern news editor George McIntosh. Both commented on reports of children mysteriously disappearing from the same area. Back in the office, they drew a circle on the map, ringing an area centred on the commuter towns of Ashton-Under-Lyne and Hyde, in the shadows of the bleak moors of the Lancashire–Yorkshire border. Jack Nott wrote a story, with a plea for public help from one of his contacts, Detective Inspector Joe Mounsey, later to become head of CID for Lancashire and an assistant chief constable. 'It's as if these children have been spirited away to the moon,' Mounsey said. At the time, it was a chilling, unconscious reference to the lunar-like landscape of the moors where bodies were later to be found.

But the disappearances remained a mystery until a teenage youth was hacked to death at a council flat right in the middle of the circle drawn by Nott and McIntosh. McIntosh and another reporter, Nick Pritchard, drove to Hyde and found the small town seething with rumours. They quickly discovered that the two people who knew more than anyone else about what had happened were Myra Hindley's sister, Maureen Smith, and her 17-year-old husband, David. The couple had gone in terror to the police after David Smith had watched Brady kill the youth, Edward Evans, while Hindley looked on.

At this time, there were no restrictions on the interviewing of potential witnesses in future trials, as long as nothing was published until after the trial was over. The pursuit of witnesses by newspapers gathering background material to publish after a trial was a highly competitive and vigorous aspect of crime reporting.

McIntosh and Pritchard went to the Smiths' third-floor council flat to try to talk to them. Other reporters had already failed but David Smith allowed the balding McIntosh inside. A *Sunday Times* reporter also sneaked in without Smith realizing and hid in an airing cupboard. Later, Smith told the other *News of the World* man, Pritchard, that he trusted McIntosh 'because he was bald'. However, McIntosh preferred to believe it was because of the power of the *News of the World*'s name and the paper's reputation for accuracy. At one stage, Smith went on to the balcony of the flat and kicked dog excrement on to the roofs of cars belonging to other reporters waiting below.

Over many months, the *News of the World* men interviewed the Smiths repeatedly until they had a detailed background of everything the couple knew about the Moors Murders. They 'minded' them and kept them away from other newspapers, who were offering blank cheques. This turned out to be the very last time under British law that such advances could be made to witnesses. The couple kept to their promise not to talk to any other newspaper.

Unable to work or earn money because of the notoriety of the case, the Smiths were given handouts of money in dribs and drabs, totalling around £600, though a total of £1,000 eventually was agreed. Much later, these payments were to land the newspaper in trouble with the then attorney general Sir Elwyn Jones QC.

At one stage, Stafford Somerfield thought the Smiths would relate better to a woman reporter, so feature writer Rosalie Shann was sent to Manchester. Shann, a warm, motherly woman with a sunny nature, was able to charm her way into the couple's confidence. Twenty-eight years later and still writing in the *News of the World*, she recalled: 'It was my first big assignment for the paper and one I shall never forget. David, who was 17, and his 16-year-old pregnant wife, Maureen, were somewhat bizarre to look at, dressed in black leather jeans and bomber jackets adorned with silver studs. But we got on well and they talked to me for hours. Because of their close associations with Brady and Hindley, then awaiting trial, the office suggested I should always be accompanied by a man, but the Smiths wouldn't hear of it. I felt safe with them and we went for long walks over the moors. The office only found out when I asked if I could charge a new pair of shoes on my expenses. They were horrified and forbade me to go on the moors with the Smiths again.'

Interviewing the Smiths in public restaurants or the smart Manchester hotel where she was staying proved a problem for Shann. Head waiters weren't too keen on the bizarre looks of the couple, their crude language or their requests for beer and butties. Shann solved the problem by interviewing them in her hotel room and ordering room service. As sometimes happens when a reporter is on a story for a long time, she became close to the family – in fact, she recalled, 'David Smith's father, who was womanless at the time, asked me to marry him!'

The young Smith, though only 17, became quite protective towards her, said Rosalie. 'Once, a male friend called to see me and I invited him in for a drink, just as Maureen and David were leaving. Fifteen minutes later, the phone rang and it was David. He said he hadn't liked the look of my friend and did I want him to come and sort him out for me? When the job was finally over, they gave me a beautiful black kitten as a present. I called it Smith.'

When Brady and Hindley finally came to trial, David Smith was the chief prosecution witness. Defence lawyers attacked him mercilessly, suggesting he was to be paid a huge sum of money by the *News of the World* if the pair were convicted. The trial judge also suggested, falsely, that the paper had paid for the Smiths' hotel and a car to take them to court every day.

When the trial was finally over and Brady and Hindley sentenced to life imprisonment, reporter Pritchard handed a cheque for £400, the balance of the £1,000 owing, to Smith. But he couldn't cash it because he didn't have a bank account, so Pritchard gave him the money in cash, the last such payment ever – legally – paid to a witness. Ironically, however, because of the huge controversy surrounding the circumstances, the *News of the World* never published any of the exclusive information given to them by the Smiths and made no more of the story than any other paper.

The implication during the case that Smith had been lying to secure Brady's and Hindley's convictions, so that he and his wife could profit, was a serious one indeed. According to Stafford Somerfield, the newspaper's own counsel was very worried and told him: 'My God, you've done it this time.' And Rosalie Shann recalled how Somerfield said to her in the office one day: 'You and I will soon be sharing a cell, darling!'

There was a government inquiry, instituted by Sir Elwyn Jones, to which Somerfield and George McIntosh were summoned to give evidence. The paper was eventually exonerated but the law was changed to outlaw the interviewing of witnesses in advance of a trial. An intriguing, though shadowy, area of reporting had come to an end.

The *News of the World* was criticized in the House of Commons over the Moors Murder case and, inevitably, yet again by the Press Council. But Stafford Somerfield, as in the Keeler affair, was unrepentant. The Press Council published a Declaration of Principle, supporting the banning of payment to witnesses before a trial and also seeking to ban payment to 'persons engaged in crime or other notorious misbehaviour where the public interest does not warrant it.'

Somerfield refused to accept the latter point. Who was to decide what was notorious behaviour and what was in the public interest? he asked. He regarded it as a blatant attempt to muzzle the press and in a leader he wrote: 'It is the duty of a newspaper to seek out and publish news and information of public interest, and especially at times, information which some people may wish suppressed. In pursuing that duty a newspaper may have to pay for the information it seeks.' The Press Council's attempt to impose a general restriction was a step on the road to censorship, he declared. Not for the first time, the *News of the World* was standing out against attempts to shackle its free-flowing style of reporting the news.

For much of the 1960s, the man in charge of the news-gathering operation was an irascible but brilliant newspaperman called Charles Markus. A short, tubby, pipe-smoking Mancunian who was almost never seen out of doors without a porkpie hat, Markus was moved to London in early 1964 from Manchester, where he had been northern editor. His predecessor as news editor, Bill Taylor, a diffident, charming man, went in the other direction to assume Markus's former role in Manchester. The two men could hardly have been more different in character if they'd tried. Whereas Taylor was urbane, easy-going and laid-back, Markus was gruff, abrasive, prone to flying off the handle and often downright rude to his staff.

He could be a slave-driver and vicious with it, if a reporter had got on the wrong side of him. Roy Stockdill, who joined the *News of the World* as a general reporter in 1967, recalls how he and another reporter had both managed to upset Markus in the same week. The news editor contrived to make both suffer for it with one double-strike. Stockdill recalled: 'There were two stories early on a Saturday morning, one in Brighton and one in Hemel Hempstead. The other reporter lived south of London and could be in Brighton in forty minutes. I lived in Watford, just down the road from Hemel Hempstead. Markus sent me to Brighton and the other chap to Hemel Hempstead, which entailed us both getting up at some ungodly hour!'

Stories about Markus were legion but here are two of the best . . .

Reporter Robert Warren – later to succeed Markus as news editor – was one of the *News of the World* team dispatched to Aberfan in South Wales to cover the terrible tragedy when a slag heap slipped down a mountainside and engulfed a school, killing 140 children. Warren found it necessary to purchase a pair of Wellington boots to traipse around in the dreadful conditions and he put the bill for them on his expenses. A couple of years or so later, Warren was sent to Iceland to cover a story about a fishing trawler from Hull that had gone down in the ocean. Only one crew member had survived and was in hospital in Reykjavik. Warren got to him and acquired his exclusive story. The reporter also found it necessary to buy another pair of wellies and again charged them to expenses when he got back to London. Markus sent for him and growled: 'You had a pair of boots on expenses when you went to Aberfan. What happened to them? Why didn't you take them to Iceland with you?'

Markus was also a one-man consumer council in the days when consumerism was in its infancy. Any shop, garage or hotel that short-changed him or gave him bad service would very quickly be trembling to its foundations as Markus conducted a campaign of complaint and vilification, usually at the top of his voice on the newsdesk telephone, to the undisguised glee of his staff.

One particular saga went on for days when he became convinced that a well-known firm of coal merchants had cheated him by delivering a bag short to his home. The affairs of the newspaper were forgotten as Markus pursued the matter relentlessly. Eventually, the local weights and measures inspector, representatives from the coal company and two men with shovels descended on his Surrey home one Saturday morning. Markus wasn't there. It being pre-publication day, he'd gone to the office to take charge of the newsdesk and left his unfortunate wife to deal with the situation.

Carefully, the coal was shovelled from the bunker on to the weights and measures inspector's scales. It corresponded almost to the last ounce to the amount that should have been there, according to the delivery note. Markus's embarrassed wife telephoned the *News of the World* office to inform him of the outcome. He grunted and replaced the phone. 'Seems like I was wrong,' he conceded to his reporters, eager to know the end of the saga. When it was suggested by a hesitant subordinate that perhaps an apology would be in order for the unnecessary fuss he'd caused, Markus exploded. 'Apologize! Why should I apologize?' he roared. 'It keeps them on their toes!'

Despite the fact that Markus was an extremely hard taskmaster, his staff had a huge respect for him as a newspaperman, and even a quiet affection which few would publicly admit to, for beneath his gruff and often irritable exterior he was good-hearted. A joke against himself which he enjoyed hugely occurred when the *News of the World* editorial staff gave Stafford Somerfield a party to mark his 59th birthday and presented him with a spoof edition of the newspaper. The lead story declared that Somerfield had had a heart transplant – heart swaps were a very new phenomenon in those days – and that Markus was meant to be the donor until, as the story put it, 'it was discovered that what the newsroom had always suspected was true – Charlie didn't have a heart!'

The year 1964 saw a tragedy for the *News of the World*. One of the paper's star writers, the ebullient and extrovert Nancy

Spain, was sadly killed in a light aircraft crash on the Grand National course at Aintree whilst on her way to cover the world's greatest horse race for the paper. Spain wasn't just an outstanding journalist, she was a novelist and major television personality as well.

She'd started her career as a sports reporter – it was a very rare thing in those days for a woman to write about sport – in her native Newcastle upon Tyne and took to freelance writing after being invalided out of the WRNS during the war. She wrote a score or more novels and worked on the *Daily Express* in the 1950s as a book critic and feature writer. She became familiar to TV audiences as a regular on panel games like *Twenty Questions* and *Juke Box Jury*.

When Spain joined the *News of the World* in the early 1960s, she started her first column with: 'Mother always said I would end up in the *News of the World*.' She was sent to cover a giant leek show in Durham, which the paper sponsored, and wrote in her report: 'Then in came a man with the biggest one I'd ever seen.' Though a star name, she was no prima donna and loved the company of the colourful collection of characters then working for the newspaper. She often joined them in boisterous singsongs in the pub behind the office.

She wrote and spoke in a fresh, somewhat breathless style and built up a strong following among the paper's readers. Only days before her death, she had finished writing a third volume of autobiography called *A Funny Thing Happened On the Way*. Because of her hasty departure for Liverpool, she'd arranged for the manuscript to be collected from a friend. In it, with what turned out to be tragic prophecy, she had written: 'I very seldom gave my own future a thought . . . I have never seriously considered I have a future at all.' Her death was a great loss to the paper.

Somerfield's editorship coincided with that period of history that will for ever be known as the Swinging Sixties. It was the era of the Beatles and the Stones, Carnaby Street and mini-skirts, hippies and flower power, meditation, sexual freedom and groupies, Vietnam War protests and a fascination amongst newspapers for investigating and reporting on the growing drugs movement.

The *News of the World* was in the forefront of the thirst for coverage of pop music and hired the 'daddy' of British guitar players, Bert Weedon, to give weekly lessons in the paper on how to play the instrument. Weedon also gave tips on how to start a pop group and encouraged amateur bands to send in demo tapes, for which prizes were awarded. In a way, the hugely popular feature was a throwback to the old *News of the World* song sheet feature that had run in the paper for so many years until its abandonment during the Second World War.

What proved to be perhaps the *News of the World*'s most dramatic brush with the permissiveness of the 1960s once again made large headlines in all the other newspapers. The paper published an investigation into allegations about the Rolling Stones and drugs, as a result of which Mick Jagger issued a libel writ. Then the newspaper was tipped off about a party at Keith Richards's Sussex home and passed the information to the police. The subsequent police raid on the party, and one particular bizarre rumour involving Jagger's then girlfriend Marianne Faithful, became virtually part of the folklore of the 1960s.

When Richards came up on drugs charges at West Sussex Quarter Sessions, his defence counsel – Michael Havers QC, later to become attorney general – alleged that the *News of the World* had planted an *agent provocateur* at the party who supplied drugs in a bid to get Jagger convicted. The allegation was fiercely denied by Somerfield in a powerful page one comment.

That Saturday night, hundreds of Rolling Stones fans laid siege to the *News of the World*'s Bouverie Street offices, protesting about the part the paper had played in the Richards trial. Delivery vans were held up by the crowds thronging Fleet Street and police carted off a number of demonstrators, including an American groupie colourfully known as Suzy Creamcheese, in Black Marias.

There was a strange sequel to the affair not long afterwards when drugs squad detectives arrived at Stafford Somerfield's London flat with a search warrant. Some anonymous Stones fan had given them a false tip about drugs being at the address as a retaliation for the *News of the World*'s role in the Richards affair. Mrs Somerfield told the policemen she must go and phone the *News of the World*. 'Why?' asked a sergeant, who was unaware whose address it was they had been tipped off about.

'Because he's the editor,' replied Mrs Somerfield.

The officer exclaimed: 'Jesus Christ!'

'Not quite,' Mrs Somerfield retorted, 'though he sometimes behaves like it.'

Somerfield, relating the story in his memoirs, wrote that the officers stayed on for some time to guard the flat in case any more false stories were spread. They made themselves thoroughly at home, brewing tea, having fry-ups and drinking his whisky. 'Eventually I got their chief to call them off, on the ground that I couldn't afford them any longer.'

Above: 'All human life is there' – an advertising campaign that became a national catchphrase.

Above: Hot metal men: printers make up a page in pre-Wapping times.

Right: Pages are cast and made ready for the printing machines.

Reginald Cudlipp, editor in the 1950s, when circulation soared to its peak of over eight million.

Rupert Murdoch at the time he won control of the *News of the World* in 1969.

Nudist welfare man's model wife fell for the Chinese hypnotist from the Co-op bacon factory

By RON MOUNT

I'VE JUST been talking to three of the most incredible people I've ever met:

● The chief welfare officer of one of London's biggest boroughs;

● His blonde wife, a part-time nude model;

● And a half-Chinese amateur hypnotist who works for a Co-op bacon factory.

The married couple spoke of their love life difficulties and the fact that they called in the hypnotist to help.

The husband alleged that his wife lacked passion. But now he is even more upset because the wife has fallen for the hypnotist.

I only heard the story in the first place because of a letter sent by the husband to the News of the World.

And after meeting all the people involved in this crazy triangle, I say:

To the husband: Put your own house in order before trying to solve the

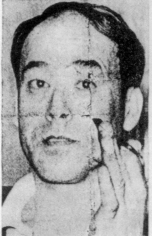

and I thought, 'That's fine. We're getting somewhere with the treatment.'

"He hypnotised her about four or five times that evening. At one stage she said she felt a choking feeling. She was asked to put on something looser.

"She returned in a negligee. After a while, without 'putting her under,' he ordered her to remove it. She refused but after being hypnotised she did so.

"I wasn't terribly shocked at my wife being naked in front of us because she and I are both nudists.

Mr Song caressed her, saying, 'You're on fire. You're responding.'

"Watching them I thought the treatment was working. He kept telling her to imagine he was me. The effects were fantastic."

Mr Austwick said his wife had had treatment sessions with Mr Song after the first visit in February, both at his home and in the north.

"I was very hopeful of results at first," he went on. "But now I want him exposed for what he is.

"I still love my wife deeply and now she's become infatuated with him I want him out of her life.

"He's a philanderer.

Danger

for all of us by making it public.

I also saw Mrs Austwick at her bungalow. She was wearing a black satin see-through mini-skirt and skin-tight orange sweater.

The walls of the room were festooned with nude pictures of her in frames shaped like keyholes.

She included them casually and said: My husband insists on those being up there. I am on show all over the house for anyone to see.

I asked her about her relationship with Mr Song, and her husband's allegations that she was frigid.

"I'm not a frigid woman if the demands made on me are normal," she said. "In fact, I'm exactly the opposite.

"It's true I'm infatuated with Mr Song, but my husband has brought this on himself.

"I don't know how it will all end."

Above: A particularly memorable *News of the World* headline.

Star names: Noyes Thomas (*left*) and Peter Earle, two of the paper's leading staff writers.

Bernard Shrimsley, who fought to go tabloid – and failed.

Crime investigator Trevor Kempson who 'made his excus and left'.

International news: a *News of the World* kiosk in Athens.

Above: Editor Nick Lloyd (*centre*) inspects the first tabloid issue.

Left: Wendy Henry, the first woman editor of a British national newspaper

Below: David Montgomery: 'Welcome to the first day of the rest of your lives.'

Four of the many front page exclusives.

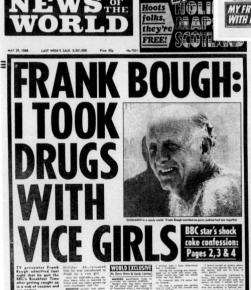

NEWS OF THE WORLD

SECRET DATES WITH TYCOON

PLUS Sunday COLOUR MAGAZINE

JULY 7, 1985   BRITAIN'S BIGGEST SALE   PRICE 28p   No. 7,380

ROYAL LOVE SENSATION

EXCLUSIVE OF THE YEAR

TOGETHER: Princess and tycoon Ward Hunt who wants to marry her

Princess Michael torn between
Prince and her Dallas millionaire

ROYAL COUPLE: Marriage problems

■ **BEAUTIFUL** Princess Michael of Kent is facing heartbreak over her love for two men.

She is torn between her husband Prince and Dallas property tycoon Ward Hunt.

■ The popular Princess, 40, has been secretly meeting millionaire Hunt, 44, it can be revealed today. They have stayed together at private homes of close friends in London, the Cotswolds, Dallas and Santa Barbara, California.

■ At one stage divorce Hunt declared his wish to marry the Princess. Ten days ago, after their last meeting she went into hospital suffering nervous exhaustion.

■ Other members of the Royal Family are said to be extremely distressed by her marriage problems.

I WANT TO MARRY HER: See Pages 2, 3 and Centre Pages

Pat Chapman, the present editor.

Below: Lethal barbed wire protected 'Fortress Wapping'.

TWENTY

Manchester

During the 1960s and early 1970s, the *News of the World* maintained district offices in various parts of the country. In the era when crime stories and coverage of the Assizes and Quarter Sessions courts were the paper's staple diet, it was vital to have men on the spot who knew their areas like the back of their hands and who had intimate contacts amongst the police and other bodies. The paper maintained staff reporters in Cardiff, Winchester, Birmingham, Newcastle and Dublin and three newsmen and a sports reporter in Glasgow.

By far the biggest operation outside London, however, was the Manchester office, which had the responsibility for printing all the northern editions of the paper, plus the Scottish and Irish editions as well – a substantial slice of the *News of the World*'s circulation, especially in the days of the mammoth eight million-plus sales.

Printing of national newspapers in Manchester, simultaneously with London, had begun during the vicious circulation wars of the 1930s. The *Daily Mail*, *Daily Express*, *Daily Herald*, *People* and *News Chronicle* all opened editorial offices and printing plants in the city, competing for regional news and the advantage of having quicker distribution to northern towns and cities. The newcomers joined established plants like that in Withy Grove, Manchester, the world's largest newspaper printing centre, home of the *Empire News* – later taken over by the *News of the World* – *Sunday Times* and long-defunct papers like the *Sunday Chronicle*, *Daily Dispatch* and the *Daily* and *Sunday Graphic*. In addition, the *Manchester Guardian* had its headquarters in Cross Street, before it went nationwide and became known simply as the *Guardian*. In all, more than 20 million copies of national newspapers were produced from Manchester, in hundreds of regional editions.

This alternative Fleet Street provided a national newspaper career for hundreds of journalists who chose to stay in the north and a stepping stone for many more with London ambitions. A rich and earthy culture thrived among them, similar to that of their Fleet Street counterparts and centred on pubs and clubs clustered around every newspaper office. Today, with the growth of electronic technology bringing instantaneous transmission of pages, and the smashing of the print unions' power, the Manchester newspaper scene is a shadow of its former glories.

The *News of the World*'s plans to print in Manchester were at first curtailed by the outbreak of war in 1939. A site had been acquired at Cheetham Hill but remained undeveloped. Then, in 1942, the paper looked again to Manchester, not at that stage as a means of building circulation but as an alternative printing centre if the London presses or the vital railway lines should be knocked out by enemy bombing.

The paper began printing on the *News Chronicle*'s presses in Derby Street, establishing a seven-day printing pattern which was of mutual benefit to both papers. The first northern editor was Harry Carr, who was being groomed to succeed his illustrious father Sir Emsley as editor and chairman. Many of the *News Chronicle*'s printing staff were Quakers of austere habits and, though Carr's professional newspaper skills won their respect, his habit of taking ladies back to the office did not. Finding the environment too dry for his taste, Harry Carr arranged for the then considerable sum of £2 to be provided each Saturday for 'editor's refreshment'. In 1942, it bought a bottle of Scotch and several beers. The same sum, never increased, was still being solemnly allowed to the last northern editor, George McIntosh, nearly fifty years later. His secretary spent it wisely – on tea.

After Carr's death in 1943, he was succeeded by a razor-witted Scot, John Milligan. The *News of the World*'s Manchester staff used the editorial offices of the *News Chronicle* to produce the paper on Saturdays and one day Milligan received in the post a parcel. On opening it, he was surprised to find a ham sandwich neatly wrapped, together with an abusive note from a *News Chronicle* executive who accused Milligan of having left it on his desk. Milligan sent back a courteous reply: 'Thank you for the kind present, it was delicious, but I cannot agree that it might originally have belonged to me.' He suggested it was more likely to have been left by a cleaner and added: 'It was quite fresh, definitely a Sunday product.' The *News Chronicle* man replied, suggesting peace and a pint.

The *News of the World* moved its Manchester printing operation to Withy Grove in 1960, on the paper's takeover of the *Empire News*. From there, it printed up to 2,300,000 copies for the north of England, Scotland and Ireland in eight main editions. This provincial printing colossus was at the height of its massive production power, spilling out the *Daily* and *Sunday Mirrors* – latecomers to the Manchester scene – the *Manchester Evening Chronicle*, *Sunday Times* and the *Sporting Chronicle*, along with a variety of smaller productions. The *Sunday Chronicle* and *Sunday Dispatch* had been sacrificed to make way for the *Mirror* newspapers and the *Empire News* was killed off to accommodate the *News of the World*'s 25-year contract. Withy Grove at that time had the biggest battery of linotype machines in the world and the largest and proudest workforce in the north of England. The game of musical chairs between London and Manchester had meant that John Milligan had gone to London, to be succeeded as northern editor for two years by Stafford Somerfield before he, too, had returned south to take over the editor's chair from Reginald Cudlipp. Somerfield's successor was Charles Markus and it was he who led the *News of the World* advance into Withy Grove, an invasion he compared to the Japanese march into China.

Markus's feisty style led him into numerous bruising encounters with the printers but also won him grudging respect before he, too, hit the road to London, where he took over as news editor. His successor in Manchester, W.G. 'Bill' Taylor, spent the remaining twenty years of his career there, first as northern editor, then later as general manager. One of Taylor's abiding interests became the Irish edition, which was a curious anomaly of the *News of the World*. The paper had not had an Irish edition for many years and there was a misconception that it had actually been banned by the Irish authorities because it was thought to be too pornographic for a country with such strict religious views.

In fact, this was not the case. Like most other British newspapers, the *News of the World* had stopped sending copies to Ireland because of the war. Under Charles Markus, the Irish edition was resumed, at first principally as a means of making use of an early edition of the paper sent mainly to the Outer Hebrides and to British expatriates overseas. Markus successfully applied for the paper to be re-admitted to Ireland but it became something of a production nightmare because complicated changes had to be made to make the contents acceptable to the Irish authorities. Large, inoffensive pictures and bland stories replaced the more racy pin-ups and court cases of the normal editions. But after an initial upsurge of interest in Ireland, mainly curiosity sales, circulation figures plummeted.

Stafford Somerfield, after he had become editor, threatened to kill off the Irish edition but was persuaded to give it one more chance. He had been told by a circulation representative of the Irish people's great fondness for a radio soap opera called the *Kennedys of Castleross* – a sort of Irish *Archers*. The technique of turning the popularity of a television series to a newspaper's advantage was still in its infancy but George McIntosh, then a news and features writer, had been among the pioneers of the genre with series on *Coronation Street* and *Z Cars*.

At the time, television had barely got a toehold in Ireland. There was no home-grown TV station and only fringe reception of British stations along the east coast, captured by giant aerials. The *Kennedys of Castleross* was Ireland's first and only soap at the time and it had the sort of grip on the whole country that *Coronation Street*, *EastEnders* and other TV soaps do in Britain today. McIntosh wrote a four-part series about the radio programme and, without any publicity or advertising, the *News of the World*'s circulation in Ireland shot up. He wrote another six features and the circulation increased again, so he wrote a further ten articles from Dublin, returning to Manchester at weekends to help produce the newspaper. The paper had a staffman in Dublin, Charles Orr, who was released to travel the country and produce other stories.

The Irish edition began to thrive but still not without immense difficulties, for it was in effect a quite separate newspaper. At one stage, an artist was employed full-time in the Manchester office whose principal role was painting bras on pictures of topless women.

So puritanical was the Irish moral climate thought to be that in one issue of the paper a charming, perfectly innocent picture of two girl toddlers, no more than 4 or 5 years old, playing naked on a beach, had pants painted on to them for the Irish edition. And a constant alert had to be kept to ensure that adverts for contraceptives did not slip through the net into the paper.

Bill Taylor travelled extensively in Ireland, sometimes with writer Gerard Fairlie, and the pair concluded that the heavy editing of the paper's main content was damaging the Irish edition's progress. In a memo to the management, Fairlie urged the need to include the latest football and racing results and to have 'bright pictures of pretty girls sprinkled about the paper'. His view was that they had leaned over too far backwards in trying not to offend the Irish censor.

Agents reported that Irish readers felt cheated by the toned-down content of their version of the *News of the World*. 'We have been too careful,' Fairlie said. 'We must brighten the paper and take chances. It is better to be banned than just fade out.' Priests often warned against buying the paper from their pulpits but then, with typical Irish logic, turned a blind eye to it being sold outside their churches.

The ripples cast by the Swinging Sixties had extended across the Irish Sea. Paying an exploratory visit to Dublin, Stafford Somerfield was told by the chairman of the Censorship Board that Ireland, though still a deeply religious country, was becoming much more broad-minded, a fact Somerfield had already established by noting the number of women in miniskirts and the amount of sexually explicit literature on sale. What the *News of the World* editor also learned was that the Irish, having perfectly good newspapers of their own, didn't buy English newspapers to read Irish news. They wanted English news and sports, photos of pretty girls and only nominal 'fig leaf' coverage of Irish affairs.

Taylor began to reduce the Irish content and the size of the words 'Irish edition' above the front page masthead. Occasionally, he 'accidentally' left them off altogether. The stratagem worked. Ironically, at a time when the *Mirror* newspapers were pushing their Irish sales at huge expense and effort, the *News of the World* spent little and did better.

In 1977, when Bernard Shrimsley was pushing for the *News of the World* to go tabloid, production man Ray Mills was appointed from the *Sun* to be northern editor of the *News of the World*. Mills, a blunt-speaking northerner whose nickname was 'Docker' because he was big and burly, left to join the *Daily Star* when Shrimsley's dream of a tabloid failed to come true.

To the seventh and last northern editor George McIntosh, who had been deputy to four of the previous six, fell the task of dismantling the editorial organization and simultaneous production in Manchester. Towards the end of the Withy Grove contract period, he stood in the vast linotype room with Robert Maxwell, then a prospective buyer of the premises. 'What do you think of all this?' McIntosh asked. Compositors whose jobs depended on the answer awaited Maxwell's booming reply. 'It's a f***ing museum!' he roared.

TWENTY-ONE

Rupert Murdoch to the Rescue

In the autumn and winter of 1968 and early 1969, Fleet Street witnessed the bloodiest takeover battle in its history. It was a bitter affair and when the mud-slinging and the financial wranglings were over, the world's largest Sunday newspaper had a thrusting new proprietor. After a span of almost eighty years at the helm of the *News of the World*, the Carr dynasty was over. In their place was a brash, ambitious young Australian that few in Fleet Street had ever heard of. His name: Rupert Murdoch.

At the heart of the battle was another would-be newspaper tycoon whose name would also continue to make headlines throughout the 1970s, 1980s and early 1990s – the man Fleet Street loved to call the 'bouncing Czech', Robert Maxwell. It was to be the first time, but not the last, that the two titans would clash head on. Nearly a quarter of a century ago, who could have predicted that one would go on to build a world-wide media empire, whilst the other would end his life in mysterious circumstances amid a financial scandal of almost unbelievable proportions?

The struggle for control of the *News of the World* began in a modest enough way. In the summer of 1968, Sir William Carr visited his eccentric cousin, the shadowy and mysterious Professor Derek Ainslie Jackson, in Paris. At that time, Jackson and his family held about twenty-five per cent of the company's shares, the Carr family controlled about thirty per cent and the rest were held by a large number of small shareholders, including *News of the World* executives and employees. It had not occurred to Carr that without a majority shareholding he and his family could be vulnerable. Though Jackson had never shown the slightest interest in the running of the paper, he had a representative on the board and Carr had always kept him fully informed.

Carr and managing director Mark Chapman-Walker were in Paris to discuss a French TV company in which the paper and Jackson, privately, had an interest. The much-married Jackson had just wed his sixth wife and invited the pair to meet her. Carr thought it was a purely social occasion but at some stage 62-year-old Jackson mentioned that he was thinking of selling his shares in the *News of the World* because he was worried about eventual death duties.

Back in London, Sir William began to realize the seriousness of the situation. He was in a dilemma. The ordinary voting shares stood at 28s (£1.40) and Carr didn't have the money to buy Jackson out at more than the market price. If he offered more, he would have to make a similar offer to all the other shareholders. The possibility of a takeover was first raised by Chapman-Walker, who noticed that there was activity in the company's shares on the stock exchange.

Carr wrote to Jackson and told him he was willing to discuss buying his shares. But by this time Jackson had made his mind up definitely to sell. He wrote to Sir William's nephew, Clive Carr, another director of the *News of the World*, and told him that he had appointed Rothschilds, the merchant bankers, to handle the sale. He refused to discuss the matter except through them.

On the morning of 16 October, Carr was taken ill in the office and went home to bed. Whilst there, he was telephoned by his friend Sir Max Aitken, chairman of the Express Group, who told him the London *Evening Standard* had a story that Robert Maxwell, then a Labour MP and head of Pergamon Press, had put in a bid of more than £26 million for the News of the World Organization. Maxwell, who had started Pergamon just after the war and built it into a leading scientific publishing firm, was a ruthlessly ambitious, intimidating man in search of power and saw ownership of a newspaper with such a huge circulation as a way of achieving it.

His shock bid put a value of 37s 6d (£1.87) on the ordinary shares and 36s (£1.80) on the non-voting shares. It was based on an exchange of Pergamon shares, with a cash alternative. The evening paper front page headline MAXWELL BIDS FOR THE NEWS OF THE WORLD was the first public indication of the coming battle and it sent the ordinary shares soaring on the stock exchange. Clearly, Maxwell had control of Professor Jackson's shares and was confident of picking up enough extra shares at the higher price to achieve victory.

An emergency board meeting was held at the News of the World Organization's West End headquarters, where Sir William Carr had a flat. He was too ill to attend but from his sickbed above the boardroom he sent a message, rejecting the bid as 'impudent'. Chapman-Walker telephoned Jackson in Paris but he wouldn't discuss it, referring him to Rothschilds. On the following Sunday, 20 October, Stafford Somerfield wrote a powerful and acerbic leader on the front page, which began: 'We are having a little local difficulty at the *News of the World*. It concerns the ownership of the paper. Mr Robert Maxwell, a Socialist MP, is trying to take it over.' Somerfield went on: 'Personally, I don't think he will and I, as Editor of your paper for more than eight years and a member of the editorial staff for nearly a quarter of a century, hope his bid will fail.'

The leader was punctuated with references to Maxwell's foreign origins as Jan Ludwig Hoch. Somerfield declared that he would not work for Maxwell and that it would not be a good thing for him to gain control of a paper that was 'as British as roast beef and Yorkshire pudding'. The paper was, Somerfield said, independent and impartial with no political affiliations. He questioned whether that attitude and policy would be continued by Maxwell, a complete stranger to Fleet Street, a man with no newspaper experience and a Socialist MP. He concluded: 'This is a British newspaper, run by British people. Let's keep it that way.'

Somerfield's leader caused a riot of comment in other newspapers. He was accused of xenophobia by the *Observer*.

A somewhat curious comment was made in the *Guardian* by David Steel, later to become leader of the Liberal Party, then an ordinary MP. He wrote: 'What a disgusting piece of chauvinism. Mr Maxwell is not everybody's cup of tea and he knows it, but he is as disgustingly British as anybody I know. He even has a Rolls Royce with a telephone in it ... Good luck, Bob.'

Despite the fact that Maxwell was a Labour MP, there was opposition to him from the trade unions, and especially those whose members produced the *News of the World*. In a rare action, the Imperial Father (senior shop steward) of the Federated House Chapel at Bouverie Street wrote to Sir William assuring him of the unions' complete solidarity with the Carr family and the board. 'Your employees feel deeply the apparent threats that the Maxwell hierarchy are making to destroy this newspaper ... We reiterate our determination to stand fast and support the management in its stubborn fight to survive the onslaught from these destructive pressures,' he wrote.

News of the World staffmen who remember the dramatic days of the takeover battle recall a more intimate and colourful incident in which the print unions were won over. On the Saturday night of the week in which Maxwell's bid was announced, Stafford Somerfield, having written his memorable leader, sent for one of their leaders, a near-legendary union figure at the *News of the World* known as 'Ginger' because of his carrot-red hair. In the chaotic world of Fleet Street industrial relations, this man had had many run-ins with the management and been responsible for causing numerous stoppages of the paper.

Normally, a summons to Somerfield's office meant a confrontation in the minds of union officials and Ginger duly arrived with a deputation of his men. But Somerfield disarmed them totally by producing a bottle of Scotch and inviting them to have a drink. A couple of hours or so later, editor and union bigwig were arm-in-arm, singing, and Ginger was promising that 'if Maxwell comes in here, he'll go straight out of that window'.

Within the square mile of the City, too, strong – and at times, suspect – moves were being made to fend off Maxwell's attack. Carr's bankers, Hambros, had placed £750,000 at the disposal of its stockbrokers to buy *News of the World* shares on the market, claiming this was an independent stake. It came close to breaching the spirit of the code of practice that had recently been introduced by a new City Takeover Panel, under which companies were forbidden to buy shares in their own business in order to fight off a takeover bid.

The brokers secured pledges of support from other shareholders, on promise of a payment of 10s each, and employees of the *News of the World* were given shares on a temporary basis. After much wheeling and dealing, the Carrs were guaranteed around forty-eight per cent of the votes.

Six days after his initial bid, Maxwell reacted by upping his offer to £34 million valuing the voting shares at exactly 50s (£2.50). By now, the man who'd started the whole snowball rolling, Professor Derek Jackson, had finally come out into the open and urged his cousin, Sir William Carr, to accept Maxwell's offer.

While the battle was going on in London, thousands of miles away in Australia, Rupert Murdoch was watching the situation closely. Murdoch, the son of newspaper owner Sir Keith Murdoch, had built up a chain of papers, radio and TV stations in Australia and was keen to expand internationally. He foresaw that new developments and media techniques would force large publishing and television companies to become international conglomerates.

Murdoch had been tipped off by the London bureau of his News Ltd organization that the *News of the World* might be up for grabs. He had already had designs on the International Publishing Corporation, then publishers of the *Daily* and *Sunday Mirror*, where Cecil King had recently been ousted as chairman after writing a mischievous article undermining the government of Labour Prime Minister Harold Wilson.

Murdoch had acquired a minor shareholding in IPC and had been trying to put together a syndicate of Canadian businessmen to help him gain control. But the deal came to nought and Murdoch's attention was diverted towards the *News of the World*. Through his friend, Lord Catto, of merchant bankers Morgan Grenfell, he bought a modest three-and-a-half per cent of the *News of the World* voting shares and asked for more details of the Pergamon offer.

On 19 October, three days after the Maxwell bid, Murdoch was at a race meeting in Melbourne, 500 miles from Sydney, when a call from Lord Catto came through. His information was urgent: Robert Maxwell was about to increase his bid for the *News of the World*. Murdoch immediately took a plane back to Sydney, where a packed suitcase and his passport were waiting. He arrived in London on the Sunday morning that Somerfield's patriotic leader appeared. The London editor of Murdoch's Australian organization later told how he walked into his office to find his boss sitting at his desk. 'What's this about the *News of the World*?' Murdoch asked.

His subordinate replied in classic Aussie style: 'If you'll get your feet off my desk and your arse out of my chair, I'll tell yer!'

The ailing Carr's advisers had been urging on him the need for an ally. Carr was unwell and ill-equipped for the rigours of a takeover battle. Murdoch was hailed by the rest of Fleet Street as the saviour of the *News of the World*, a white knight charging to the rescue. Carr was too ill to meet Murdoch initially, but Clive Carr and Sir William's son, another William, had dinner with the Australian. Both Carrs reported back favourably to Sir William and next day, 22 October, Carr and Murdoch breakfasted together at Carr's apartment at Cliveden Place, Westminster. There, they thrashed out an agreement under which the News of the World Organization would acquire part of Murdoch's publishing interests in Australia and, through an issue of new shares allotted to News Ltd, his Australian company, Murdoch would acquire the majority shareholding and become joint managing director, with Carr continuing as chairman. Approval of the new share issue would have to be sought at an extraordinary general meeting of shareholders.

Murdoch produced a written record of the agreement, in which he told Carr he looked forward 'with keen anticipation to working with you and your colleagues for many years to add to the strength and prosperity of the *News of the World* and further the interests of its shareholders.'

Two days later, the stock exchange suspended dealings in the company's shares to enable shareholders to make up their own minds on the Maxwell and Murdoch offers. However, by this time Carr and Murdoch between them had almost fifty per cent of the shares. Maxwell fought on, telephoning and sending telegrams to uncommitted shareholders. He also complained to the City Takeover Panel about the ethics of the *News of the World*'s tactics in buying its own shares.

The Panel was coming in for criticism from financial writers, too, and there were questions in the House of Commons. After several days of charge and countercharge, the Panel finally announced there had been no breach of the takeover code but Maxwell secured a concession that votes acquired by either side since his original bid was announced would not be used at the decisive extraordinary general meeting. Clive Carr and a representative of Hambros flew to Australia to work out the fine detail of the proposed agreement in advance of the meeting. Then there was a period of hiatus until after Christmas 1968, though as a sideline to the main battle, Maxwell issued a writ against some of Rupert Murdoch's papers in Australia over stories alleging dubious doorstep methods of encyclopedia salesmen employed by Pergamon.

Arrangements for the crucial meeting, held in the Edinburgh suite of the Connaught Rooms, Great Queen Street, London, on 2 January 1969, were handled like a military operation. At a briefing beforehand in an adjoining room to the main hall, various formal roles and so-called 'spontaneous' questions were allotted to selected senior *News of the World* staff and shareholders. A number of employees had each been given shares, in order to allow them to attend the meeting and vote for the Murdoch plan. They had to hand them back later. Sir William Carr was supplied with cue cards containing his replies to specific questions and an adviser sat beside him to provide advice on any unforeseen or difficult ones.

After an introductory speech by Carr, he called on Murdoch, who spoke for three minutes, urging the proposed linkup between the *News of the World* and his company. Anti-Maxwell feeling was strong when he rose to address the meeting and he was heckled throughout his speech. When Carr put the motion – approving the linkup with News Ltd of Australia by issuing a further 5,100,000 ordinary shares of 5s each and enabling Murdoch to put six directors on a reconstituted board – the deal was overwhelmingly carried on a show of hands, by 299 votes to 20. Carr then announced that because of the importance of the matter, a poll was necessary. The result this time was closer, 4,526,822 votes to 3,246,937, but still the same.

The *News of the World* had beaten off the raid by Robert Maxwell but there was no doubt now as to who was the new boss. Rupert Murdoch had acquired the base on which his future worldwide communications empire was to be built. By March 1969 he had control of a virtual majority of the voting shares to add to the executive control he already held.

Carr's health had declined severely and he had had an operation. Murdoch let him know forthrightly that there could be only one executive boss and that person had to be him. He alone would be responsible to the board for the management of the company. Carr stayed on for another three months as chairman but in June Murdoch drove down to Carr's Sussex home, where he was convalescing, and asked for his resignation.

Carr handed over the reins to Murdoch and accepted the sinecure role of life president and consultant. Within less than a year, his cosy, comfortable world had collapsed and a dynasty that had ruled over the *News of the World* for almost eighty years was ended. Carr never recovered his old style and enthusiasm for life. He lived on for another seven years but his health continued to decline and he died on 14 November 1977, at the age of 65. Stafford Somerfield wrote in his memoirs ten years after the takeover battle that had Carr not been an ill man, the *News of the World* would have beaten off Maxwell without Murdoch's help.

The two main protagonists in the *News of the World* takeover battle, Robert Maxwell and Rupert Murdoch, had crossed paths on a previous occasion when Maxwell had offered to sell Murdoch part of his Australian Pergamon operation. The writs against Murdoch's Australian papers over the stories about Maxwell's encyclopedia salesmen were still outstanding.

Three months after the battle for the *News of the World*, the two men met again when, at Maxwell's invitation, Murdoch visited him at his apartment in Fitzroy Square. Maxwell was then negotiating with IPC with a view to buying the *Sun*, the former *Daily Herald* which Hugh Cudlipp had renamed and relaunched but without much success. Maxwell wanted to explore the possibility of printing the *Sun* daily on the *News of the World* presses, which were idle during the week.

At the meeting, Maxwell told Murdoch that, though he had not liked losing the *News of the World* battle to him, he accepted it was a *fait accompli* and he didn't like crying over spilt milk. Both agreed that as they would be living and working in the communications industry for many years to come, it was foolish and a waste of time and money to continue with the litigation in Australia. They agreed to call off their respective lawyers, Maxwell giving an assurance to Murdoch that anyone who might have been concerned in any of the malpractices alleged in the articles was no longer employed by Maxwell or any of his companies.

Ironically, it was Murdoch, not Maxwell, who ended up buying the *Sun* from an IPC anxious to be rid of it and turning it into a highly successful daily newspaper that eventually overtook the *Daily Mirror* in circulation.

Maxwell eventually achieved his ambition of Fleet Street proprietorship when in 1984 he gained control of Mirror Group Newspapers from Reed International, who had acquired it from IPC. In November 1991, the 'bouncing Czech' drowned in circumstances which still await a convincing explanation when he disappeared from his luxury yacht off Tenerife.

The *News of the World* was left to reflect on what a narrow escape the paper had had twenty-two years previously when, in the days following Maxwell's death, it emerged that he had perpetrated the biggest fraud in history, ripping off his company's pension fund for over £400 million.

TWENTY-TWO

Another Keeler Affair

The new owner of the *News of the World* had a reputation for getting involved in the editorial side of his newspapers as well as management. The editor he had inherited from the Carr regime had an equally strong reputation for brooking no interference from any quarter, including the board and the chairman. A clash between Ruper Murdoch and Stafford Somerfield was inevitable and it would not be long in coming.

Murdoch's meteoric arrival in Fleet Street had surprised many but he gave an insight into his reasons when he addressed a conference of newspaper executives. 'You might be surprised to learn that sentiment played a part,' he said. 'My father learned about journalism here and he loved it. Anyone interested in journalism and mass newspapers realizes that Fleet Street is the heart of it all.' And he gave a glimpse into the expansion that he was already planning when he added: 'What most people don't realize is that publishing empires are going out beyond national boundaries. Whether it be in the transmission of news between countries or satellite programmes, you have got to think in terms of numbers much greater than you can achieve in Australia.

'Secondly, the world is getting smaller and at the same time literacy is increasing with living standards. To be in the communications business means you are in a growth industry.'

Everybody wanted to talk to the new, powerful force in Fleet Street and in a radio interview Murdoch was asked if he were a new, dynamic type of newspaper proprietor. 'I do get involved in the newspaper I am responsible for,' he responded. 'I am not a backroom businessman or simply chairman of the company. I am the chief executive.' Did he believe a newspaper proprietor should have day-to-day editorial control? 'Well, he must be prepared to take responsibility for it,' was Murdoch's reply. 'You must have editors whom you work closely with, whom you have trust in and who know your mind on things because in the end you are going to take responsibility for what is in the paper. You cannot pass it on to editors. If they make mistakes they damage the newspaper. These days, newspapers are big business in every way. If the product suddenly goes wrong, everything is finished. So, the man at the head of the company must remain interested in the product.'

Later, he was to answer the same question more bluntly: 'Yes, of course I intervene whenever I have the time and think it helpful.'

This was a far cry from the working atmosphere Somerfield had been accustomed to in the near-decade he had been editing the *News of the World*. Sir William Carr had assured a Royal Commission on the Press: 'I cannot remember issuing a directive to the editor. The policy of this paper is laid down by the board and the editor interprets it.' Somerfield's view was that the editor was engaged to edit the paper and no one else.

Somerfield felt himself to be comfortably entrenched, despite the upheaval at the *News of the World*. He had negotiated a new, seven-year contract with Carr just before the takeover situation. He was good friends with Lord Goodman, the leading lawyer who had had offices in the *News of the World* building in Bouverie Street. Somerfield was fond of relating how the first time Murdoch had met Goodman he had remarked, jokingly: 'Good chap, that, we must get him to break your contract,' to which Somerfield replied: 'Too late, he drafted it.'

A confrontation was on the cards sooner or later and it was no surprise to anyone when it came. In May, just a few months after Murdoch's takeover, the new proprietor decided to make changes to the paper's layout, especially the leader page, which disappeared. Somerfield was on holiday in Spain but was tipped off by a colleague by telephone and caught the first plane back to London. He went straight to Murdoch, as the presses were about to roll, and insisted the leader page must go back in the paper. It did.

Somerfield then sat down and wrote a memo to the chairman, in which he said:

The episode sharply pinpoints a number of issues which urgently call for clarification. As Editor, I am responsible for the newspaper and its contents. The responsibility is both traditional and inveterate. Whether the editor is present or absent or whether he has actual knowledge of the particular contents of the paper, his responsibility remains. This is true in law or in ethics or morality or generally in accordance with long-established custom in Fleet Street.

The editor is the servant of the board and contractually answerable to the board and the managing director. But this does not mean that the chief executive, acting independently of the board, can take his chair or seek to discharge his functions or introduce fundamental editorial changes in the paper without consultation.

Murdoch suspected Somerfield was deliberately seeking dismissal and a large payoff. In a note to Sir William Carr, he said: 'I am delighted about the first part of this proposition but wary of the second. It is obvious what Stafford is after and he won't get it from me.'

A month later, on his return from Australia, Murdoch proposed to Somerfield that he should become editorial director and warned that he might ask him to leave the main board in a future reconstruction but added that he could stay on the board of the newspaper. Somerfield asked for time to think it over and nothing further happened for some months.

Meanwhile, yet another *cause célèbre* was about to break around the *News of the World* in the shapely form of Christine Keeler – for a second time. The woman around whom the original Profumo Affair of six years earlier had centred had written a book rehashing her memoirs, with some extra morsels. Since the original scandal, John Profumo, the disgraced minister whose sexual liaison with Keeler had sparked off the affair, had been rebuilding his life by quietly burying himself in social work in East London.

Extracts from the book were offered to the *News of the World*. Somerfield showed them to Rupert Murdoch who was aware of the risk of attracting criticism but agreed to their publication, with some deletions. Mark Chapman-Walker alone, of the small committee that discussed the memoirs, opposed publication on the grounds that Profumo had paid for his mistakes. However, Chapman-Walker didn't dissent when both Murdoch and Somerfield suggested he was motivated by his loyalty to the Conservative Party.

Chapman-Walker was on the verge of leaving, anyway, to become joint managing director of British Lion, the film production and distribution company. In an ironic footnote to the affair, he was later involved in a potentially embarrassing situation when some of his new colleagues at British Lion, the top film-makers John Boulting, Sidney Gilliatt and Frank Launder, wrote a letter to *The Times* expressing their abhorrence at the *News of the World*'s publication of the Keeler memoirs. Their views were almost identical to Chapman-Walker's but they hadn't told him of their letter to avoid him embarrassment. Chapman-Walker had remained a *News of the World* director but offered to resign in case it was thought there had been a breach of loyalty on his part. The board declined to accept his resignation but he left, anyway, at the end of the year.

The serialization of the memoirs was condemned – as it had been the first time round – by the Press Council. A large company withdrew its advertisements from the *News of the World* and the Independent Television Authority banned all TV adverts for the paper until the memoirs were either withdrawn or finished.

No member of the public had complained, in fact, but the Press Council decided to lay its own complaint. It held that publication of 'sordid' details of Christine Keeler's life story was damaging to the morals of young people and an exploitation of sex and vice for commercial purposes. Keeler had been paid £21,000 for the serialization the second time round. The Press Council declared that such payment, where the public interest didn't warrant it, was unethical and that the raking up of unsavoury scandals and the dragging up of a man's past in his lifetime was also unethical.

Stafford Somerfield's response was just as spirited as it had been six years earlier, though neither he nor Murdoch attended the Press Council hearing. In a written defence, Somerfield pointed out that when the complaint was made, only one instalment had actually been published and he doubted how the council could arrive at an opinion without having seen all the material. The Press Council was again acting as a censor, Somerfield declared.

Because of the furore over the Keeler memoirs, Cardinal John Heenan, the Catholic Archbishop of Westminster, withdrew from a commission to write an article for the paper on 'the Permissive Society'. His reason, he explained, was sympathy for Profumo who had redeemed the past. Somerfield was quoted in the *Daily Mail* as saying he would have thought the Archbishop would have welcomed the opportunity of talking to 15 million sinners.

This remark appalled Rupert Murdoch, who was anxious that the public outcry over Keeler should not jeopardize other business activities he was engaged in, like the purchase of the *Sun*. He told Somerfield: 'We will win this debate, I am sure, but there can only be one spokesman and that's me. In future, please say nothing or clear it with me first. I must be firm about this – there is a lot more at stake than one newspaper.'

Murdoch wrote a personal note to Heenan apologizing for the editor's remarks, which he regarded as 'tasteless and unnecessary'. However, no permanent damage was done to relations between the Cardinal and the *News of the World*. Heenan said he was not offended by Somerfield's remarks, merely that it would have been more accurate to have said 'fellow sinners'. A month later, the Cardinal and Murdoch met for lunch at Archbishop's House, when they discussed the subject of newspaper ethics.

What went unrecorded at the time was the fact that the Archbishop of Canterbury, Dr Michael Ramsay, had also been commissioned to write an article for the *News of the World* and he also backed out because he was unhappy about the Keeler serialization. However, Dr Ramsay did not make his decision public, so it went unreported.

Rupert Murdoch appeared on London Weekend Television with David Frost and Frost gave him a hard time over the Keeler memoirs. Though the show gave valuable publicity to the *News of the World*, Murdoch was not pleased at coming off second best in the encounter. He and his aides complained that Murdoch had been the victim of an 'unscrupulous ambush,' that Frost hadn't stuck to agreed questions, that the studio audience had been loaded against Murdoch and that a filmed interview with Cardinal Heenan had been screened unexpectedly. Frost denied the allegations and claimed Murdoch had had full knowledge of the content of the programme beforehand.

There was an angry exchange of correspondence in which both agreed to differ. 'Let us not worry too much,' Murdoch wrote. 'It is in the past and I certainly won't fall for it again.' Later, they bumped into each other at Les Ambassadeurs Restaurant and agreed to re-establish social contact.

The second Keeler affair caused widespread mixed reactions. Whilst some of the letters received by the *News of the World* were critical, other correspondents who thought there had been over-concern for Profumo's feelings said they were sickened by the hypocrisy of some of the criticism. Could a politician who had besmirched his position ever become immune from publicity? they asked. One woman, who described herself as 'a strait-laced, middle-aged lady', applauded Murdoch's performance on the Frost programme and wrote: 'I have always maintained a public life is a public life and a minister with the responsibilities that accompany that post should be especially careful to lead a blameless life.'

The public argument over publication of the Keeler memoirs, together with Murdoch's preoccupation with the *Sun* takeover and a long visit to Australia, delayed any action on his part involving Somerfield. However, with the dust of those matters settled, he was able to concentrate his mind on the editorship of the *News of the World*. In February 1970, Murdoch sent for Somerfield and asked for his resignation. Somerfield's response was swift and pointed. 'I never resign,' he said. No reason was given for his dismissal, Somerfield later claimed, and no mention made of his twenty-five years' service to the paper.

The whole episode took just three minutes and entered the folklore of Fleet Street. Somerfield's departure was the splash story on the front page of both evening papers – London had two then, the *Evening Standard* and the *Evening News* – and it was said he had left with a golden handshake of £100,000. In fact, he got a payoff of £50,000 and a consultancy agreement worth £5,000 a year for the remaining six years of his contract. Somerfield's brief interview with Murdoch inspired an old friend, another sacked editor, to send him a cable: 'Why did it take three minutes, you talkative bastard?'

Somerfield left the *News of the World* in the style in which he had spent much of his ten-year editorship. He went to the long bar of the Falstaff and held court. Smoking a cigar, clutching a glass of champagne and surrounded by colleagues, he gave interviews to reporters from other newspapers. He was still plugging the *News of the World*, mentioning that it was over a million ahead of its nearest rival, the *People*.

That night he went on television to give his account of his dismissal. Still the flamboyant editor, he had the studio technicians in fits of laughter with his wisecracks. He declared: 'Mummy told me never to resign.' And when one interviewer accidentally called him 'Mr Murdoch,' he responded: 'I'm not Murdoch, I'm the sacked one!'

Stafford Somerfield went off after a decade of editorship to indulge in his other great passion, breeding pedigree dogs. He wrote a column for a canine newspaper, *Dogs' World*, which inspired a wit writing in the *Guardian* to dub the paper 'Woofs of the World'. Another colourful era in the history of the *News of the World* had ended.

TWENTY-THREE

More Scandal in High Places

There are good headlines, there are great headlines – and there are *News of the World* headlines. A new decade, the 1970s, started off in Bouverie Street with a new editor and possibly the most wonderful banner headline the paper had published since the classic of the 1880s, 'Awful Discovery In Drury Lane: A Child Found Pickled In A Jar.'

In early 1970 there appeared the following masterpiece, sprawling four lines deep across five columns of a whole page: NUDIST WELFARE MAN'S MODEL WIFE FELL FOR THE CHINESE HYPNOTIST FROM THE CO-OP BACON FACTORY. Fifteen words of pure magic that yet again had the whole country spluttering into its beer in every pub in the land on Sunday lunchtime. Even today, it is still fondly recalled by many journalists and *News of the World* readers.

The name of the man who created what became the most talked-about headline of the era deserves to be recorded. He was Monty Levy, a popular subeditor and long-serving member of the staff who retired a few years ago with the knowledge that his little niche in newspaper history was secured. The story beneath the extraordinary banner occupied a whole page – and this was in the days when the *News of the World* was a full-size broadsheet newspaper, not the compact tabloid of today. Written by reporter Ron Mount, one of the paper's veteran foot-in-the-door men, it had all the elements of a Whitehall farce.

The story concerned the welfare services chief of a major London borough who was, indeed, a keen naturist. His pretty wife, a model, had had an extra-marital relationship with a gentleman of Oriental extraction who worked in a Co-op bacon factory and who was also an amateur hypnotist in his spare time. To make the story even more bizarre, assiduous readers who waded through the whole saga discovered that the one fact the otherwise admirable headline had omitted was that the cuckolded husband also had two artificial legs, so he was a legless nudist welfare chief! According to reporter Mount, the man had encouraged his wife's friendship with her Oriental paramour in the belief that the hypnotist was treating her for problems in the marriage.

Who else but the good old *News of the World* could possibly have carried such a story and had the whole country laughing with it? It was a great start to the decade and readers could be assured that, whatever the behind-the-scenes turmoil created by having a new owner, the paper would go on dishing up the kind of fodder they loved.

Under the Carr regime, everything had ticked away smoothly like an old grandfather clock. Perhaps too smoothly. The old-style paternalistic management of the Carrs and the paper's huge circulation had created complacency. Rupert Murdoch didn't care for much of what he saw and began scything away at the deadwood. One of his earliest acts was to order a review of all the paper's subscriptions and charitable donations, which swallowed up thousands of pounds every year. Many of the sponsored events, so close to Bill Carr's heart, were for the chop as well. The John Hilton Bureau, with offices and a largish staff in Cambridge, was another casualty.

Murdoch instructed Mark Chapman-Walker: 'Get some money in.' So, the managing director began selling off some of the unprofitable subsidiaries. Chapman-Walker quit a few months into the new regime, though not, he was at pains to point out, because he was at odds with Murdoch but because he fancied a new challenge at British Lion films.

As his successor, Murdoch recruited from IPC a fellow Australian, Alick McKay. Soon after joining the *News of the World*, McKay was to be at the heart of one of the most bizarre and tragic episodes in the paper's history when his wife was kidnapped and murdered, probably the victim of a case of mistaken identity. Her body was never found and it was believed that as the McKays had been using Murdoch's Rolls whilst he was away, the kidnappers had bungled their operation and taken Mrs McKay captive instead of Murdoch's wife, Anna. Two West Indian-born brothers were subsequently found guilty of the murder at the Old Bailey and sentenced to life imprisonment.

For the staff of the *News of the World*, the change to a different way of life post-Murdoch was very noticeable. The old paternalistic days of the Carrs had gone for ever. No more strawberries-and-champagne teas served by butlers on Sir William's Sussex lawn. No more Leg o'Mutton suppers. And the new proprietor was certainly not one to buy drinks for the lads in the Falstaff. There was a substantial up-side, however. There was a new realism in the place and, as part of that, one of the first things that happened under Murdoch was that the journalists' salaries were increased fairly rapidly to levels approaching others in Fleet Street.

Industrial correspondent David Roxan, who was Father of Chapel (senior shop steward) of the journalists' union, recalled: 'In the Carr days it had been a question of grace and favour. Only in the very last year of that regime did I sit down to negotiate a pay and conditions agreement for the first time in the paper's long history. It all changed when Murdoch arrived. My main recollection of those early days post-Murdoch is that I was in the office early one Tuesday morning and there was hardly anyone else about. We were in the middle of our first wage talks with the new owner and they were settled, not through hours of sitting round a table, but by him coming in and shouting a figure across an empty newsroom and my shouting back acceptance.'

Somerfield's replacement as editor was his deputy, Cyril Lear, a placid, pipe-smoking West Country man who was never known by any other name than his nickname, 'Tiny' — earned because he was around 6 foot 5 inches tall. Lear was as quiet and unassuming as his predecessor was flamboyant. He had eased his way to the top via the subeditor's desk, having earned a reputation as a man who could dress up a mundane story into the paper's own entertaining style. 'Tiny' Lear was the sort of man liked by everyone, from the chairman to the office boy, but there were some on the staff who found him indecisive and thought he was too gentle to occupy the editor's chair of a paper like the *News of the World*.

Lear, a devout Catholic, had a son who was a priest and who was reputed to tell penitents: 'You think you've got problems? My father's editor of the *News of the World*.'

Editorially, the paper was changing in content. It had to keep pace with the times and changing values of society. Much of its successful formula had been copied by other newspapers and the *News of the World* had to find new ways of showing it was still out in front. One of the areas it had been expanding for some time was that of investigative journalism.

Stafford Somerfield had begun the process when he had brought in as an assistant editor Michael Gabbert, a top man from the *People*. This was probably the first time there had been any crossover of staff between the two largest Sunday newspapers, who were deadly rivals. It was Gabbert who had orchestrated the Rolling Stones drugs inquiry in 1967. In any newspaper office there is often keen rivalry between the news and features departments but at the *News of the World* at that time it was particularly intense. The formidable Charles Markus resented the introduction of a new department running parallel to his newsroom team and there was frequent friction between him and Gabbert, not always to the paper's benefit.

With Gabbert from the *People* came Trevor Kempson, who became the *News of the World*'s chief investigative reporter and who was to become one of Fleet Street's best-known exposé specialists for more than two decades. One of Kempson's earliest successes had been in 1968 when Stafford Somerfield sent him to Brazil to cover a scandal in which 131 members of the country's Indian Protection Service were accused of atrocities and virtual genocide against the backward people they were supposed to be protecting. Kempson, refused the funds to hire a light aircraft and fly into the Amazon jungle as other reporters were doing, got a five-part series by bribing a government official to let him photostat the official files on the case, then hiring an interpreter to translate them from Portuguese into English.

In early 1971, Kempson led an investigation into what became known as the BBC Payola scandal, in which disc jockeys and producers were allegedly offered cash and sex inducements to plug records on the radio. The *News of the World* told of call girls being laid on for DJs and of orgies involving a two-way mirror. At the centre of the affair was the pop singer Janie Jones, who later went to jail for seven years for controlling prostitutes and attempting to pervert justice.

To get the necessary evidence, Kempson and a freelance journalist set up an elaborate cover story, posing as wealthy businessmen anxious to break into the record industry. They used false names and rented expensive apartments and employed sensitive tape recorders to record conversations covertly – one of the earliest occasions on which such methods had been used.

That the new owner of the *News of the World* approved of such campaigning journalism was evident in a lecture Rupert Murdoch gave at Melbourne University in 1973. He said: 'When things go wrong it is in the interest of those in power to conceal and it is in the interest of the press to reveal. The muck-raking tradition in popular journalism is an honourable one.'

It was in the same year, 1973, that another sex scandal involving people in high places erupted. And once again the *News of the World* was right in the thick of it. While Stafford Somerfield rated the Profumo affair as the greatest story of his editorship, another potential government-wrecking scandal exactly a decade later presented a traumatic situation for his successor, 'Tiny' Lear, who agonized for days over publication of the latest revelations. The story involved the exposure of the then Under Secretary of State at the Ministry of Defence, Lord Lambton, and later another minister, Lord Jellicoe, the

Lord Privy Seal and Leader of the House of Lords. Aspects of the affair were yet again to bring the paper into conflict with the Press Council and a Security Commission headed by Lord Diplock. The Prime Minister at the time, Edward Heath, determined not to fall into the embarrassing trap in which his predecessor, Harold Macmillan, had found himself in over Profumo and demanded to be kept fully informed.

Lear's editorial style was quite different to Somerfield's 'Publish and be damned' approach. Throughout the Lambton affair, he adopted a cautious attitude that did not entirely endear him to his subordinates. Though he was understandably worried about the possibility of libel writs, and also that Lambton might have been the victim of blackmailers, there were some who felt his caution went too far and that the paper did not make the most of the sort of scandal story at which it excelled.

Running more or less parallel to the Lambton affair were three other investigations the *News of the World* was pursuing. One involved alleged corruption amongst high-ranking Scotland Yard policemen who were accused of taking bribes from Soho club owners. A second inquiry was being conducted by Peter Earle, who had heard stories of another call-girl ring patronized by prominent people, and the third involved a vice ring organized by a Maltese businessman.

The paper had had the latter story for some time but Lear had agreed to withhold it at the request of police, who were still making their own investigations. However, when by April 1973 no police action had been taken, the newspaper began running the story. A week later, two men called at the *News of the World* offices and were interviewed by Trevor Kempson. They told a startling tale . . . that they had cine film incriminating Lord Lambton, who was then the minister responsible for the Air Force, in sexual acts with a call girl.

The men, Colin Levy and Peter Goodsell, revealed that the woman involved was Levy's wife, Irish-born Norma Levy, and asked for £30,000 for the story. They handed over two rolls of colour cine film, which later proved insufficiently clear to

positively identify the minister. Levy and Goodsell were pan-
icking because they reckoned the police and MI5 were out to
silence them and they wanted the money to enable them to
get out of the country.

Kempson spent several days checking out the men's information. Then it was decided that more evidence was needed
before any story naming Lambton's involvement could be published. A staff photographer from the *News of the World* went
to the Levys' flat in Maida Vale and they showed him how
they had concealed a cine camera behind a two-way mirror,
pointing into a bedroom through a hole in the wall from
another bedroom next door. A black tent had been fixed up
as a light trap around the hole. The two men had also rigged
up a tape recorder, with a wire stretching along the carpet
edge between the two rooms and into a microphone concealed
in the nose of a large teddy bear sitting in a chair.

The photographer set up a stills camera on a tripod and
showed Levy and Goodsell how to operate it, then took some
shots of them and Mrs Levy lounging on a bed. One of the
pictures subsequently appeared on the front page of the *News
of the World*.

Next day, Kempson and the photographer returned to the
flat, believing Lambton was expected. They were hastily ushered into the side bedroom, as the minister was already on his
way. When Lambton arrived, he went into the main bedroom
with Norma Levy and another girl, a black woman. It had
never been intended, in fact, that the *News of the World* photographer would take the incriminating pictures of Lambton.
He was there merely to show Levy and Goodsell how to operate the camera. But Levy stepped into the black tent, then
emerged moments later, saying that the photographer would
have to take the shots himself. The photographer fired off
several exposures which showed Lambton lying on the bed
with Norma Levy, with the other woman standing alongside,
and smoking what later turned out to be cannabis.

Back at the *News of the World* offices, 'Tiny' Lear continued
to agonize over the story. In the end, it was decided not to

buy anything from Levy and Goodsell. The possibility of payment had been held out in order to get their cooperation
but no money was handed over. Instead, the paper passed
on to the police everything that Levy and Goodsell had told
them.

However, the photographs and tape recordings were handed
to the two men, who promptly took the material to the *News
of the World*'s principal rival, the *People*. When the tapes were
played in the *People*'s offices, the first words to be heard on
the recordings were: 'Testing, testing, testing . . . this is Trevor
Kempson, *News of the World*.' Lambton already knew the story
was about to break and promptly resigned from the government. He was rapidly followed by Lord Jellicoe who, ironically,
was not involved with Norma Levy at all but who had obtained
the services of prostitutes through advertisements for escort
agencies. Though underworld gossip was linking him with call
girls, there was no direct evidence and it was his own conscience that forced him to resign.

When the story did, indeed, break all over the front pages
of the daily papers, both the *News of the World* and the *People*
ran similar stories on the following Sunday. The *News of the
World* was able to claim it had had the story before anyone
else and it also named the 'madam' who was head of the vice
ring for which Norma Levy worked. The article revealed also
that Lambton had been remarkably indiscreet in his relationship with Norma. On one occasion he'd arrived at her flat
in a chauffeur-driven car, flying a government pennant and
bearing a military number plate.

Yet another fierce public debate blew up over the Lambton
affair, involving the limits to which newspapers might go in
their attempts to expose matters of legitimate public concern.
The *News of the World*'s defence in relation to the pictures was
that they could not obtain corroboration in any other way.
They were taken as legal evidence and were never intended
for publication.

Inevitably, the paper was censured, though not for the clan-
destine photographs and tape recordings. Its alleged error was

in handing over incriminating and potential blackmail material to 'persons of ill repute'.

His career ruined, Lord Lambton was eventually fined £300 for possessing cannabis and amphetamines. The question remained, was the *News of the World*'s investigation of Lord Lambton of legitimate public interest? The subsequent report by Lord Diplock's Security Commission gave a clue as to the answer. 'When we turn to what might have happened if he had continued in the same course of conduct, we consider that a potential risk to security would have been involved such as would have compelled us to recommend that Lord Lambton should be denied further access to classified information,' the report said.

Lambton's use of drugs and prostitutes had left him open to blackmail and that would have disqualified him from secret work if he had been a civil servant subject to positive vetting, Diplock added.

There was an ironic footnote to the Lambton saga five years later in 1978. Just as it had done so before in the Profumo affair by republishing Christine Keeler's story, the *News of the World* was able to have a second bite at the cherry when it serialized the memoirs of Commander Bert Wickstead, Scotland Yard's top gangbuster and head of the Serious Crimes Squad. Wickstead, known to fellow coppers, villains and pressmen alike as 'the Old Grey Fox', had led the police investigation into the Lambton–Norma Levy affair and devoted a two-page article to it. Wickstead was retiring after thirty years in the police force to take up a new appointment – as chief security officer for News International, publishers of the *News of the World*.

TWENTY-FOUR

Swappers, Swingers and Madam Cyn

In the late 1960s, the *News of the World* discovered a new national sport in Britain which was to provide a rich source of material for the next couple of decades. A good bout of it still fills the odd double-page spread in the paper today. It was a sport with few ground rules and any number from two upwards could participate. It was called Wife-Swapping or, more picturesquely, Swinging. All over the country, couples were flinging themselves with wild abandon into illicit liaisons with their neighbours' spouses – or so the constant stream of stories throughout the 1970s and 1980s would suggest.

The paper's long-time bread and butter, the court cases – what old-timers on the staff called 'trad' *News of the World* material – had all but been dropped altogether by the late 1970s. What took their place was a stream of stories and investigations into wife-swapping, vice rings, escort agency call girls, sex contact magazines and massage parlours. It was the new staple diet and the readers loved it. They were hungry for titbits about what might be going on behind the neighbours' lace curtains.

The genre had begun with a series called 'Sex In the Suburbs' in 1968. From London to Liverpool, from Southampton to Skegness, the new craze for changing partners was changing the sexual pattern of British society. And the *News of the World* was there to chronicle it.

Many of the investigations were carried out by Trevor Kempson and a woman reporter, Tina Dalgleish. Kempson and Dalgleish were to become a remarkable team for years, travelling the length and breadth of the country posing as husband and wife in order to infiltrate wife-swapping circles.

Dalgleish, an attractive redhead who could hold her drink as well as any man, also spent much of her seventeen years with the *News of the World* working undercover as an escort agency girl or nightclub hostess.

She got into the whole scenario by accident when working as Kempson's temporary secretary. One day, he asked her to go and register with an escort agency he wanted to expose. Dalgleish, dressed outrageously in a mini-skirt, fur coat and big floppy hat and with a reel-to-reel tape recorder – then state-of-the-art – concealed in a huge handbag, did so. Later, on the way to meet Kempson, she was propositioned in Mayfair's notorious Shepherd Market and asked how much she charged. She was hooked on investigative journalism.

Dalgleish, now a housewife and mother-of-two, recalled: 'It was my very first assignment and Trevor was accused of leading me into prostitution. Not long after registering with the escort agency, police came to see me about some shooting outside the office. My mother was frantic with worry. She went to Scotland Yard and told them her daughter was being coerced into a life of vice. Fortunately, Trevor was well known to them as an investigative reporter and the whole thing was sorted out.'

One of the more sordid episodes she recalled was when she and Kempson went to expose what they thought, from the address they'd been given, was a pair of wife-swappers who were in the upper echelons of society. It turned out to be a tiny council house on Merseyside, occupied by a pot-bellied man of around 45 and his wife, a much younger petite brunette. The *News of the World* investigators had taken a bottle of Scotch and a bottle of vodka to break the ice but their hosts produced a bottle of VP wine. Then they proceeded to reveal the wife's sexual needs in graphic detail. 'What she really liked,' said Dalgleish, 'was having sex with disabled men or amputees. She would dress up in sexy underwear and then stand provocatively at the top of the stairs and invite wheelchair-bound men at the bottom to come and get her. She would denigrate them as they tried to climb the stairs. Her husband got his kicks from watching her perform with disabled men.'

The inquiries were not always so sordid and frequently had their funny side. Dalgleish recalled how on one wife-swapping story, she and a freelance male reporter stayed overnight at a pub in Suffolk, where the landlord and his wife had advertised for 'broad-minded couples' to join them. They took a photographer with them and introduced him as a friend whose turn-on was taking pictures of the frolics. Having acquired the verbal evidence they needed for their story and persuaded the couple to pose for pictures, in the time-honoured tradition they made their excuses and retired for the night. However, to maintain the illusion that they were a married couple, Dalgleish and the male reporter had to share a twin-bedded room, while the photographer was given a room on his own.

Dalgleish takes up the story: 'In the early hours, the photographer hammered on the door, shouting: "For God's sake, let me in." He was standing in his underpants, holding his suit on a coat-hanger. He explained that he'd woken up and found the landlord's wife in the room, dressed in frilly red knickers and a suspender belt. Then she'd taken her false teeth out, put them on the bedside cabinet and jumped on him! The photographer spent the night in our room. He was too scared even to go to the bathroom in case she set on him again, so when a call of nature came he opened the bedroom window and watered the flowers below!'

Once, Tina and another male reporter spent three weeks 'on the road', posing as wife-swappers in the West Country. Feeling they deserved a break, they booked into a posh hotel in Cheltenham. Seeking some relaxation, they were directed to a nightclub by a river, where they were offered a splendid meal and champagne and no one asked them to pay. 'This young lad of about 19 asked me to dance,' Dalgleish recalled. 'He asked me my name and I told him my name depended on where I was working and who I was with. Puzzled, he asked me if I was married. I said that, too, depended on what job I was doing at the time. He was so intrigued he asked to see me again, so I invited him to have breakfast with me the next day.

'At breakfast, the male reporter joined us. The young lad asked us whether we'd been guests of the bride or groom the previous evening. It turned out we'd accidentally gatecrashed a wedding party! Then the male reporter and I started planning our tactics for another wife-swapping meeting we were going to later that day. The lad was now totally confused. He asked if the male reporter was my husband. I said: "He wasn't yesterday but from lunchtime today he will be. Tomorrow he isn't but on Wednesday he is." The male reporter agreed, at which the poor lad jumped up and said: "I've had enough of this! You lot are kinky. I think I'll stick to football!" He fled, never knowing we were telling the truth.'

The couple that Dalgleish and her male companion met later turned out to be both teachers. They had advertised in a contact magazine for 'swinging couples'. After a chat in a country pub, Dalgleish and her colleague had enough material for their story. Then they were faced with the usual problem of making their excuses and leaving. On this occasion, Tina came up with a really original one. As the four were chatting outside in the sunshine, the teachers asked the two reporters if they had any particular sexual dislikes. Dalgleish, having noticed that the male teacher was quite hairy, responded: 'I can't stand hairy bodies. If you're hairy, I'll have to shave you.' The male reporter almost choked on his drink. This time, it was the would-be swappers who made THEIR excuses and left.

When the *News of the World* is about to expose someone, they are always given an opportunity to answer the allegations before the story is printed. In the case of wife-swapping stories, reactions frequently varied. Some subjects would disappear for a few days, others would be indifferent. One case that caused anguish in the *News of the World* offices concerned a Welsh schoolteacher who was indulging in extramarital swapping with a couple, unknown to his wife. The man killed himself when he found out his activities were to be exposed.

Tina Dalgleish was called to give evidence at the inquest and faced a hostile barrister acting for the wife. He forced Dalgleish to read the man's suicide note in court and asked her: 'Does that not upset you?'

She replied: 'No, not really. I can see how it would upset his wife but it doesn't upset me.'

She later explained her attitude towards the man's death. 'He was not only a liar but a coward,' she said, 'a coward who could not take on the responsibility of what he'd done and face his wife. The distress he caused his wife and children by killing himself was far greater than by being exposed about some nookie.' Quite the reverse reaction was the man who, when told he was about to be exposed, said: 'Be sure to send me the pictures, mate!'

Dalgleish often found herself working undercover in night-clubs as a hostess, talking to the other girls about how they were expected to provide sexual services for the male punters. She recalled working in one club whilst she was five months pregnant with her first child. 'I wore a flowing gown to cover the bulge,' she recalled, 'and had a tape recorder taped to my expanding waist to catch all the salacious talk by the other hostesses. The man I was sitting with had ordered three bottles of champagne. Though I was a hardened drinker, I didn't actu-ally like champagne, so I kept going to the loo to throw up. I also secretly tipped the champagne from my glass into the plants.

'Anyway, this man kept pestering me for sex and I kept refusing him. He got angry, insisting it was his right, so I tipped what was left of the last champagne bottle over his head and walked out. Even working for the most successful newspaper in the world had to have its limits!'

On another occasion Dalgleish became a Bunny Girl in order to check out whether girls at the Playboy Club were offering sex to clients. Kitted out in her black Bunny costume and named Scarlet because of her red hair, she convincingly looked the part. So much so that when the *News of the World*'s sister paper, the *Sun*, wanted a picture of a Bunny Girl to illustrate another story several years later, they pulled her picture out of the picture library's files and put it on the front page. Said

Tina: 'I'd left the *News of the World* by then. My brother had been playing rugby and was having a pint in the pub after-wards when he saw the picture in the *Sun*. He said to his mates: "I know that face." All his mates said, "Introduce us and we'll buy you a pint." "No problem," my brother said, "she's my sister!"'

A far more dangerous and deadly assignment for Dalgleish was when, whilst exposing drug dealers, she found herself in a situation in which she had no choice than to allow herself to have heroin injected into her arm. It was a case of going along with the charade that she was an addict or having her cover blown and possibly risking physical violence. Afterwards she became violently ill and recalled vaguely sitting in the foyer of Bouverie Street at 2.00 a.m., waiting for a taxi. Bruce Matthews, the managing director, came across her sitting in a stupor. 'What on earth are you doing, Tina?' he asked. 'You look dreadful.'

Dalgleish replied: 'Read about it on Sunday.'

When her story appeared in the paper exposing the dealers, Scotland Yard's drugs squad arrived at the paper's offices and cautioned her for drugs possession, using and dealing. 'There was an outcry from the rest of Fleet Street and the *News of the World*'s lawyers sorted it out,' said Dalgleish.'I loved all the years I spent working for the paper but that was the one time I asked myself whether it was all worth it!'

Trevor Kempson, who died in 1990 after a long battle against cancer, used to say his motto was: 'Scotch, sex, cigarettes and sunshine', and he enjoyed all with equal enthusiasm. Kemp-son was a fully qualified first-degree witch, having been initiated into a coven for an exposé. He had to be naked for the ceremony, so found it impossible to employ his usual tech-nique of having a secret tape recorder concealed about his person. He solved the problem by having a special briefcase made with a high-powered microphone in the handle, linked to a long-running recorder inside. Like any investigative reporter who gets involved in highly charged sexual situations, Kempson was often asked how he dealt with the problem of getting . . . well, a physical response. 'Never happens,' he used to reply. 'You remind yourself you're just doing a job and think of the most unsexy thing you can, like the car needs servicing or something.' Kempson also became famous for his convenient migraine attacks at the critical moment when an excuse was needed.

Another Kempson investigation in the 1970s involved the exposure of a prostitution ring in Mayfair, operated by a team of vice kings known as the 'Maltese Mafia'. After weeks of inquiries, Kempson was asked to lay off by the police, who were also investigating the gang. But their investigations were going nowhere either, as the gang leaders had covered their tracks by concealing their ownership of properties in which the prostitutes were operating.

Kempson eventually managed to become friendly with some of the gang's collectors who collected the money from the girls. Every night, they took thousands of pounds back to the chief ringleader's flat, where it was counted, and next day took the cash to the bank. However, one night Kempson sent out a team of more than a dozen reporters, armed with banknotes that had been photographed in the *News of the World* offices and had the serial numbers recorded. The reporters went round the prostitutes, made their excuses and left but paid the money. Later, some of the collectors took the money back to Kempson's office, where the serial numbers were checked. Some tallied with notes that had been given to the reporters earlier.

After the *News of the World* published the story, Kempson gave evidence for the police when the gang came up at the Old Bailey. The leaders got a total of thirty-five years' jail between them. Much later, after the chief ringleader had come out of prison, he used to get someone to telephone Kempson with the occasional message at Christmas, sending his regards. Kempson, not knowing whether it was a veiled threat, would suggest meeting for a drink. Once he was told on behalf of the gang leader: 'He still thinks you owe him money for getting such a good story.'

A tale Kempson used to tell cheerfully against himself was

about the day he became the first reporter to expose the notorious Lindi St Clair, the vice girl who is rarely out of the headlines. St Clair, who wages a long-running battle with the Inland Revenue and who claims to have scores of MPs and peers among her clients, hit the front pages in early 1993 when she faked her own disappearance, then turned up on a luxury cruise liner in Florida.

However, she was unknown when Kempson went along to her house in Earl's Court in 1977 to sample her wares. After observing a brass plaque with the warning 'Abandon hope all ye who enter here', Kempson was ushered into St Clair's torture chamber, which was furnished with rubber suits, medieval costumes, a mortarboard and gown, schoolgirl gym slips and whips and canes. He paid her £200 and picked out rubberwear, thinking it was the safest. But Lindi St Clair had other ideas. 'You're into bondage, aren't you?' she demanded.

Kempson protested: 'No, I just like wearing rubber.'

She wouldn't listen. 'The more you protest, the more they think you like it,' Kempson explained. 'She put this dog collar around my neck, buckled one of the straps up top, one at the bottom, then tied my wrists behind my back, put a rubber mask over my head, tied my ankles up and threw me on the couch. She left me there for twenty minutes. I was wetting myself with fear. When she came back, she untied my legs but then put a rubber cloak on me and strung me up on a rack with handcuffs that cut into my skin. Finally, after I'd paid her another £200, she took me into another room and showed me a two-way mirror looking into the room I'd been in. I thought, bloody hell, who's been looking through at me?'

Kempson's exposé of St Clair described her as 'an evil woman who trades in torture'. For years afterwards, when she had become infamous, he used to get phone calls from her in which she told him: 'I have a lot to thank you for, Trevor.'

As the sexual climate of the 1970s became ever more relaxed, the scene changed from straightforward partner-swapping and three-in-a-bed sessions – the *News of the World* dubbed it 'troilism' – to full-scale orgies. Investigator Ray Chapman gave this hilarious account of a mass sex session attended by himself and a woman reporter at a semi-detached house in East London:

> The room was a mass of heaving, naked bodies. One beautiful Asian girl was intimate with three men in half-an-hour. Some girls paired off together.
>
> Except for myself and the girl reporter, the only other person fully dressed was a female midget. It had been a stipulation that every man should bring a female partner – no singles were allowed. An old boy had turned up with the midget as his partner, just so he could get into the orgy. After all, she was a female. The old fellow couldn't believe his luck when the action started. He was grabbing and fondling every woman he could lay his hands on. Meanwhile, his tiny companion sat on a sofa watching the writhing throng. A couple were making love directly in front of her. The man looked up at the midget, then back at his partner and said: 'I don't think we should be doing this in front of the children.'

Chapman subsequently achieved a kind of instant fame in the *News of the World* office as the man who turned down one of the world's most celebrated prostitutes, Xaviera Hollander, who called herself the Happy Hooker. The notorious vice girl was supposedly in London to promote her memoirs but an investigation by the paper quickly proved that she was also plying her trade from a luxury flat in Chelsea, a fact that investigators established by taking short-let apartments in the same block.

Chapman was deputed to take the lady out to dinner and get her to offer her favours. This she did back in her apartment, making sure to ask for the money first. She went off for a shower and returned naked, except for a gold waist chain with a heart-shaped medallion. When she lay on the bed, the intrepid investigator used a classic, time-honoured excuse and told her he'd had too much to drink to oblige her. Miss

Hollander was amazed. 'But I'm Xaviera Hollander and you've paid your money. Lots of men would give their right arm to be where you are right now. I can't believe you won't come to bed with me,' she trilled.

'And nor will my mates,' muttered the conscientious Chapman as he slipped out of the apartment. A few days later, the romantic reporter went out and bought his wife a chain with a heart-shaped medallion, just like Miss Hollander's. 'I told her where I'd got the idea from,' he recalled. 'Very understanding, she was.'

The sleazy world of saunas and massage parlours was another favourite haunt of *News of the World* investigators. One series involved visiting scores of massage parlours all over the country in order to establish in which ones the girl masseurs offered 'extra' services. That turned out to be pretty well all of them. Because it was difficult to conceal a tape recorder when lying near-naked on a bed, it was decided to send two reporters into each establishment in order to get the necessary corroborative evidence. It added up to a lot of massages – but at least the *News of the World* men were the cleanest bunch of investigators in the business.

The star of the sauna spies was a freelance journalist from the Midlands called David Potts, who was used extensively on such inquiries because there were few who looked less like a reporter. He was an elegantly dressed, distinguished-looking man with grey hair in his fifties who looked more like a typical provincial bank manager or businessman. His gentle charm and benign manner earned him the nickname of 'the vicar' in the office. It was a standing joke that Potts had had so much baby oil rubbed into his body in the course of his massage parlour inquiries that he became known as 'the man with the softest skin in Fleet Street'.

In the late 1970s, the nation was agog with another saucy saga of suburban sex. Ranking with Lindi St Clair and Xaviera Hollander in the annals of prostitution was Cynthia Payne, whose exploits as the madam of what became famous as the 'luncheon voucher brothel' were even turned into a hit film. *News of the World* feature writer Rosalie Shann spent an evening at Madam Cyn's in order to sample the atmosphere. This is her entertaining and often hilarious account of what went on at Cynthia's Edwardian house in Streatham, South London . . .

No doubt about it, Cynthia Payne was the funniest person I've ever interviewed. Cyn, as she was affectionately called, was the woman who ran Britain's most amazing 'knocking shop'. It was known as the 'luncheon voucher brothel' because the customers used to buy £25 luncheon vouchers in exchange for having sex. The nicest thing about the setup was that it was homely rather than sleazy. The cash was kept in a pressure cooker in the broom cupboard. The vouchers were stored in a cardboard box in the kitchen and a large Bisto tin housed dirty videos with titles like *Casanova and the Nuns* and *Naughty Girl Guides*.

The men were all middle-aged. Cyn set a minimum age limit of 40 'because young men are far less appreciative than older ones'. They all seemed to know each other and were, outwardly at any rate, very respectable. Most of the girls were not tarts such as you'd find standing on street corners but bored housewives anxious for some fun, free booze and pin money. For their £25 voucher, the men were entertained in an elegant drawing room, with salmon and cucumber sandwiches tastefully arranged on lettuce leaves, a wide range of drinks, a live sex show and, of course, a trip upstairs with the woman of their choice. Plus, at 6.00 p.m. a high tea of poached eggs on toast in the kitchen.

I was sent along to find out what it was all about and write it up in good old *News of the World* style. I liked Cyn from the start. A short – only 4 foot 10 inches – bundle of energy who was convinced she was doing the country a valuable service. 'You know, darling, the Queen should really give me the MBE,' she used to say. 'I'm not doing anything wicked, just making people happy by providing sex in nice, cosy surroundings. I consider myself a social worker.'

It was obvious that to find out how the whole thing worked, I would have to attend a few parties but in what capacity? 'Perhaps I could pretend to be your maid and just hang around and see what happens,' I suggested.

'Maid!' cried Cynthia. 'Don't be silly, darling, the slaves would hate me to import a maid.'

Slaves, what slaves? They apparently were the handsome young men who looked after the guests, handing round drinks and cucumber sandwiches while being verbally abused at the same time. 'They're marvellous and you don't have to pay them a bean,' Cynthia explained. 'All you have to do is yell at them in a nasty way and they love it.'

Finally, it was agreed that I would just be one of Cynthia's friends who would talk to the clients – very useful, seeing as it gave me a chance to interview them – and not participate. We decided I'd be called Sally, which was fine, seeing as that is what I am called at home anyway (Sally being short for Rosalie), and if any chaps thought I might be a prostitute, too, I'd say I couldn't do anything because I was recovering from an operation. It was true – I had just undergone a hysterectomy and by now I was a friend of Cyn's.

She then told me the procedure. Parties took place once a month and clients were invited by a note in the post. 'Dear Mr ***,' Cynthia would write in her quaint fashion. 'The next union meeting will be held at 2.00 p.m. on ***. Please let me know if you'll be there because of the catering.' 'Catering', of course, meant how many women to call in as well as how many poached eggs to order.

On the appointed day, I arrived early in time to help with the sandwiches. I was carrying with me a little gift for our hostess, an egg poacher with enough room for six eggs to be done at one time (all on *News of the World* expenses, of course). The slaves, Cyn and I all rushed round the kitchen preparing the food and saw that the flowers were all right in the drawing room. Then the door-bell began ringing and the men started to arrive, about twenty or thirty of them. They were all smart-suited and well spoken and most of them greeted each other like old friends. These, I presumed, were the regulars. 'Not surprising,' explained Cyn, 'they've been coming to my union meetings for years.'

The men mostly ignored the alcohol and grabbed orange juices and sat around chatting, not about sex, I noticed, but mostly about gardening! Half-an-hour before kick-off time, 2.00 p.m., I noticed Cynthia getting agitated. 'Where are the girls?' she hissed at me. 'Only three have arrived so far. Why are they always so late?' She soon relaxed, however, when another six arrived. All were well over 30, I noticed, and not particularly glamorous, except for a sexy-looking blonde and a sultry coloured girl.

Exactly at 2.00 p.m. the curtains were drawn, the lights turned low and the black girl and a white girl came dan-cing into the room, stripped off and then performed a les-bian scene on a duvet spread out on the carpet. All the men, looking very serious, gazed at them, whilst most of we females stared at the curtains, wondering where Cyn had got the fabric and how much it had cost.

Then everyone seemed much more relaxed and started chatting. Cyn had already introduced me as 'Mistress Sally' who'd just come out of hospital but had come round to help. In other words, the message to the men was, 'Don't ask her. Keep off.' I noticed some of the men going over to the woman of their choice and asking: 'Would you care to come upstairs?' And the woman replying, politely: 'Thank you.' It seemed to me a bit like being asked to dance at the Palais.

As there were only four bedrooms, a queue soon formed on the stairs. 'Nothing to worry about,' Cyn smiled. 'You know how the British love queuing.' Suddenly the door-bell rang and a man of about 50 rushed in, apologizing to Cyn for being late. He looked round the room, stared at me for a moment, then obviously thinking he recognized me, rushed over and kissed me. 'Darling,' he cried, 'where have you been? It must be at least three years since you were last here.' Talk about mistaken identity! but I couldn't let Cyn down, so I said quickly:

'I've been ill. I've had an operation. I'm not here for THAT this time.' Suddenly Cynthia was at my side. Bending down, she whispered:

'Look, you can go upstairs if you want to, I promise not to tell the *News of the World*.'

'Thanks, Cyn,' I replied, 'but it's nearly six o'clock and you know how good I am at poached eggs, so I'd better get out to the kitchen.'

Before I went to the kitchen, though, I felt I needed a drink. I hailed a passing slave: 'Philip, do you think you could get me a gin and tonic, please?' Cyn overheard me and was furious.

'THAT'S not the way to talk to a slave, Sally, as you should know,' she cried. Then turning to the cowering young man, she shouted at him: 'Slave Philip, get Mistress Sally a gin and tonic immediately!'

Later, dancing with some of the clients, they talked to me about how much they appreciated Cynthia's 'union meetings'. 'You can be unfaithful to the wife without any emotional commitment,' seemed their most common remark. Other observations included: 'Cyn actually saves marriages. She's fantastic.'

I struck up quite a friendship with Cynthia Payne. she seemed to be a lonely person, perhaps because although most people thought she did a fine job, they didn't care to associate with her outside the parties. She visited my home, met my family and, having discovered that my house had two bathrooms, even asked me if I'd like to run a 'branch office'! I made an excuse and said no. But

I did like her and I had to agree with her and her clients
that she was providing a worthwhile service. Later, after
she'd been convicted and sent to prison, we still occasionally met. Her conversation inevitably turned to sex and
the injustice of not allowing her to continue to run her
'union meetings'.

'Every man wants another woman,' she used to say,
'even if he loves his wife. It's inevitable he'll go off with
someone else, just to prove he can still do it.'

I only had one criticism of Cynthia. She would keep on
and on about who she was – and she had the most raucous
voice. We'd go out for a meal together and I would always
ring up in advance and ask for a secluded table. But however secluded, the evening always ended in the same way.
We'd get up to leave and then, just before we left, Cyn
would pause dramatically at the door and turn to face the
other diners. Suddenly, that raucous voice would blare
out. 'In case you're wondering who I am,' she would
declare, 'I'm Cynthia Payne, the queen of British brothels.
And this is Rosalie Shann of the *News of the World*!' Ah,
dear Madame Cyn . . .

TWENTY-FIVE

Bludgers and Badgers

It wasn't all wife-swapping, saunas and massage parlours, of course. As always, and no matter who was editing it, the *News of the World* sought to satisfy its readers with a well-balanced diet. Several other areas of investigations proved to be generous sources of stories – two in particular. Dole scroungers who were fiddling the nation's social security system were one. Another was cruelty to animals, in which the paper built up a lengthy and honourable record of exposing scandals.

Dole fiddlers – people who were drawing their unemployment and social security benefits and working on the side – became a particular *bête noire* of the paper from around the mid 1970s onwards. A string of stories and investigations appeared, encouraged by the proprietor, Rupert Murdoch, whose papers had exposed similar cheats in Australia, where they called them 'bludgers'.

One particular story, which made a front page splash in the *News of the World*, was obtained after the paper had set up an elaborate 'Sting' operation. Reporter Ray Chapman, who was responsible for many of the scrounger stories, learned from a contact about a crooked roofing and building contractor in North London who recruited his entire workforce from the queue at the dole offices. The contractor had been heard boasting that he used men who were on the dole because he didn't have to pay them the full rate for the job and that he hadn't paid income tax or VAT himself for five years. As Chapman remarked: 'He'd pulled more strokes than the Oxford boat crew.' But how to catch him out?

It was decided to rent a rundown house and work a

con-in-reverse by offering the prospect of doing some work on the property as bait to lure the cunning contractor. After some searching round estate agents, Chapman eventually found an empty house that had been converted into flats and with a roof that was in need of repair. Then he met the conniving contractor at his 'office' – a pub – with three of his men, all of whom he introduced as being on the dole.

Chapman took them to the house, where they clambered about on the roof, unaware that their every move was being photographed by a *News of the World* cameraman with a telescopic lens. The contractor told Chapman the roof repairs were going to cost £1,500 for wages alone, with materials extra. The reporter obtained another quote from a reputable builder of only £1,200, including materials, for the same work. Then he chatted to the workmen and got them to admit they were drawing social security payments and working on the side.

Confronted by the evidence, the crooked contractor uttered a classic admission on a par with 'It's a fair cop, guv.' Shaken, he told reporter Chapman: 'You done me up like a kipper!' The story appeared on the front page under the headline: FIDDLERS ON THE ROOF.

Another story which made the front page was headlined THE SPAGHETTI SCROUNGERS. This was about a bunch of young Italians who had taken advantage of the new freedom of movement within Common Market countries and were squatting in a block of flats in Islington and claiming social security benefits. They told reporter Chapman: 'We don't like you or your country but as long as you keep giving us money we'll stay here.' The newspaper wanted a large group photograph of the Italian squatters. But, cheeky to the end, they said they'd only agree on condition that Chapman bought them a meal – all twenty of them. The reporter did a deal with a friend who owned an Italian restaurant and a large photo of what the paper called the 'Latin layabouts' living it up at the expense of the good old British taxpayer appeared on the front page. Immediately after the exposé appeared, the Department of Health and Social Security moved in to make its own inquiries.

Chapman recalled another amusing incident when he was exposing a slum landlord who owned a couple of rat-infested bed-and-breakfast hostels for homeless people. Protesting that there was nothing wrong with the premises, the landlord waved his arms and said: 'The food is good and the furniture is nearly new.' As he spoke, the chair he was sitting on collapsed under him and he crashed to the floor.

The reporter, having captured everything on his tape recorder, couldn't help remarking: 'I'm sorry but I don't think you've got a leg to stand on.'

In exposing animal cruelty, the *News of the World* has led the field. Three times the paper's reporters won awards from the League Against Cruel Sports, two of them to the same writer, Maureen Lawless. Reporter Ron Mount won an award for the journalist who had done most to expose cruelty to animals, for a fox-hunting story in the 1970s, and Lawless was honoured twice during the 1980s, once for a story on stag-hunting and again for a hard-hitting exposé of evil badger-baiters.

Often the *News of the World* investigators worked under cover, alongside League Against Cruel Sports members, to get the evidence they needed. They frequently put themselves into dangerous situations, risking physical violence and even receiving threats to their lives.

Lawless, a lifelong animal lover who combined her work for the *News of the World* with running a sanctuary for unwanted farm animals in the Midlands, began her crusade with an investigation into a Welsh farm where beagles were being bred in horrific conditions for laboratory research. To complete the necessary evidence, another reporter, Wendy Henry – later to become editor of the *News of the World* – was sent to get a job at the farm. Henry freely admitted she was a city girl, knew nothing about animals and especially hated dogs. However, to her amazement, she was taken on as a supervisor. Her first job was to segregate the puppies according to sex. 'I didn't know how to tell one from the other, so I just guessed,' she told Lawless after her first day.

However, by the end of the week Henry was so incensed by the plight of the beagles that she aided Lawless in rescuing two of the puppies. She pushed them through a gap in the fence to Lawless, who ran with one dog in a carrier bag and the other under her jumper across a field to her waiting car. Maureen kept the beagles in her home as pets for years afterwards.

Much later, when Henry was appointed editor of the *News of the World*, she got a telegram from Lawless which said: 'I always knew when you were made supervisor of the beagle farm that you were destined for higher things.'

Maureen Lawless's next major story actually brought about government legislation. She and another reporter, Janet Taylor, followed truckloads of sheep being illegally dispatched from Britain to slaughterhouses on the Continent in appallingly cramped conditions. They followed the trucks across France and Belgium and their front-page report resulted in the banning of live animals from being exported.

In one undercover operation, Lawless and an investigator from the League Against Cruel Sports infiltrated a West Country stag hunt, posing as tourists and hunt followers. They witnessed a terrified stag being torn to pieces by hounds and the barbaric ritual of cutting out the liver and heart and handing them to the watching crowd. It was for this exposé that Lawless won the League's Peter Wilson award for the campaigning journalist of the year.

Later, Lawless was to team up with a reformed criminal, Graham Hall, a self-confessed petty thief whose knowledge of the underworld enabled him to blend in easily with poachers, dog fighters and badger baiters. Hall was prepared to put himself into situations of extreme risk in order to help the *News of the World* expose the animal abusers.

One of the most dangerous assignments involved infiltrating the bizarre world of the dog fighters, a web of evil men based in Liverpool who enjoyed watching specially bred pit bull terriers tearing each other to pieces for so-called 'sport'. On one trip over to Dublin, Hall found himself in a gang of around fifty men, including IRA supporters, watching seven hours of dog fighting. He had gained the men's confidence to the extent that they let him take pictures. It was these, and tape record-ings, that eventually led to six men being convicted, the first successful prosecution of its kind in Ireland.

Back in Liverpool, Hall had established himself amongst known dog fighters. They even showed him a bloody video of a fight between two bull terriers, one of which was kept in a barrel used as a kennel behind one of the gang's homes. Hall managed to steal the video, which provided vital evidence leading to the conviction of three of the men. The *News of the World* team realized, however, that once their story had been published, the dog, called Sykes, was doomed. The animal had had half its face torn away and had been crudely stitched by its owner. Two days before the story was due to appear, a rescue operation was launched.

Lawless and Hall made attempts to retrieve the dog from its barrel in a back garden but the barking of other pit bulls alerted the owner. They returned next day with a tough ex-paratrooper who was a member of an animal rescue organiz-ation. That attempt looked doomed to failure also when the team were stopped by a police patrol, who searched the car and found SAS-style balaclavas. The *News of the World* investigators were hauled off to the police station. But once they'd explained the situation, an understanding sergeant offered them steam-ing mugs of tea, then insisted on accompanying them to the house and removed the injured dog himself.

The triumph had sinister repercussions. Somehow, the gang obtained Hall's home address and for months he received threatening phone calls. Then, one day he was lured to a meet-ing at a motorway service station, where he was overpowered by four men, bound and blindfolded and taken to a field where he was tarred and feathered. He was highly fortunate to escape with his life when three of the men went away – to fetch a gun, he heard them say – leaving one man alone to guard him.

Others in the team have had death threats, too. One arrived

in the form of a sinister video showing a dead badger. A man with his back to the camera hacked at it with a meat cleaver, saying: 'You bastards, we know who you are. This is what is going to happen to you.' It was the badger-baiting story that became the *News of the World* investigative team's most successful and dramatic exposé. As a result of months of investigations, eighteen men were convicted of badger digging and baiting, and causing unnecessary cruelty. As a result of the paper's Save the Badger campaign, legislation was introduced to outlaw the barbaric practices.

Amongst the evidence produced in a magistrates' court was a video taken by Graham Hall of men digging out young badgers and throwing them to dogs before kicking, stabbing and shooting them. Another bloody battle captured on film by Hall was of an unequal fight between an ordinary terrier dog and a pit bull. One of the badger baiters, annoyed with his terrier because it didn't fight fiercely enough against a badger, matched it with the pit bull. The poor animal was dead within seconds, crushed by the jaws of its fearsome adversary.

Some of the sadistic men found guilty in the various court cases went to jail. Once again the *News of the World* had triumphed in its campaigns against the evil animal abusers.

TWENTY-SIX

Murder

Twice within the last two decades the *News of the World* has been instrumental in solving murder cases. Given the paper's long fascination with crime stories, it was perhaps no surprise that the tradition should continue into the modern era. It's a tradition that goes back to the paper's connections with the wife-murderer Dr Buck Ruxton in the 1930s and the acid bath killer, Haigh, in the late 1940s. In the more recent cases, one of the murders was an unsolved, 42-year-old killing. In the other, the paper cooperated with the latest wonders of forensic science to solve the brutal murder of a young mother.

In 1976, a man called Tony Mancini telephoned the *News of the World*'s Manchester editorial office and reporter Alan Hart took the call. Mancini's story was extraordinary. He said he had got away with a murder in 1934 but now wanted to confess to the crime. Reporter Hart agreed to meet him. He found an elderly man of 68.

The Brighton Trunk Murder had been a *cause célèbre* in 1934. During a five-day trial at Lewes Assizes, Mancini, then a petty crook of 26, had denied murdering his lover, a 42-year-old dancer-prostitute, Violet Kaye. Crowds in the public gallery booed and hissed Mancini every time he was led into the dock. He told the jury he had come home to the couple's rented flat and found Violet's lifeless body. He panicked, he claimed, thinking nobody would believe in his innocence, so he stuffed the body into a trunk and paid two strangers 10s to transport it to his new lodgings.

Before he could decide what to do with her body, his hand was forced by an amazing coincidence. Another trunk containing a young girl's torso was deposited at Brighton railway station and a suitcase containing two legs was left at King's Cross station in London. That gruesome murder – unsolved to this day – was totally unconnected with Violet Kaye's death but it was enough to make Mancini flee Brighton, leaving his grisly secret behind. Violet's body was discovered and Mancini was shopped to police by gangland friends.

Mancini faced the gallows if he was found guilty. But he stuck to his story about having come home and found the woman already dead and panicked. He had the greatest King's Counsel of the day, Norman Birkett, as his defence lawyer and Mancini was acquitted. He had to be smuggled out of the court building to avoid a mob outside who were baying for his blood. With extraordinary brazenness, he then worked with a travelling fair in an act in which he pretended to chop off a pretty girl's head with a guillotine. He was billed as Tony Mancini, the Brighton Trunk Murder Man.

Over the years, Mancini faded into obscurity and might never have been heard of again but for his call to the *News of the World* that day in 1976. With staff photographer Boyd Milligan, Alan Hart went to Liverpool and chatted to Mancini in a pub. Mancini said he was thinking of writing a book and wanted some advice. After a few pints, he confessed he had killed Violet Kaye and lied to the jury to escape the hangman's noose.

The *News of the World* men listened with fascinated horror as the elderly Mancini gave his version of the events that led to his lover's death. He told them he'd been trying to break away from her because she was an alcoholic and a drug addict. She'd gone to a restaurant in which he was working and got him the sack because she was 'legless and doped up to the eyeballs'. Later, back at their flat, the couple had quarrelled and Violet had hit him on the head with a coal hammer. He'd managed to get the hammer off her, then thrown it at her and she had fallen down on to the brass fireplace surround. Mancini said he found himself banging the woman's head on the surround until blood began to trickle from her mouth. 'I honestly didn't mean to kill her,' he claimed, 'I just lost control in the heat of the moment.'

The rest of the story was the version he told at his trial. He told the two *News of the World* men how he had carefully rehearsed his evidence, even to the extent of practising crying to gain the jury's sympathy. He added: 'Of course, I feel ashamed and guilty about what happened. But although I told lies to get off the murder charge, there were mitigating circumstances. Under today's laws I would probably have got away with manslaughter but not then. In those days it would have been impossible to tell the truth and escape the gallows.'

Mancini claimed he had wandered the world ever since with his guilty conscience pricking him. He had had two broken marriages but was now married to a wonderful woman who knew the full story. 'When you harbour a guilty secret like mine all these years, it's a great relief to tell someone,' he said.

In telling his story, Mancini knew he could not be charged again with a murder of which he'd been acquitted. His belated confession, together with a picture of him in dark glasses, appeared on the front page of the *News of the World* . . . and a 42-year-old mystery was solved.

The second murder mystery in which the paper played a major role unfolded at an Old Bailey trial in January 1993. And it was like an Agatha Christie-type detective story. A young mother was brutally battered to death with a hammer at her flat in Fulham in May 1992, whilst her 2-year-old daughter was in the next room. The girl's ex-lover was the principal suspect but the police could not find his fingerprints in the flat and the murder weapon had been cleaned. Added to which, the man claimed he had spent the day of the murder with his mother in Kent, miles away from the death scene.

However, the vital piece of evidence that was to put the ex-boyfriend behind bars for a life sentence was lying just yards away from the dead girl's body. It was a blood-stained copy of that Sunday's *News of the World*, which the killer had picked up and thumbed through as he contemplated his dreadful crime. When the pages were dipped in a chemical solution, perfect prints of his left forefinger were revealed on five pages of the newspaper. More prints were on the cover and inside pages of the accompanying *Sunday* magazine.

However, police then had to convince the jury that the copy of the *News of the World* could only have been handled by the suspect at the girl's flat on the day of the murder, for the defendant claimed the only copy of the paper he had touched was at his mum's home. Detectives also feared the defence lawyers might suggest they had planted a doctored newspaper at the scene of the crime, inserting pages with the man's prints on them inside the bloodstained front cover.

That was where *News of the World* production experts came in. Police visited the paper's offices at Wapping with the vital pages. The experts studied them carefully and were able to tell by deciphering the code at the top of each page exactly when the edition was printed and where it was sold. They also confirmed that the pages all came from one edition. It was a special edition that had been printed at 1.00 a.m. on the Sunday morning. Earlier editions of the paper had carried an exclusive story about Princess Anne's planned wedding to Tim Laurence. But the front page had been changed at midnight to cover, ironically, another murder story. The edition was available in Fulham, where the dead girl had lived, but not in the area of Kent where the accused man said he'd been with his mother. The *News of the World* production experts also identified a printing error which had occurred only in that edition.

One of the experts said: 'The police were amazed by how much we could tell them just by looking at the pages.' It was enough for an Old Bailey jury to find the ex-lover guilty of a horrific murder.

TWENTY-SEVEN

Editorial Musical Chairs

From 1891 to 1970, a span of almost eighty years, the *News of the World* had just six editors. In the twenty-three years since Stafford Somerfield was fired, no fewer than ten incumbents followed him into the chair that was stoutly occupied by Emsley Carr alone for an amazing half-century. It's a turnover rate probably surpassed only by that of football club managers.

The 1980s saw three momentous changes for the newspaper. First was the launch of the colour magazine, *Sunday*, in September 1981. Then came the transformation of the paper into a tabloid in May 1984. Finally, there was the traumatic move to a new plant at Wapping, with the introduction of electronic typesetting and the smashing of the power of the print unions, in early 1986.

There were other factors at work which made being editor of the *News of the World* a relatively high-risk occupation. Rupert Murdoch had taken over in 1969 with a reputation for getting through editors fairly swiftly. The massive 8 million circulation of the *News of the World* of the 1950s had long gone, eroded by the unwillingness of younger readers to follow family tradition in their choice of newspaper. The success of the newly risen tabloid *Sun* under Murdoch had brought to daily journalism a fresher, livelier and more irreverent style, some of which spilled over into the Sunday paper stable.

There was heavy competition from other entertainments and other media, especially television. Realizing the futility of trying to compete with the latter, newspapers developed a new phenomenon during the 1970s and 1980s of writing fervently about the private lives of the TV stars, especially those in soap operas, to the extent that it sometimes became difficult to distinguish between their personal lives and those of the on-screen characters they portrayed. And there was another, real-life soap opera which was increasingly grabbing the headlines – the extraordinary shenanigans of the Royal Family, especially its younger members.

These developments were taking place against a background of ever-fiercer competition in Fleet Street and worsening industrial relations, which were little short of shambolic. The *News of the World* was as badly hit as any other paper by the truculent gestures of the print unions. Disputes were rife. Once, the paper lost hundreds of thousands of copies when printers took exception to a phrase in an article by the Labour peer Lord George Brown, himself a champion of trade unions. On another occasion, a union official demanded that the editor join him in a Christmas drink. When the editor suggested it might wait until after the main edition had gone to press, the offended printer immediately brought production to a standstill.

Despite having lost almost half of its 1950s circulation, the newspaper continued to outsell its rivals throughout the 1970s and 1980s by a substantial margin. The unique Sunday formula, with sex scandals, the love lives of the stars and sport being major ingredients, was still irresistible to millions of readers. But the toll in editors was a bit like a game of musical chairs.

One steadying influence for some years was the presence of Sir Larry Lamb, the man behind the amazing success story of the *Sun*. He had overlordship of both newspapers for a while as group editorial director. The appointment of the placid, pipe-smoking 'Tiny' Lear as editor had been regarded as a stopgap by some of his colleagues, though they had high regard for him. But he remained for almost four years, until the end of 1973, when he was made editorial manager, responsible for the editorial administration of both the *News of the World* and the *Sun*. His reign had been successful: during his editorship the paper's margin of circulation over its nearest rival had almost doubled to 1,700,000.

For the next year, the editorial chair was occupied by Peter Stephens, who had been recruited to the *Sun* after a career in the provinces during which he edited the *Newcastle Journal* and the *Evening Chronicle*. He had been deputy editor of the *Sun* before joining the *News of the World* as associate editor. After a shortish reign at the *News of the World*, he moved back to the *Sun* in 1975 as associate editor and later became editorial director of News Group Newspapers.

Stephens's successor was Bernard Shrimsley, who had also been one of Larry Lamb's launch team for the *Sun* in 1969. He had been recruited as deputy editor from the editorship of the *Liverpool Daily Post*, moving up to edit the *Sun* after Lamb's appointment as editorial director. On being offered the editorship of the *News of the World*, Shrimsley stipulated that he should have sole charge of the week-to-week editing and that Lamb should not interfere.

Shrimsley's first action on taking the job was to go to the old files and read back numbers of the paper, from when the circulation had been over 8 million, to try and discover the magic formula of that era. He was surprised to find the front page consisted of straightforward sober news reporting. 'It contained nothing rude, sensational or even marginally naughty,' he recalled. 'The front page was like a Sunday edition of the *Daily Telegraph*. Inside court stories were only what the *Telegraph* would publish.'

Tall and fastidious in appearance, Shrimsley was regarded in the office as a perfectionist in newspaper design and layout. He fretted about a column rule out of place or too much, or too little, white space around a headline. He would cast his experienced eye over the final product on the stone – the table on which pages were made up in type – and, if satisfied, would sometimes burst into a short refrain from a song from the musical, *Kiss Me Kate*: 'Something appealing, something appalling, something for everyone, it's comedy tonight.' To Shrimsley, it summed up the appeal of the paper.

One of the stories of which Shrimsley was most proud during his five years of editorship occurred in 1977 when the

News of the World published a front-page attack on the leaders of the extreme right-wing political party, the National Front. The party was putting up candidates at by-elections and gaining a substantial number of votes. Shrimsley felt it right to reveal the Nazi background of some of the party's leaders.

However, more significantly he chose deliberately to break the law by publishing the criminal records – including jail sentences – of the two principal leaders, John Tyndall and Martin Webster. At the time, a relatively new law, the Rehabilitation of Offenders Act, had been in operation for just over two years. The law, intended to help petty criminals live down their past, banned the publication of convictions if the person concerned had gone straight for seven years or more. But Shrimsley didn't think the Act should apply to people seeking public office, so he wrote a powerful front-page leader telling readers just why the *News of the World* was revealing the crime records of the National Front men.

Shrimsley's view was that the overriding public interest demanded that the electorate should be made aware of what sort of people they were being asked to vote for. He was proved to be justified in his decision to publish the criminal records, for there were no comebacks from the government law officers, nor did the two men sue the paper. The episode became enshrined in the newspaperman's legal bible, *Essential Law For Journalists*, as the classic case of a paper justifiably defying an act of parliament. Recalled Shrimsley: 'It was the *News of the World* at its bold best.'

Shrimsley was a strong advocate of the paper going tabloid and twice during his editorship he negotiated big-money deals for sensational kiss 'n' tell memoirs with which to launch what would be virtually a new newspaper. Both occurred in 1978, the first being the life story of actress Joan Collins, who was spilling the beans in a book about her colourful love life.

The second serialization, the memoirs of the Swedish actress Britt Ekland, cost the *News of the World* what was then a world record fee of £110,000, negotiated by Ekland's London agent, ex-newspaperman Don Short. The series was spicy, for the lady told all about her relationships with the likes of Rod Stewart, George Hamilton and Peter Sellers, and boosted circulation. However, there was a story behind the story which was unknown to the readers . . .

Shrimsley had bought the memoirs on the basis of a synopsis but when the finished manuscript came into the office it failed somewhat to live up to its initial promise, having been penned by a ghostwriter. The paper's top woman's writer Unity Hall – who, besides being the agony aunt, was a tough-as-nails experienced reporter – was dispatched to re-interview the actress at her home in New York. When Unity arrived at Miss Ekland's apartment, she discovered that the actress had decided to play the prima donna and kept her waiting for half-an-hour. Hall, too much of an old Fleet Street hand to be fazed by such behaviour, sent a maid to the errant Miss Ekland's bedroom with the brief but effective message: 'Tell the lady that if she doesn't get her arse down here in five minutes, I'm on the next plane back to London and she can forget about the money!'

So outstanding was Unity Hall's version of the Ekland memoirs that Shrimsley sent her what he called a 'herogram'. In it, he told her: 'I have never seen a more successful transformation of a very, very ordinary manuscript into a quite superb series. Thank you for proving that when it comes to newspaper serialization, one should never judge a cover by its book.' (Many years later, there was an ironic footnote to this incident. When the *News of the World* tragically lost Unity Hall in 1992, Bernard Shrimsley gave the address at her memorial service and referred to his 'herogram' of fourteen years previously. So admired was Unity that the ghostwriter of the original Ekland manuscript turned up to the service, heard the reference and accepted it with gracious good humour.)

Despite having two such outstanding properties with which to launch a tabloid newspaper, Rupert Murdoch had misgivings about such a drastic change to the *News of the World*'s format, fearing many older, established readers would be alienated. Shrimsley argued forcibly and persistently that modern readers were used to tabloid papers every day and that nothing would be lost. However, the issue came between the two and Shrimsley departed after five years of editorship, soon afterwards becoming the first editor of the new *Mail on Sunday*. It was to be another six years and four more editors later before the tabloid plunge was finally taken.

There followed two editorships of short duration. Kenneth Donlan, a devout Catholic family man with vast experience in news-gathering techniques at the *Daily Mail* and, more latterly, the *Sun* succeeded Shrimsley and edited the *News of the World* from 1980 to 1981 until returning to the *Sun* as editor of news and pictures when Murdoch and Larry Lamb parted company. A decade or so later, Donlan was to secure a niche in Fleet Street history by being made the *Sun*'s Ombudsman, with a brief to look into readers' complaints against the newspaper, the first such appointment to a popular paper.

After Donlan, the editor's chair was briefly filled by Barry Askew, who arrived in Fleet Street from the editorship of the *Lancashire Evening Post*, where he had won an award as campaigning journalist of the year for exposing a certain chief constable as fiddling his expenses and misusing police vehicles. Askew's period of editorship at the *News of the World* lasted for only a few months but is still recalled by some of the longer-serving journalists as one of the more colourful periods in the paper's history. A newcomer to Fleet Street, he arrived with a northern brashness that did not endear him to some of his senior subordinates.

However, it was his private life that became the centre of office gossip and entertainment. His liking for Scotch whisky and his forays into the clubs of the capital assured him an almost permanent starring role in the satirical magazine *Private Eye*'s Street of Shame spot. The magazine dubbed him 'The Beast of Bouverie Street' and it was a label that was to pass into Fleet Street folklore, a nickname by which he was still remembered long after his brief editorship was over.

Askew had a virtual obsession with Sonia Sutcliffe, the wife of Peter Sutcliffe, the Yorkshire Ripper. Even when he was editor-designate of the *News of the World*, before he had taken up the appointment, he was cultivating Mrs Sutcliffe's friendship. He attempted to make behind-the-scenes payments to Mrs Sutcliffe, which were later quashed on Rupert Murdoch's orders. An echo of the close relationship between Askew and the Ripper's wife were to surface over a decade later, when a book written by a former *Mail on Sunday* reporter, Barbara Jones, revealed that Askew had pretended to cooperate with Mrs Sutcliffe in a bizarre plot to 'spring' the Ripper out of Broadmoor. Ironically, the book was serialized last year in Askew's old paper, the *News of the World*.

It was under Askew that the paper's colour supplement, *Sunday*, was launched (see chapter 29 for the whole story) and, as a result, the circulation soared by over half a million. However, Askew's editorship on the whole was not a successful experience and he was replaced at the end of 1981 by the chirpy Cockney Derek Jameson.

Jameson, a Fleet Street old hand who had already edited the *Daily Express* and *Daily Star* and been northern editor of the *Daily Mirror*, had made his name as a tabloid journalist. However, throughout his three-year editorship the paper was to remain a broadsheet. 'The last thing I expected was to be editor of the *News of the World*,' Jameson recalled. 'The paper reeked of sanctimonious hypocrisy. Now here I was editing a paper that had become a national institution. I wanted to maintain the paper's tradition whilst bringing it up to date. I wanted to go tabloid but Rupert Murdoch and Bruce Matthews felt it was a dangerous course because it was tampering with success – if you have a winning formula do you radically change it? My view was that we lived in an age of tabloid newspapers.'

Jameson added: 'It was eventually forced on them by a technicality. With the long-term prospect of a move to Wapping, they couldn't be messing about from having a tabloid *Sun* during the week to a broadsheet *News of the World* on Sunday. When it did become a tabloid later, it was not visibly different from the other tabloids. Instead of being alone in its field as a national institution with nothing quite like it, it suddenly became another tabloid looking for bigger sensations, bigger buy-ups.

'When I took over it was still writing about potty peers and scoutmasters on grave charges. There was a strange dignity about the coverage of those sort of things. Changes in the law had some effect but I think they just went out of fashion. After the permissive society of the sixties, it took a great deal more to shock the public.'

The paper, Jameson recalled, was still very strong on crime stories. 'You relied on people like Peter Earle and Trevor Kempson to keep their eyes and ears open. They knew clubland, they knew the police officers and security service people. They also knew the hostesses, the Christine Keelers and the villains. They were out and about.'

Jameson's own dismissal, after three years as editor, was a mystery to him, he said. 'I was one of the great tabloid experts but officially they didn't think I was the man for the tabloid challenge. This didn't make sense to me. I had made my name as a tabloid editor.' There were possibly other factors in his demise. During his editorship he unsuccessfully sued the BBC for libel in a radio programme, an action which Rupert Murdoch had advised him to settle out of court. In his autobiography published after he had left the *News of the World*, Jameson claimed another reason was that he had published a story about the disappearance of an Australian politician who was a friend of Rupert Murdoch's mother, Dame Elisabeth Murdoch. Whatever the reasons, Jameson's career didn't suffer in the long term, for he went off to make a new name for himself as a radio and television personality.

Rupert Murdoch had finally bowed to those who were pushing him to turn the *News of the World* into a tabloid newspaper. It was still well ahead in the circulation stakes at this point, but the initial boost it had been given by the launch of *Sunday* magazine in 1981 had run out of steam and the circulation had dipped again, dangerously close to the 4 million mark. It had a smaller percentage of younger readers compared to its rivals and fewer women readers. It was also the only mass-market Sunday paper that was still a broadsheet. It had even lost readers to the *Mail on Sunday*, which had been relaunched as an aggressive middle-market tabloid with a strong colour magazine, *YOU*.

The man finally entrusted with overseeing the transformation of the newspaper from a broadsheet to a tabloid was Nicholas Lloyd (later to become Sir Nicholas), who had worked for the paper before. He was in a different journalistic mould from some of his predecessors. An Oxford history graduate, Lloyd had hovered between popular tabloids and broadsheet 'quality' papers. He had been education correspondent and news editor of the *Sunday Times* in the late 1960s before joining the *Sun* as news editor and then transferring to the *News of the World* as features editor. Later, he went off to the opposition camp for a spell, first as deputy editor of the *Sunday Mirror* and then editor of the *Sunday People*.

When Lloyd was recruited to join the *News of the World*, cynical Fleet Street observers claimed he had the most thankless task in the business – taking the paper down market. However, he had a crucial weapon at his disposal – an entirely new format.

The long-awaited change to tabloid finally came about on 20 May 1984. The very last issue of the *News of the World* as a broadsheet on the previous Sunday announced the news with banner headlines across the top of the front page, with the slogan: 'New Size, New Shape, New Look.' After 141 years, it was out with the old and ring in the new. The front page blurb, though, still carried an echo of the paper's old traditional slogan when it announced: 'All human life is here.'

The tabloid *News of the World* had to have a sensational story on which to pin a successful launch. Sure enough, it did. Most of the front page was taken up with an exclusive royal story about Prince Andrew – then a bachelor – and his love affair with a model and playgirl, Vicki Hodge, thirteen years his senior. On pages two and three the full account, by feature writer Sharon Ring, told of the couple's frolics on the island of Barbados, under the headline: WE MADE LOVE AMONG THE SCENTED TROPICAL FLOWERS.

Other goodies blurbed on the front page were stories about two high-profile marriages, those of the Prince and Princess of Wales and of singer Elton John and his new wife Renate; news that *Coronation Street* star Pat Phoenix was to marry her lover, actor Tony Booth; a picture of TV personality Michael Aspel with his new baby son; and a report on 'Love Today: The Naked Truth', a reference to a two-page report on sex and marriage by Unity Hall. On the back page and the immediate inside sports pages, there was only one story that took the lion's share of the coverage – the defeat of Elton John's team, Watford, by Everton in the FA Cup final at Wembley the previous day.

To be in a position to launch the new tabloid *News of the World*, the News International management had had to do some heavy negotiating with the print unions. As always, their only interest was a mercenary one. The negotiations had dragged on and on and been responsible for a number of delays in previous plans to launch the tabloid. Arthur Brittenden, the company's spokesman, told *The Times*:

> The intention to take the *News of the World* tabloid has been there for some years but we were dealing with the unions on a realistic basis and were not going to give money away just because we were making a change.
>
> We do now have a deal with the unions where some people will be paid more but only within areas where they are definitely going to be doing more work.

A principal aim, said Brittenden, was to get the paper into the hands of readers who had not looked at it for years.

Lengthy problems with the unions there may have been but a totally unforeseen hitch to the launch of the new-look paper occurred at the very last moment. The paper had agreed a payment of £25,000 to Vicki Hodge for the story of her affair with Prince Andrew and a contract was on the verge of being signed. Then the lawyer acting for Miss Hodge telephoned managing editor Stuart Kuttner to clinch the deal but informed him, almost as an afterthought, that the price had been trebled. Hurried and fevered negotiations ensued until a compromise agreement was reached.

There were those journalists on the paper, especially the longer-serving ones, who had some qualms about the whole notion of going tabloid. They felt the paper's circulation had been eroded because it had already departed too far from the traditional style and content. There was also a certain amount of resentment because the ordinary, non-executive journalists felt they should have been consulted through their union chapel, as the print unions had been. However, once the tabloid *News of the World* had become a *fait accompli*, any resistance quickly petered out.

After the successful launch of the tabloid, Nicholas Lloyd's term as editor was relatively short. He was being groomed within the organization for top-level management and, sponsored by Rupert Murdoch, he went off for a spell at the Harvard Business School. However, after the move to Wapping in 1986, Lloyd became frustrated because there did not appear to be a significant role for him in the company and he accepted an invitation to become editor of the *Daily Express*.

Lloyd was followed at the *News of the World* by two more shortish editorships. First in the chair was David Montgomery, a thrusting young Ulsterman whom Lloyd had brought over with him from the *People*. He was an experienced tabloid journalist who had honed his skills on the *Daily Mirror*, to which he was later to return in controversial circumstances as chief executive in the post-Robert Maxwell era.

Some of the *News of the World* staff found Montgomery cold and aloof and not an easy person to get on with. However, one of his observations will surely find a permanent place in the annals of the paper. Montgomery was editor during the move to Wapping – which is detailed fully in the next chapter – and he welcomed staff to a special meeting in the Bouverie

Street offices with the opening remark: 'Welcome to the first day of the rest of your lives.'

When Rupert Murdoch took over the ailing newspaper *Today*, having bought out the ninety per cent interest in it that Tiny Rowland's Lonrho Corporation had acquired from the paper's founder, Eddie Shah, David Montgomery moved over to become its editor. He was succeeded at the *News of the World* by a character as flamboyant as he was cold and unemotional.

Wendy Henry made journalistic history as the first female editor of a national newspaper. In becoming editor of the *News of the World* she had gone full circle, for she had worked for the paper twenty years earlier on casual shifts when first arriving in London as an ambitious freelance reporter from Manchester. She had become a staff feature writer, then gone off to become an executive on a woman's magazine before returning to News International as *Sun* features editor and then editor of the *News of the World*'s *Sunday* magazine.

Henry, whose well-endowed form, amply displayed with plunging necklines and mini-skirted dress style, made her an instantly recognizable figure, had a reputation for the earthy, go-get-'em journalism that had made the *Sun* such a success. Whilst on the daily paper she had concentrated heavily on revealing the sex lives of the show biz stars. She also had a penchant for the macabre – one of her favourite role models was the American scandal newspaper, the *National Enquirer* – and whilst editor of *Sunday* had gained the magazine the nickname 'Freaks of the week', with stories about dwarfs, two-headed babies and other peculiarities. Her ingenuity and nose for a good story was unchallenged, though strict accuracy was not always her forte.

Henry believed fervently that people wanted to read about the peccadilloes of the famous. One of the more celebrated stories of her reign was an exposé of the popular TV presenter Frank Bough (of which more later) for indulging in orgies with prostitutes and taking cocaine.

Henry's cavalier attitude to the way in which stories were

presented sometimes brought her into conflict with her most senior lieutenants. She invariably wanted to push the facts as far as possible – sometimes a little too far – against the advice of her executives.

Once, when the paper had exclusive pictures of septuplets born to a mother in Liverpool – none of which, tragically, survived – she planned to run them across the top of the story, all seven of them. However, the parents had been able to take shots of only six of the babies. No matter, Henry insisted on having pictures of SEVEN babies, so the story appeared with one of the infants pictured twice.

She found herself in outright conflict with Murdoch when a complaint was made by Sir Ralph Halpern, the former Burton boss whose 'five-times-a-night' sexploits with his girlfriend, Fiona Wright, hit the headlines. The *News of the World* ran extracts from Miss Wright's diary, in which she revealed that one of her lover's fantasies was to 'goose' Maggie Thatcher at No. 10. Henry changed the story in such a way as to suggest that the fantasy had actually occurred, despite the entreaties of hard-nosed senior executives. Halpern complained personally to Murdoch, who hit the roof.

This was a factor in the eventual parting of the ways between Murdoch and his exotic editor. Henry's continued strong emphasis on sex scandals offended many and Murdoch finally demanded that she should tone the paper down. She refused, pointing to the fact that under her the *News of the World*'s circulation had increased substantially. Murdoch and Wendy Henry finally parted company after she had edited the *News of the World* for sixteen months. Some who admired her talents as a tabloid journalist but who had sought to persuade her against some of her own excesses, were not too unhappy to see her go.

Henry later went to work for Murdoch's great rival, Maxwell, as editor of the *People*. But he, too, found her style unacceptable and fired her as well. She then crossed the Atlantic to become editor of a tabloid supermarket newspaper in Florida, the *Globe*.

The repercussions of Wendy Henry's reign at the *News of the World* continued to be felt well after her departure in the form of writs arriving at the paper's legal department and libel actions being settled. Henry's successor, Patricia Chapman, became so disconcerted with the number of apologies and announcements of actions being settled that she insisted on having the words: 'This story was published under a previous editor', inserted into them.

So, one woman editor followed another. Chapman, known universally to her staff as Patsy, moved across to take over the *News of the World* from the deputy editorship of the *Sun*. At the time of writing, she has held the job for four years and is the longest-serving *News of the World* editor since Bernard Shrimsley in the 1970s. Under her leadership, the paper has continued to maintain its substantial lead in the readership battle, sometimes outselling its principal rivals, the *Sunday Mirror* and the *People*, with a sale of more than their combined circulations.

During her editorship, she has expanded the paper's coverage of crime and investigations, with campaigns against animal cruelty, child molesters and fraudsters. The paper has continued the tradition of offering substantial rewards for the apprehension of villains and also of setting up trust funds for the victims of crime and other injustices.

A wonderful example of reader generosity occurred early in 1993 when, in January, the *News of the World* told the story of a blind baby, Karen Seasman, whose parents couldn't afford to take her to America for pioneering surgery which might restore her sight. In just four weeks more than £52,000 poured into a special fund set up by the newspaper. Donations ranged from £1 from pensioners to an anonymous gift of £1,000.

In 1991, an appeal for Louise Duddy, the victim of an acid attack that left her horribly scarred and blinded, raised £15,000. The cheque was handed over on behalf of the newspaper by TV comedian Ronnie Corbett.

The most astonishing response of all, however, was that to

the Simon Weston Children of Bosnia appeal, which the *News of the World* launched in August 1992 to help the young victims of the war-ravaged land. In conjunction with other newspapers who joined in, a total of £400,000 was raised – at least £250,000 of it from *News of the World* readers.

Patsy Chapman's own introduction to the *News of the World* came at a young age when her mother featured in a typical story in the paper after helping to trap a thief who was stealing women's underwear from clotheslines. 'That taught me that a minor sex crime can have a pretty powerful effect,' she says.

Her recipe for the paper today differs little in essence from that of her predecessors: 'I have tried to get back to the crime aspect, a bit of froth and show biz, something sexy – a bit of this and a bit of that.' She adds: 'Stories sell newspapers. On a Sunday morning people will look at the headline on the front page and if it is a grabber they buy it.'

Whilst editors may come and go, a paper like the *News of the World* tends to generate considerable loyalty amongst a nucleus of the staff who provide the continuity between eras. Several of the paper's senior journalists have clocked up well over twenty years' service. They include the assistant editor in charge of news, Robert Warren, who has been running the news-gathering operation for much longer than any of his counterparts on other national newspapers, and the boisterous Bill Bateson, assistant editor heading the sports department, whose devotion and service to the paper is probably rivalled only by his affection for Arsenal football team.

However, one long-serving journalist who watched the procession of editors with a keener eye than most is the avuncular Philip Wrack, known as 'Uncle Phil' to younger colleagues to whom he was ever willing to lend a word of wisdom from his long experience in newspapers. Wrack, now the *News of the World*'s Ombudsman and all too briefly married in the 1990s to the late Unity Hall, was deputy to no fewer than nine editors. It was a long-standing office joke, which might not have been too far from the truth, that if one included all the times he'd stood in as acting editor, either waiting for the new incumbent to arrive or as a holiday deputy, then he was probably the *News of the World*'s longest-serving editor!

TWENTY-EIGHT

Escape to Wapping

During the summer and autumn of 1985, a curious complaint afflicted a number of key members of the *News of the World* editorial staff. It was highly contagious, spread swiftly and silently and passed into instant office folklore. Some wag dubbed it the 'Wapping cough'.

What was this strange ailment unknown to any doctor or medical dictionary? It was not, of course, a genuine illness at all. Rather, a conveniently vague and – to those in the know – significant way of explaining the absence of certain personnel who were engaged elsewhere on more pressing duties. In the main subeditor's room at Bouverie Street, casual inquiries of 'Where's so-and-so?' would be met with muttered replies of 'He's got the Wapping cough.' The questioner would then indicate by a mere quizzical raise of the eyebrows that he had got the message: that the absentee, far from being confined to a sick bed, was actually beavering conscientiously away at an establishment some two miles to the east.

This went on for some months and was at first little more than an office in-joke to provoke a bit of conspiratorial conversation in the pub at lunchtime. Journalists, after all, love conspiracy, gossip and speculation. It's their lifeblood. However, as the rumours grew and the regularity of absenteeism of certain senior staff from Bouverie Street became more marked, it became obvious to any employee not living on Mars that something major was happening. Though what perhaps even the shrewdest and astutest among them could not have imagined was that within a few weeks they would be involved in the most momentous events Fleet Street had witnessed in many decades and that, indeed, they would be facing a whole year that for many of them would be the most traumatic of their entire working lives.

What became known as the Battle of Wapping, or the Battle of the Barbed Wire, was to turn out to be not just a watershed in the history of national newspapers but a monumental landmark also for the trade union movement in Britain. After Wapping, the traditional relationships between management and employees, especially in the newspaper business, could never be the same again.

How little the *News of the World* journalists realized, as they light-heartedly discussed in those weeks towards the end of 1985 who was the latest victim of the 'Wapping cough', that they would soon be engulfed in violence and hatred on a scale few of them had ever encountered before. Who amongst them could have imagined that they would soon be working flat out to produce the newspaper inside a high-tech plant bristling with security cameras and surrounded by barbed wire fencing, while outside in the streets a baying, howling mob, 3,000-strong, fought a pitched battle with mounted police in riot gear?

To the journalists, especially those who had worked in Fleet Street for many years, Wapping, though only a couple of miles eastwards, a short stroll from the Tower of London and a ten-minute ride in a black cab, might as well have been at the north pole. Newspapermen, though they often travel the world in the pursuit of their story, are a parochial bunch at heart and when not actively working rarely tend to stray far from their own back yard. The Fleet Street they knew and loved was a village, with all the attributes one would expect from a village community. It was a place of familiar everyday sights and sounds. And, like any village, it was a hotbed of gossip and intrigue. So parochial was 'the Street', in the days before all the newspapers upped and fled to different parts of London, that the journalists from different papers tended to stick to their own favourite restaurants, pubs and wine bars and rarely encroached on each others' territory. *News of the World* journalists drank in one hostelry, whilst their counterparts on their principal competitors, the *Sunday People* and *Sunday Mirror*, frequented another.

It was traditionally part of the Fleet Street game that if journalists from one newspaper got wind that one of their rivals had a major scoop, some of them would pop into the enemy's pub and do a spot of what was politely called 'ear-wigging' to try and find out what the opposition were up to. Or, if in a particularly mischievous mood, they might go to the rivals' hostelry and spread disinformation about some imaginary, spectacular story of their own. The mere appearance of two or three *News of the World* men in the opposition's camp, and vice versa, had often been known to send panic-stricken reporters scurrying to the telephone to alert their newsdesks.

The journalists regarded Fleet Street as the nerve centre of their world. It was cosy and familiar, like a favourite armchair, a place of warmth and friendliness that welcomed them back to its bosom when they returned after some particularly arduous or irksome out-of-town assignment. But Fleet Street was about to become part of newspaper history and for the journalists their lives would be changed drastically for ever. This, then, was part of the background to the cataclysmic events that were about to unfold in early 1986 . . .

What those senior editorial staff afflicted with the jokingly named 'Wapping cough' were actually up to was undergoing training in the use of new computers and electronic typesetting equipment that had been installed in conditions of great secrecy at an eleven-acre site in London's Docklands, close by the Tower. They were in the vanguard of a newspaper revolution that was about to shatter the print unions' long-standing grip on the throat of Fleet Street for ever more.

Bosses and trade unions in other industries had long looked with unconcealed amazement at the state of relations in the newspaper business – which the columnist Bernard Levin had once described as being like 'a protection racket within a lunatic asylum'. From the 1950s, weak managements had successively given in to the demands of the Fleet Street printers, not caring about the restrictive practices and extortionate demands as long as the newspapers were making buckets of money. Which indeed they were. With the lifting of wartime newsprint restrictions, circulations and advertising revenues had rocketed and the newspaper proprietors were content to let the print unions get away with murder.

But cut-throat competition, produced by the end of price-fixing for newspapers in 1964, eventually meant the overall cake had grown smaller. And managements, finding themselves stuck with outdated technology and outmoded working practices, instead of taking the bull by the horns simply opted out. Print chapels (the union branches inside newspaper offices) had become so powerful that managements had handed over to them the responsibility for employing labour within the offices.

Mark Chapman-Walker, managing director of the *News of the World*, presented the new proprietor with a gloomy view of the situation in Fleet Street, just before he departed for fresh fields in the film industry. 'There has been a shift of emphasis in bargaining from what was formerly national level to the shop floor or, in our case, the House,' he told Rupert Murdoch. 'National control of unions is rapidly disappearing . . . the general secretaries no longer have the control which they used to have and this particularly applies to the printing unions. Earnings structures in Fleet Street are now in a state of chaos. As a result, traditional differentials have been fractured.'

Chapman-Walker's comments reflected an extraordinary malaise that existed in the whole of Fleet Street. Print union barons virtually ran the newspapers, especially in the vital production and distribution departments like the machine room, where the huge presses roared, and the warehouse where the papers were packed into bundles, ready to be sent out.

Bizarre and colourful practices, extortionate fiddles known as 'old Spanish customs', had developed and become accepted as routine. Amongst these were the so-called Mickey Mouse shifts, where men took extra pay packets in fictitious names for ghost workers who didn't exist but whom managements had agreed to put on the payroll to maintain the unions' demanded jobs quota. The real workers simply shared out the extra money amongst themselves in return for a bit more work. Such practices were especially rampant on a Sunday paper like the *News of the World* which required a large amount of casual labour on one night of the week only.

An indication of the printers' own cynical view of the 'system' is revealed in an anecdote from the late 1960s. One Saturday night, the cashiers' office in Bouverie Street was raided by a couple of armed bandits, who sped off with a tidy sum of money meant for the casual workers' wages. Two printers were overheard in a nearby pub, discussing the matter. 'How much did they get, then?' demanded one.

'About five grand,' replied his mate.

'Don't know why they bothered,' the first printer muttered, laconically. 'They'd have been better off doing a shift down the machine room!'

It was a black joke but too uncomfortably close to a ludicrous situation to be totally funny. And as the years went by, things didn't improve. Restrictive practices, blackmailing demands in return for accepting new technology, expensive strikes, often over trivial issues, and endless negotiations that sometimes dragged on for years, all contrived to increase Murdoch's frustration.

There was an added complication in Bouverie Street, caused by the arrival of the *News of the World*'s newly born sister paper the *Sun* in November 1969. Murdoch had acquired the paper – then a dying broadsheet – from IPC, the former owners of the Mirror group, for a bargain basement price and proposed to print it as a tabloid on the *News of the World* presses.

Besides fighting management, the print unions were constantly at loggerheads with each other and there was bitter rivalry between the National Society of Operative Printers and Assistants (NATSOPA, later to merge with the Society of Graphic and Allied Trades, SOGAT) and the National Graphical Association, which regarded itself as the superior, skilled union. In most Fleet Street offices, NGA men controlled the machine room but at the *News of the World* it was the other way round. The Bouverie Street machine room was a one hundred per cent NATSOPA shop, whilst the incoming machinists from the *Sun* were NGA. There was rivalry over job possession and, whilst in the end a compromise was reached, it added to the murky waters of already appalling industrial relations.

An opportunity to tackle the overall problem head on was finally presented by a combination of factors. Firstly, trade union legislation passed by Margaret Thatcher's government in 1980 and 1982, which required secret ballots to be held before strikes and outlawed secondary picketing. A second factor was the stand by a newcomer to the newspaper scene, Eddie Shah, who had stood out against the print unions in a violent dispute at Warrington and who had signed a one-union, no-strike deal with the electricians' union, the EETPU, to start a new national daily newspaper, *Today*. Thirdly, there was the desperate need to leave Bouverie Street. The building was over fifty years old, dilapidated, with clapped-out machinery, and was in danger of failing to meet health and safety regulations. Reporters who worked in the paper's second-floor newsroom still recall the day that acid started dripping from the floor above, right through the ceiling, and burned holes in their desks. And the memory of the grimy, first-floor canteen, complete with rats and giant cockroaches, still brings a shudder to those who worked in the building.

The Wapping site had been bought as early as 1977 to provide a printing plant, equipped with the very latest machinery, on which to print the *News of the World* and the *Sun*. The site was a historic one, occupying part of the old Western dock where from the early 1800s imports of wine, brandy and rum were stored in great vaults beneath the quays and warehouses. The docks had shut down in 1969, killed off by the twin effects of the dockers' militancy and changes in the seafaring trade.

The cost of developing and equipping the site was around £80 million, while another parallel development was going on at Kinning Park, south of Glasgow, from where it was planned to produce Scottish, Border and Irish editions of the papers from pages transmitted electronically from Wapping.

Rupert Murdoch wanted guarantees of uninterrupted production of his newspapers and also the unions' acceptance of new technology. In the case of Wapping, this meant 'single key stroking', by which journalists and advertising staff could set type on computer screens, doing away with the need for traditional, hot metal printing methods. Such technology had been commonplace in provincial newspapers since the 1970s but Fleet Street proprietors, with their long-standing fear of the power of the print unions, had shied away from it.

Murdoch was becoming increasingly impatient with the intransigence of the printers, who insisted that if they were ever to move to Wapping, all their old cherished (but outmoded) agreements and practices must go with them. All pleas to see sense and accept the realities of the 1980s, computers and all, had fallen on deaf ears.

The thankless task of trying to reach agreement with the print unions fell on the shoulders of Bruce Matthews, managing director of News International, a tough but genial fellow Aussie and Murdoch's right-hand man in Britain. Matthews spent much of 1984 attempting to negotiate deals but the talks broke down just before Christmas. One stroppy union leader remarked that the best thing Murdoch could do with Wapping was burn it down.

Contingency plans were put into action in case the talks went out of the window altogether. Plans were announced for a new London evening newspaper to be produced at Wapping, to be called the *London Post*. This presented the unions with a different set of circumstances and was essentially a cover plan, for in the end the new paper never happened.

Early in 1985, Bruce Matthews went to Murdoch with a bold and daring plan to smash the power of the unions once and for all. Mindful of the experience of Shah at Warrington, he had been having quiet talks with an official of the electricians' union. At this time, the Fleet Street branch of the

EETPU were an extremely militant group, far to the Left of the national officials. They had started merger talks with SOGAT, which irritated Eric Hammond, the maverick general secretary of the EETPU, and his national officer for Fleet Street, the man with whom Matthews was dealing.

Matthews and a small, select group of executives flew to New York and persuaded Rupert Murdoch to go for the ultimate gamble, a radical new operation at Wapping and Kinning Park to produce his newspapers without the print unions. It was, indeed, a risky gamble, for his worldwide empire depended on the cash flow from his British newspapers and the prospect of disruption was huge.

Murdoch sought a meeting with Eric Hammond, who was a pioneer of single-union, no-strike deals – a policy which later earned him expulsion from the Trades Union Congress. The *News of the World*'s outspoken political columnist Woodrow Wyatt, a former Labour MP, was a friend of both Hammond and Murdoch and brought them together at a discreet private meeting at Murdoch's elegant London home on the top floor of a block of flats in St James's, overlooking Green Park. Wyatt had himself suffered at the hands of the print unions when they'd refused to print a piece he'd written about union behaviour with which they had disagreed.

On a subsequent occasion, Hammond was flown to California for another meeting with Murdoch. He guaranteed that his men could help set up the plant at Wapping and operate it as well. Now, Murdoch saw an exciting opportunity to break the stranglehold of the print unions which, he said, had given him 'seventeen years of hell' in Fleet Street. For Hammond and his electricians, the prospect was equally enticing. Opportunists also, they saw a chance to establish themselves as top dogs in the printing industry and settle old scores with SOGAT and the NGA.

Murdoch decided to go for broke and take all his UK newspapers to Wapping, not just the *News of the World* and the *Sun* but also *The Times* and *Sunday Times* as well, for he'd had just as much trouble with the print unions at Gray's Inn Road, where those newspapers were produced, as he had at Bouverie Street.

Ostensibly, the company was still talking to the print unions, with Murdoch's top negotiator from Australia, Bill O'Neill, a former union hard man himself, leading the parleying. But while O'Neill continued his pow-wow with SOGAT and the NGA, a top-secret operation was going on to get Wapping operational.

O'Neill put Murdoch's terms bluntly to the unions. He wanted a single-union, no-strike deal that was legally binding, no closed shops, lower manning levels, more flexible working practices and direct computer input by journalists and tele-ad salesgirls. The print unions countered with demands for secure jobs for life for their members and regular, index-linked pay rises. Predictably, no deal looked remotely likely.

Meanwhile, the secret contingency plans were going full steam ahead. Quietly, a team of top specialists from an American computer company, Atex, began arriving in London and moving into addresses in fashionable areas like Chelsea and Belgravia. So vital was it that the print unions didn't find out what was going on that both News International and Atex set up separate companies, with unfamiliar names, to do business with each other in a way that wouldn't cause any comment. Atex even changed their normal shippers and sprayed out its company name on the outside of packing cases.

The giant computer system was put together in extreme secrecy in a disused factory in South London, then moved into Wapping equally discreetly in three lorries. Next came the printing presses, which were installed in the vast new printing hall. Eric Hammond's electricians' union recruited men in Southampton to run the new plant. They were bussed up to Wapping every day and sworn to secrecy about what they were doing.

Bruce Matthews set about recruiting a team of girls, mostly Australians and New Zealanders who were only in Britain on a short-term basis, to train on the Atex computers and then train other people. 'They did a fantastic job,' says Matthews.

'There was no question of using local London girls because they might easily have had relatives who were printworkers.'

It was soon after this that a few key journalists became involved in the operation for the first time, disappearing discreetly to Wapping to be trained on the new system in which, for the first time in Fleet Street history, they would be doing work that had always been the exclusive preserve of the printers. Inevitably, gossip began circulating in the pubs and wine bars of Fleet Street but it was still on the jokey level, hence the sly references to what had become known as the 'Wapping cough'.

On the night of Saturday, 18 January 1986, Rupert Murdoch pressed a button at Wapping to start the dormant presses roaring for a print run of a special section of the *Sunday Times*. The revolution had started and now there was no stopping it. The print unions still hadn't woken up to the reality of the situation – that they had been out-thought and out-manoeuvred.

Said Murdoch on the historic occasion: 'If nothing else, we have at last driven a truck through their wall of obstinacy and ignorance. People will remember tonight's events.'

For the *News of the World* journalists, though, it was not that night but one just six days later that was to be the momentous one. On the following Friday, the print unions finally picked up the gauntlet that Murdoch had thrown down and walked out on strike at both Bouverie Street and Gray's Inn Road. By doing so, they played straight into Murdoch's hands, for by going on strike they were legally deemed to have sacked themselves and, therefore, were not entitled to any redundancy money. In all, around 5,000 printworkers had lost their jobs.

So confident, however, were they that their previously all-conquering power would prevail yet again, that two SOGAT Chapel officers who knew and liked Bruce Matthews, stopped him on the steps of Bouverie Street and said: 'Shame, Bruce, but we'll be back in a couple of weeks.'

Within minutes, they were gathering in force outside the

Bouverie Street main entrance, either cajoling and urging editorial staff to join them or jeering at the departing journalists with catcalls of: 'Off to Wapping, then?' There were extraordinary scenes, as the editorial staff walked out of the building through the lines of chanting pickets, their arms piled high with personal belongings. Some of the women reporters and secretaries were even dragging large plants in pots behind them.

The wine bars and hostelries of Fleet Street probably broke all records that night, as the shell-shocked journalists repaired to their favourite watering holes to discuss this astonishing twist in their lives. In their hearts they knew that, after more than a century of production in the most glamorous heart of newspaperland in the world, it was finally The End of The Street – as a subsequent book was indeed titled.

For the time being, though, the journalists had little time to assimilate the true significance of the momentous events they were now caught up in. From standing in the wings for so long, they now suddenly assumed centre stage. Their attitude was crucial if Rupert Murdoch's Wapping gamble was to succeed. After all, there was not a lot of point in being able to produce a newspaper without printers if you had no stories to put in it.

On the Saturday morning, most of the editorial staff reported to Bouverie Street early, threading their way through the now burgeoning picket lines, and were addressed by editor David Montgomery at a mass meeting in the subeditor's room. His opening remarks contained the aforementioned memorable statement: 'Welcome to the first day of the rest of your lives.' Montgomery urged the journalists to seize the opportunity they had been given to become at long last the most important people in the newspaper industry.

For most of the journalists, the prospect of possessing real power was a rare novelty and their attitude towards it was ambivalent. Though the vast majority were members of the National Union of Journalists, they were notoriously unmilitant and, on the rare occasions they had taken industrial

action, had been regarded with slightly pitying amusement by
the printworkers.

Added to this was the fact that many of the editorial staff
resented not only the huge wages – far outstripping theirs
– and the outrageous practices of the printers, but also the
bloody-mined way in which they had for many years sabo-
taged the journalists' own work by sometimes refusing to
print the newspaper. For these reasons, there was little love
lost between the editorial staff and the 'inkies', as the journalists called the printworkers.

Even so, an anguished debate ensued that Saturday morning, with some members of the NUJ Chapel urging caution.
The journalists had been offered a one-off payment of £2,000,
plus an extra £2,000 a year on their salaries to go to Wapping.
There were those who believed that by sticking their heels in
they might get more, while others were worried about defying
their national union officials, who had ordered them not to
go to Wapping until a deal with the printworkers had been
settled. In the end, an overwhelming vote was taken to accept
the management's offer and produce the newspaper.

Many of the editorial staff remained in Bouverie Street that
Saturday, while others went to Wapping. The following day's
News of the World was produced partly from both places, with
copy being transmitted by telephone and messenger and electronically typed in at the Wapping end. In between producing
the newspaper, journalists were desperately piling their important files and belongings into black plastic binliners – in some
cases the residue of twenty years or more on the paper – for
transmission to their new home over the weekend.

The paper's royal reporter Fiona Macdonald Hull, and several others, did something that up to that day would have
been regarded as impossible; indeed, would have been treated
as akin to blasphemy by the print unions who had guarded
their territory so jealously for so long. She recalled: 'We walked
into the composing room and touched our by-lines set in metal
type. In fact, we nicked them. I got my own by-line, plus a
line with "News of the World exclusive" and one with "Royal

exclusive" and a crown on it. They remain my most treasured possessions.'

That night, one of the great wakes of all time took place in a bar/restaurant on the corner of Fleet Street and Bouverie Street, called appropriately the First Edition, where *News of the World* journalists had traditionally dined every Saturday night for years. Says Macdonald Hull again: 'One of the production managers had salvaged a unique picture of all the *News of the World* employees who had fought in the First World War, with a cross against each one who died. He said: "We can't leave this here. Look after it." I still have it.'

Down the road in the East End, the Battle of Wapping had already started. The pickets were massing in their thousands but they didn't manage to prevent a huge convoy of trucks from leaving the plant, carrying copies of the *News of the World*, which sped away to distribution centres outside London where, ironically, they were handled by provincial members of SOGAT, such was their lack of support and sympathy for their Fleet Street colleagues. At the same time, more lorries left Kinning Park, Glasgow, and a print run of more than 4 million was delivered to homes throughout Britain next day. In another far-sighted move, Rupert Murdoch had dispensed with the traditional distribution of newspapers by rail, because that would have meant dealing with the unions again. Instead, he decided to create a new distribution system by a vast truck network.

News of the World journalists who had never been to Wapping before were bussed in through the picket lines the following week. For many, it was a real culture shock to see for the first time the ugly barbed wire, the searchlights and video cameras of what had become known as Fort Wapping, and to be accosted by security guards demanding identification. Yet the protection was necessary because outside the gates was a howling, seething, angry mob baying for blood.

Those who hoped it would soon be over were doomed to be disappointed. The picketing dragged on for a whole year and produced some of the most horrific scenes of violence ever seen in an industrial dispute in Britain, with angry demonstrators hurling rocks, bottles and smoke bombs at police, who charged the crowd in riot gear. The worst violence was over two successive weekends in May, when 250 people were injured on one Saturday night alone.

Inevitably, there were allegations from the far Left that the police were on the side of Rupert Murdoch. These were strenuously denied by the police commanders, who pointed out that their function was to be impartial, to protect the rights of both sides and to keep the peace. However, an important legal principle had been established at Warrington during the Shah dispute.

Said Bruce Matthews: 'It was the right and responsibility of the police to keep the public highways open. Whilst they were cognisant of the rights of the pickets, they did not allow them to prevent the lorries from coming out.'

For *News of the World* staff who had gone to work at Wapping, many found it one of the most traumatic periods of their lives. Every day for twelve months they were abused and reviled by shouting, jeering pickets. Those brave souls who walked through the picket lines were abused from close up, spat at and sometimes kicked. Some staff were threatened at their homes by telephone and had their cars vandalized. *News of the World* deputy editor Paul Connew once had to strip off his clothes and have them wiped down after being soaked in spittle.

However, the dispute was not without its moments of comic relief. One hilarious story was of the two American girl tourists who accidentally boarded one of the buses bound for Wapping.

The procedure was that every day staff going to Wapping had to ring a special telephone number in the security department and quote their name and pass number. They would then be told where the buses would be leaving from that day. The pick-up places were changed daily, in order to stop the pickets finding out where they were and picketing staff at these points, which were almost always either a main-line railway station or tube station.

The buses, with specially strengthened glass and surrounded by heavy wire-mesh cages, were driven by tough Scots who were veterans of the miners' dispute. With due irreverence, the Wapping staff christened them battle-buses or – as they were constantly being called 'scabs' by the pickets – the Scabmobiles!

One morning, the pick-up point was the Embankment tube station, where dozens of other buses regularly lined up by the roadside for tourists. On this particular day, two pretty young American girls got on and began gaily chatting away. Someone overheard one girl say to her companion: 'Gee, I wonder what all the wire's for?' When her companion replied 'I guess it's to keep the animals off,' it was thought best to politely inquire whether they were sure they were on the right bus. It transpired the young women thought they were bound for a day out at Windsor Safari Park, upon which there was a loud chorus from the rest of the bus of: 'Stay with us, girls, you'll see lots of animals where we're going!'

Another amusing incident told of the reporter going to Wapping to do a Saturday casual shift on the *News of the World* who was picketed while waiting at a bus stop in Milton Keynes, some fifty miles away.

Sometimes the picketing took on even more bizarre forms. For months after the start of the dispute, many of the paper's journalists continued to return to Fleet Street to their old drinking haunts to socialize, rather than risk confrontations with the pickets in the pubs around Wapping. Some of the printers got wise to this and began to hunt them down in Fleet Street, too.

News of the World books editor Roy Stockdill, who had once had a two-year stint as FoC (Father of Chapel) of the journalists' union, recalled how one printer confronted him in a wine bar one night: 'I knew the chap vaguely. Having held union office, I knew some of the printers rather better than a lot of my colleagues. Many of them weren't bad guys, they had just been led by the nose by the militants for too long.

'Though I recognized they had only themselves to blame for

killing the golden goose, I did have a slight sympathy in that
they were faced with the loss of their livelihoods and the effective end of an honourable craft that stretched back to Caxton.

'This picket was a bit drunk and very aggressive. I'd had a
couple of glasses of vino myself, so I took him on in verbal
combat and pointed out that they hadn't done so badly, compared with we journalists, over the years. He agreed with me
eventually, so much so that he started boasting about his two
BMWs, his wife's boutique and his villa in Spain, and ended
up by inviting me to Cheltenham at his expense to watch his
racehorse run in the Gold Cup meeting! My sympathy was a
bit dissipated after that.'

Eventually, the dismal truth dawned on the pickets that
their cause was hopeless. Virtually a year to the day after the
dispute had begun, they settled for a total sum that was
between a third and a half of what they would have been
entitled to had Murdoch been forced to make them redundant.
The Battle of Wapping was over and the face of British newspapers was changed for ever.

But the bitterness lingered long afterwards. Bruce Matthews
told how some years later he hailed a taxi in central London.
The cabbie took him to his destination and the fare was £2.50.
Matthews gave him £3 and told him to keep the change. The
taxi driver replied: 'I have to take you, Mr Matthews, but I
won't accept a tip from you.' He was, of course, a former
printer.

After the move to Wapping, the much-acclaimed Bouverie
Street printing palace of the early 1930s was sold off for
redevelopment for £73 million. Almost as soon as the Wapping
plant was up and running, work began on adding two more
storeys to the building and construction began on the second
phase of the site's development, making it the largest
newspaper production plant in Europe. This second phase,
completed in September 1990, was equipped with £500-
million-worth of new machinery, including twenty-six Ger-
man-built printing presses, the fastest colour presses in

the world, capable of printing 80,000 copies an hour.

The new equipment gave the Murdoch papers an opportunity to exploit the full potential of colour printing. Another step forward came in August 1990, when 1.4 million copies of the *News of the World* were produced in colour. It is in the sections of the paper devoted to show biz stories and features where the glitz and glamour is best exploited.

Rupert Murdoch's faith in newspapers was clearly affirmed (though he was by then deeply involved in satellite broadcasting through his B-SKY-B company) when in an interview marking the completion of the Wapping Phase Two extension, he said: 'There has been a slight downward trend in newspapers over the last thirty years – a million copies lost in the last ten years at the popular end of the market alone. But considering the amount of competition media, it amazes me how strong newspapers remain in the United Kingdom. And as far as I can see, they will continue to flourish.

'People like the intimacy of a newspaper, the one-to-oneness. They like the convenience, too. People recall what they read in newspapers more than what they see on television.'

TWENTY-NINE

Sunday, Sunday

The millions of readers of mass-market Sunday newspapers expect as a matter of routine these days to get a colour magazine with the paper for their 50p. It's an important part of the overall package, a major selling point in the cut-throat scramble for circulation. A colour supplement is not just a glossy advertising vehicle. It acts as a complement to the main newspaper and its editorial pages have to be lively, entertaining, informative, eye-catching and, well . . . colourful.

The good old days of newspaper circulations, when people habitually went out and bought all the Sunday papers for a few shillings, have long gone. The cost, for one thing, would be prohibitive for the average family. The sheer size of present-day Sunday newspapers is another factor that compels millions of people to buy only one paper, whereas once they might have bought two or three. The *News of the World*, for instance, is normally well over a hundred pages when its colour magazine, *Sunday*, is included in the pagination count.

This means that many readers may make their newspaper last for several days, perhaps putting the colour supplement to one side to enjoy at a more leisurely moment. Therefore, the content of a magazine often varies in subtle ways from that of the main newspaper. Its articles, whilst still topical, usually have a slightly more timeless quality about them. It's not always an easy balance to get right.

Popular newspapers like the *News of the World* were late developers in the Sunday supplement market. The first ever colour magazine had appeared in the *Sunday Times* in the early 1960s. In fact, the idea of a magazine for the *News of the World* had been looked at by a small committee of senior executives as far back as 1964. The project even got as far as having a dummy front page produced, the original of which still exists in the *News of the World*'s archive section. It is a crude scissors-and-paste job, entitled *NOW*. The page features a full-length photograph of soccer star George Best stripped to the waist. Under the heading THE BLOOD AND GUTS OF BEING A SOCCER STAR, the photo had little arrows pointing to various parts of Best's body, illustrating the numerous injuries he'd suffered.

Also on the front page were two items that would certainly not be out of place on the front of any magazine today – an offer for a pair of large, jangly earrings – for the princely sum of 3s 6d (17½p) – and a panel headed: SLIM CHANCE: HOW SAFE ARE INJECTIONS? HOW POTENT ARE PILLS?

However, the board of that time was unable to make up its mind about whether or not to have a magazine to go with the newspaper and the project died a death for another seventeen years. It came back on the agenda in a much more serious manner in 1981, prompted by a drastic slump in the *News of the World*'s circulation to below 4 million. The paper's readership was bleeding away and something had to be done.

There was a second factor in the decision to go for a maga-zine. One of the companies that Rupert Murdoch's News Inter-national organization had inherited from the Carr regime was the Liverpool printing outfit Eric Bemrose. Bemrose employed around 1,500 people and its principal work – around sixty-five per cent of its output, in fact – was a contract to print the *TV Times*. There were fears that *TV Times* was going to take the contract elsewhere, which would put Bemrose in a very seri-ous position. Bruce Matthews, the Australian managing direc-tor of News International, was also chairman of Bemrose and he formed a committee, which included outside consultants, circulation representatives and advertising people, to make contingency plans. One of the possibilities considered was to launch a new weekly newspaper, to be printed on the Bemrose presses. Also in the background was the idea of a colour maga-zine for the *News of the World*, though there was deep concern about the size of circulation the new magazine would have

302 THE NEWS OF THE WORLD STORY

and, hence, the advertising rates that would have to be charged.

Matthews recalled: 'Many people also reminded us of the short-lived *Daily Mirror* colour magazine that had been launched some years earlier and had folded fairly quickly. However, an aspect in our thinking was that there was some resentment at the *News of the World* that they had been neglected as far as promotion was concerned, especially ever since the *Sun* had arrived.'

The company's hand was finally forced when *TV Times* did, in fact, announce its decision to take the printing contract away from Bemrose and place it with Robert Maxwell's Sun Printers at Watford. Matthews informed Rupert Murdoch of the problem and put the alternatives to him. Murdoch's initial response was that it would not be right to take a decision to launch a *News of the World* magazine – a publishing decision – from a strictly printing point of view; i.e., just to create something to fill the gap left by the *TV Times* decision to quit Bemrose.

However, after much pondering, Murdoch finally agreed to the launch of a photogravure colour magazine which would possibly have the largest print order in the world for such a publication. It didn't strike anyone at the time but an extraordinary prediction of history was being fulfilled. Almost half a century earlier in 1932, as described in chapter 6, the legendary *News of the World* editor Sir Emsley Carr had predicted: 'If I were asked to give a forecast of what will happen fifty years hence . . . I see larger and brighter papers. And I see the introduction not only of coloured supplements but the advancement of illustration by means of photogravure, colour and additional line and artistic work.' Sir Emsley had turned out to be right, almost to the exact year.

When the firm go-ahead was given for a *News of the World* magazine, Bruce Matthews approached Peter Jackson, the editor of *TV Times*, to be the editor of the new baby. One of the first people Jackson recruited from *TV Times*, in turn, was production man John Cunningham, still with *Sunday* and the only employee to have remained with the magazine through-out its twelve-year history. 'Peter told us he had Rupert's guar-antee that it would not be tits and bum,' Cunningham says. 'We were open-mouthed!'

Sunday was launched on 6 September 1981 – and, contrary to Jackson's possibly tongue-in-cheek remark about tits and bum, there *was* nudity in it. The front cover was given over entirely to a near-naked Bo Derek cuddling an ape. It was a shot from her new movie, *Tarzan the Ape Man*, and inside the magazine was a seven-page feature, with more earthy jungle shots of Derek, including one of her sprawling starkers in a gushing stream. Other features included glamour shots of Britt Ekland displaying clothes from her wardrobe, pictures from a dog show, a World Cup soccer story and a royal feature on Princess Margaret. In its first few issues the *Sunday* formula was that each story was linked to a particular day of the week, but this was later dropped.

A heavy television advertising campaign accompanied the launch, featuring the hit pop song 'Monday, Monday', the title of which was changed to 'Sunday, Sunday'. The name of the magazine was the result of an extremely careful market research study. Bruce Matthews explained: 'It had two mean-ings. Apart from the obvious one of Sunday, the day of the week, the idea was also to link it in people's minds with the *Sun* daily newspaper. We had not been very successful in get-ting *Sun* readers to buy the *News of the World* on Sundays, thus we hoped that the name of the magazine would have connotations with the *Sun* as well by association. The magazine was especially aimed at young women and mothers.'

The magazine was an instant success and sent the *News of the World* circulation soaring by 600,000, a substantial turn-around in the paper's fortunes. However, the magazine itself would be unable to break even for many years because the advertising rate that had to be charged, due to the huge sales of the paper, was too high for the marketplace. 'It had to be regarded as a promotional cost,' Matthews said.

*   *   *

Over the years since its launch, *Sunday* has often broken new ground. Serialization of novels by bestselling writers was used to boost reader interest and sales, with adaptations of books like Joan Collins's *Sins*, the American civil war saga *North And South*, and more recently a first novel by actress Kate O'Mara. In 1991, to accompany a major relaunch of *Sunday* with a new formula, a six-figure sum was paid to serialize the latest blockbuster from the queen of the sex writers, Jackie Collins. The serialization put an extra 360,000 copies on to the circulation of the *News of the World* for the three weeks it ran.

Other bestsellers have proved to be partworks – a sort of supplement inside a supplement. A gardening partwork produced a circulation increase of 241,000 in 1992, another on caravanning and camping 191,000 and a dream homes supplement upped the circulation by 104,000 in 1990. One of the most popular partwork subjects was on antiques and other collectable items, producing a circulation increase of 158,000 in 1991 and of 101,000 when repeated last year.

Perhaps the most astonishing response of all occurred when the magazine launched a Save the Seals campaign during the mid 1980s, at the time the national conscience was being pricked by the terrible stories of the Arctic seal slaughters. An incredible 2¼ MILLION – yes, that's right! – readers signed a petition to Downing Street, begging the government to bring pressure to bear on the Canadian government to stop the killing.

Sunday newspaper supplements are a major vehicle for reader offers and, with a circulation the size of the *News of the World*, a huge reader response is usually guaranteed. In the spring of 1991, a Spot the Difference competition in *Sunday* to win six Metros, featuring boxer Frank Bruno, pulled in three-quarters of a million entries.

Earlier this year, *Sunday* also entered the field of book publishing. For months the magazine had been running a series of true life crime stories, mostly of horrific and bizarre murder cases from the United States. Some of the most fascinating ones were published in book form under the title *Sunday*,

Bloody Sunday. A special reader offer was made and 8,000 copies of the book were sold as a result.

However, perhaps the most amazing success story of *Sunday* is that of Mystic Meg, the magazine's astrologer, who has become something of a national cult figure with her predictions, written in an entertaining and often sensual style. Launched by the then editor of *Sunday*, Wendy Henry, in 1986, Mystic Meg – real name Meg Lake and a former executive on the magazine – was an immediate success. Within a couple of days of her first column appearing, she had received over 2,000 letters. Two years later, she went on to the 0898 phone-in lines and broke all British Telecom records with the number of *News of the World* readers who wanted to hear her predictions.

Born into a family of fortune-tellers, she had been giving private consultations for twenty years under the name of Meg Markova. The column in *Sunday* was the first time her star forecasts had been published anywhere. However, she had no doubts about agreeing to do it. 'My own chart showed a definite move from working in private for a few clients to working for a great number,' she recalled. 'And I was getting the same message from the tarot cards and the runes.' And the name Mystic Meg? 'I saw that in my crystal ball. It is appropriate because I study all the mystic arts.'

Meg also claims a strong psychic link with her readers. She says: 'In 1987, I did a drawing of a cat wearing a star medallion. The drawing was locked in a safe at Securicor. When I asked readers to tune into my mind to see what I'd drawn, 20,000 people sent me a drawing and over half were right.'

In its early days, *Sunday* was often quite upmarket of the newspaper, a fact which didn't always make for complete harmony between the respective staffs. But in more recent times the two have come closer together. *Sunday* is particularly strong in its coverage of pop music and show business, appealing to younger readers.

The magazine has had six editors since its original launch twelve years ago, four of them women. The current incumbent, Sue Carroll, a voluptuous, red-headed Geordie, says: 'We try and appeal to the whole family. The magazine has to complement the newspaper.' Carroll adds: 'We maintain excellent standards of journalism. We aim not to be predictable. The whole Sunday supplement area is going through changes and the sands are constantly shifting, especially with the *People* having a TV listings magazine. We want people to be surprised, amused, entertained and fascinated.' And, echoing the slogan that appears on the magazine's front cover every Sunday, she declared: 'We like to think we are a proper magazine with plenty to read.'

A relatively recent plus factor is that since the beginning of 1992, the magazine has been making money, too. 'We think of it as a family magazine for readers but a good environment for advertisers, too,' says Sue Carroll.

The sheer logistics of getting a magazine with a circulation the size of *Sunday* printed and distributed are almost mind-boggling, especially as these days the journal is printed at Daarmstadt in West Germany on the presses of the Burda organization, in which Rupert Murdoch has an interest. The pages are prepared in the magazine's offices at Wapping, then sent on film to Germany, where cylinders are made and put on to the presses. Then, a veritable army of trucks is pressed into service to transport the magazines across the Continent to Britain. The whole operation takes several days to ensure that every *News of the World* reader gets their magazine with the newspaper on Sunday morning.

A major and familiar problem faced by all magazines is that, because of their lengthy 'lead' times, copy has to be prepared around six weeks in advance of the actual publication date. This is one good reason why the material, on the whole, has to be of a more timeless nature than that appearing in the newspaper. That way, the risk of being caught out by a sudden change in the circumstances of a story are less.

At *Sunday*, they still recall with shudders the time when they were running a major article about Morecambe and Wise. With the presses due to roll at any moment, the news came through that Eric Morecambe had died. Panic calls were made to the printers and new copy was phoned, updating the story. A new printing cylinder was made, at a cost of over £1,000, and put on the machines. Midway through the crisis, there was a change of shift at the printing plant and the old cylinder got put back on again! Naturally, it was all sorted out in the end. Just another day in the life of a Sunday colour supplement . . .

THIRTY

Promotions

It's not enough to have a good newspaper – you have to tell people it's good and sell it to them as well. This is where the promotions department of a newspaper comes in. Promotions are the marketing division, who work closely with the editorial team to ensure the paper maintains a high profile in the public eye.

At the *News of the World*, promoting the paper has always been a vital part of the operation, going right back to the Emsley Carr–Riddell days when reader competitions and giveaway stunts were pioneered. The pattern continued and grew throughout the reign of Sir Emsley's son, Bill Carr, under whose chairmanship the newspaper went sponsorship-crazy.

Today, it's a sophisticated operation, with all kinds of competitions and reader offers being promoted, often supported by television advertising. Chances to win motor cars and holidays in the sun are among the regular bait used to attract new readers. Some of the best ideas, though, are still the old ones. In February 1993, the *News of the World* signalled a return to the giveaway insurance schemes of the 1930s when it offered its readers £10,000 worth of free life insurance for a year.

In the same way as the journalists strive to make their stories and pictures better than those of other newspapers, the promotions staff are out to beat the competition as well. That means bigger and better prizes and more exotic giveaway offers. The mechanics of a promotional operation can be daunting. In January this year, for instance, the *News of the World* ran an offer aimed at soccer fans. By buying the paper, dads taking their youngsters to a football match could get free tickets for them. Almost half the clubs in the Football League took part in the promotion, involving thousands of tickets. The giveaway was advertised on TV, adding substantially to the investment. This sort of offer can cost hundreds of thousands of pounds in order to add perhaps another 50,000 or 100,000 readers on one particular day. However, the hope is that enough new readers will be tempted to start taking the paper on a regular basis to make it worthwhile in the long run.

The pattern of competitions and offers has changed over the years. In the 1960s, there was an emphasis on products and services aimed mainly at women readers, especially of the latest fashions, at costs substantially below those of high street stores. In 1968, an offer of real hairpieces at 45s 6d (£2.27½p) was so popular that the paper was having to print an apology a month later, imploring readers to be patient. Presumably, the Post Office was overwhelmed with thousands of sacks of envelopes containing locks of hair.

In 1969 the paper had a promotional scoop that made the record industry sit up and take notice. On 20 July the *News of the World* announced an exclusive offer of a fifteen-minute recording of astronaut Neil Armstrong's historic words as the first man to set foot on the moon. Recorded by Philips, the 'as it happens' collectors' item was available only to the paper's readers at a cost of 12s each. The actual moon landing did not take place until the following day.

In 1970, a major competition offered twenty readers the chance to win a trip to the World Cup in Mexico that summer. It wasn't a particularly outstanding promotion by today's standards but the prize, worth £800, including flights, hotels and tickets to all England's matches, plus the semi-finals and final, was a good one in those days, when £800 would buy a new Hillman Avenger motor car. These days, the cost of such a promotion would be partly shared through a tie-up with a travel or sports company. But in 1970, the cost was met entirely by the paper.

During the 1970s, competitions in the *News of the World* were largely dominated by two long-running favourites. The Spot the Ball contest offered a prize of £5,000 every week. The other popular feature was a competition in which readers had to place examples of new fashions in a likely order of best-sellers. There was a top prize of £7,500 for anyone whose choice exactly matched that of the judges. However, in both contests competitors had to pay a small charge to enter, so they actually made money for the paper.

The 1980s heralded the bingo era, which offered ever-soaring sums of money to be won, culminating in the ultimate £1 million game run in conjunction with the *Sun*. Bingo was far and away the biggest promotional and marketing tool of the 1980s, the fierce competition between newspapers carrying echoes of the bitter circulation wars of the 1930s. However, if bingo was king, then the bread-and-butter of the *News of the World*'s promotional efforts was still that good old standby, dress patterns. Reader loyalty to newspapers is a curious thing sometimes and research by the promotions department suggested that those buying dress patterns through the paper in the 1960s were still buying them through the same source fifteen to twenty years later.

One fact only sharp-eyed readers might spot concerns some of the London addresses used by the newspaper for competition entries. A couple of them are Brittons Court and Ashentree Court. You would have a hard time finding these addresses in the London A–Z. They are, in fact, fictitious and were devised by the Post Office as a way of instantly recognizing mass mail from the regular, domestic stuff.

After the *News of the World* went tabloid, promotions became an even more important element of the newspaper. There were headlines like 100,000 FREE PAGE 3 GIRL POSTERS, FREE PANINI SOCCER STICKERS AND ALBUM and WIN A SKIRT LIKE DI'S. *Sunday* magazine, too, was increasingly used as a promotions vehicle, with the added bonus of full colour . . . free colour holiday maps, free pint of Skol and free private health care were just a few examples.

A saucy promotional idea in April 1989, ran:

> C'mon, folks! Now you can go bonkers with Sex Aid. Do
> it for charity. Your favourite Sunday paper is backing a
> charity appeal to raise funds for health and family plan-
> ning in the Third World. All you have to do is put aside
> 25p every time you make love and send the money to a
> special Bonk Account.

Page 3 girl Maria Whittaker hailed the idea with: 'Smashing!
My boyfriend and I will start straight away,' whilst telly comic
Lennie Bennett quipped: 'At my time of life, I might just have
10p in the kitty by the end of the month!'

Promotions that offered something for free for everybody
escalated to new heights in the 1990s, becoming more complex
in organization and also giving a greater boost to circulation.
An example was in December 1990, when *Sunday* had
mounted on the front cover of every copy a Teenage Mutant
Ninja Turtles coin, cashing in on the latest craze amongst the
young. This was a classic case of the new kind of giveaway
offer whereby the reader got a free gift at the point of sale,
rather than have the bother of writing in and waiting for it to
arrive by post.

Outstanding categories for promotions are still the good old
standbys like sex, money and astrology, especially when
they're advertised on television.

But the *News of the World* also pulls in healthy circulation
increases with promotions aimed at the kids, like a Free Toy
Monster offer in April 1990 which, with strong editorial
factors, produced a circulation rise of six per cent. And
when the paper tied up with Woolworths for an offer of free
Cadbury's creme eggs, the nationwide chain of stores had
over 150,000 youngsters through its doors in the following
few days.

And another top promotional favourite is travel. When the
paper offered holidays for just £8.50 in August last year, more
than 120,000 readers took part. The *News of the World* and its

sister paper the *Sun* are together responsible for sending an extra half a million passengers across the Channel every year.

It's all part of a multimillion pound promotional effort aimed at helping the paper stay ahead in the circulation stakes and giving the readers some fun.

THIRTY-ONE

Tabloid Tales

Since making the bold leap to tabloid in 1986, the *News of the World* has had to compete in a Sunday newspaper market that grows ever more fiercely competitive. To stay ahead of its rivals at the sharp end of the circulation war, the paper assailed its readers throughout the 1980s and early 1990s with a constant stream of exclusive stories. Big headlines, big pictures and sensational disclosures are the meat and drink of popular tabloid newspapers.

What the ordinary reader in the street never hears about, though, is what goes on behind the scenes when a paper's journalists are stalking a really big story. Sometimes, an exclusive might land by chance in a newspaper's lap that needs very little checking out – but rarely. More often, it's a case of painstaking investigations and surveillance, sometimes lasting for many weeks, and delicate negotiations with contacts, informants and lawyers. Here, readers will find a rare glimpse of some of the stories-behind-the-stories of a major news-gathering operation such as the *News of the World* employs, with the highly professional skills of its reporting team at its disposal.

In the spring of 1985, Stuart Kuttner, then an assistant editor on the paper, met one of his regular contacts for a routine lunch. Afterwards, they took a stroll by the River Thames. Suddenly, the contact asked casually: 'Have any of your people noticed how often Princess Michael of Kent visits America?'

Kuttner replied: 'I'm not sure that they have. Why? Should they?'

After a short silence, the contact said: 'It might just be worth examining the record of her visits. Particularly this year. She seems to be going quite often. And they are private visits.'

'Is she playing away from home?' Kuttner asked.The contact was silent for a moment, then nodded. 'I'll need a name,' said Kuttner.

'Try Hunt,' came the reply.

'Do you mean Hunt as in Texas?' Kuttner asked.

'Exactly,' was the response.

Back at the *News of the World* office, Stuart Kuttner made some inquiries and found that the mega-rich Hunt oil dynasty of Texas had many members, all of them wealthy. He was unable to pin down a specific name, so turned again to his contact. 'The answer to your question is Ward,' said the contact.

'As in hospital?' Kuttner asked. The answer was in the affirmative. At that precise moment, the blonde Princess Michael was preparing to fly back to London after a week in California, staying at the Santa Monica ranch of her friend, Princess Esra of Hyderabad. Princess Esra was not there, nor was Prince Michael of Kent. But Ward Hunt, a Dallas property tycoon, was.

When this information had been established, the paper sent reporters to America to check on Princess Michael's movements during earlier trips that year. They discovered that in January she had insisted on staying in Dallas for an extra night whilst her husband, Prince Michael, flew to New York for a business meeting. Next day, instead of going to the airport she had ordered a chauffeur to take her to an exclusive apartment block where Ward Hunt had a flat.

Stuart Kuttner's original information had been gleaned in May. The following month, his contact called him again to say that Ward Hunt was about to arrive in Britain. Enterprising digging revealed that Hunt had been booked into the luxury Carlton Tower Hotel and that the booking had been made, indiscreetly, by Princess Michael's office. For the next few weeks, a virtual round-the-clock surveillance operation was mounted on both of them. Then Kuttner received another message which said there had been a change of plan, that the hotel booking had been cancelled and Princess Michael had arranged a private flat for Hunt belonging to Princess Esra's brother in posh Eaton Square, Belgravia. But one element of the unsuspecting Ward Hunt's arrangements had not been changed – his flight plans. Sitting close by on American Airlines Flight 50 when he arrived at Gatwick Airport on Monday 24 June 1985, from Texas was one of the paper's top foreign correspondents, Washington-based Margaret Hall, who had been detailed to 'accompany' Hunt from the moment he slipped out of Dallas Fort Worth Airport for his secret tryst to Britain.

En route, she had chatted innocently to him, discussing business and the Royal Family as the aircraft descended past Windsor Castle after the long overnight haul. At Gatwick, the *News of the World* photographed the Princess's admirer as he headed with two cases through the arrival lounge to buy a ticket for the train to Victoria station.

From there the tycoon was trailed to the mansions of Belgravia's Eaton Square. Princess Michael was already installed in a magnificent borrowed apartment. The paper had observed and photographed her arrival, too. The next day, Tuesday 25 June, the two were spotted leaving the flat. And the day after that the Princess and her Texan friend drove to the Cotswolds, where the Princess's close friend, Rosie, Marchioness of Northampton, was their hostess at her secluded country home. The pair had no idea at that stage that virtually every move they made had been observed and photographed.

However, two days before the *News of the World* was due to publish the story, somebody tipped off Princess Michael that it was about to break. She panicked and went into hospital, said to be suffering from exhaustion, and Hunt was hurriedly flown by helicopter to Manchester for a flight to New York and Dallas. So detailed was the *News of the World*'s inside information that the newspaper was even able to get a reporter into the next seat to the property tycoon on the flight from New York to Dallas on Hunt's escape home.

Once again, there was a conversation. This time, as the plane approached Texas, reporter Mike Graham introduced himself and asked about Hunt's friendship with the Princess. Both Prince and Princess Michael were his friends, he responded. Graham pressed on. Had Mr Hunt seen the Princess on his visit to England? No, it was a business trip, the tycoon replied. Though the newspaper was entirely satisfied with the accuracy of its story and supporting evidence, the unnecessary lie gave the paper a little extra boost of confidence. After all, why fib if there was nothing to cover up?

The story, on 7 July, began on page one under the headline ROYAL LOVE SENSATION, and continued on four further pages inside. It carried the by-lines of ten reporters and six photographers. Next day, the daily papers devoted page after page to following up a classic scoop in the best tradition of the *News of the World*. Ward Hunt was said to have wanted to marry Princess Michael, but after the story broke the affair was over.

Another sensational story that involved sensitive surveillance techniques hit the headlines in October 1986, when bestselling novelist Jeffrey Archer was exposed by the *News of the World* for attempting to pay money to vice girl Monica Coughlan to leave the country. Archer, then deputy chairman of the Conservative Party and said to be Margaret Thatcher's blue-eyed boy, resigned after the story appeared.

The story, covering five pages of the *News of the World*, described how Archer had instructed the prostitute to go to London's Victoria Station, where she would be met by an aide. It was like a scene from one of the author's own books when he told her: 'You will wear a green suit. I have a friend who will pass the package over.' Observed by *News of the World* reporters, Archer's emissary handed over a brown envelope which Coughlan tore open. It contained around £2,000 in £50 notes.

There was a near-farcical episode, however, when the messenger, public relations man Michael Stacpoole, recognized one of the *News of the World* team who had been observing the transaction, investigative reporter Gerry Brown who was an old acquaintance. The two accidentally bumped into one another outside a hotel where Stacpoole had been talking to the vice girl and Stacpoole and Brown ended up having a drink together. Despite this, Archer did not appear to know until the very last moment that the story was about to appear, for the *News of the World* had sent a woman reporter to interview Archer on the Friday before publication on the pretext of talking about his latest book. Archer telephoned the paper's offices to complain that the reporter had not arrived, so the opportunity was taken to ask him where he would be on the following day, the Saturday, when the story was going to be written.

Later, in a celebrated libel case, Archer sued the *Daily Star* and won £½ million pound damages. The *Star* had made the fatal error, in following up the *News of the World*'s story, of claiming that Archer and Monica Coughlan had had a sexual relationship – a claim the *News of the World* had never published. Archer also sued the *News of the World*, who eventually settled out of court for a tenth of the damages against the *Star*.

. Sometimes, newspapers find themselves faced with eleventh-hour applications for High Court injunctions to stop the presses. The *News of the World* was faced with such a challenge in September 1987, when it was printing a story about Left-wing London Labour MP Jeremy Corbyn, who had employed as his House of Commons researcher a well-known IRA supporter who had stood trial for killing a policeman and for bomb charges.

Corbyn alerted his lawyers and, on his behalf, they applied for an injunction to halt the publication of the report. Sometimes at night, or weekends, judges hear such emergency actions in their own homes, around their dining room tables. But on this Saturday night, the duty judge happened to live just across the street from the vast, darkened Royal Courts of Justice building in London's Strand. A few minutes before midnight, the building was opened up and the journalist who'd written the story, Alex Marunchak, was led through the corridors to the judge's private room. With him was the paper's assistant editor, Stuart Kuttner. The two newspapermen found themselves facing a solicitor and barrister arguing their client's case to stop the presses. But of Corbyn himself there was no sign.

In turn, the paper argued that their story was true and, perhaps somewhat cheekily, reminded the judge of a ruling by the distinguished lawyer, Lord Denning, that if a publisher says he will 'justify' – that is to say, prove a report – no injunction should be granted. The judge listened patiently to both sides, then swiftly pronounced his decision. There was to be no injunction – the *News of the World* was legally entitled to carry its story and the presses, thundering out more than 10,000 copies a minute, would not be halted.

As the parties rose at around 1.00 a.m., the judge had a final word. Noting that the assistant editor had an early edition of the *News of the World* with him, he diffidently inquired: 'I wonder whether you might be able to spare that paper? It's for my wife, of course.' The paper was happy to oblige Her Ladyship.

In January 1988, Marunchak and his colleague, Greg Miskiw, exposed a star of the hit soap opera *EastEnders*, Pakistani-born Aftab Sachak, for supplying girls and cocaine to clients at a trendy West End club where he was restaurant manager. To get their story, Marunchak and Miskiw posed as Ukrainian diplomats from the Soviet Embassy – a cover which was not too taxing, as both journalists are genuinely of Ukrainian extraction.

The *News of the World* subsequently exposed Sachak a second time, on the next occasion for the more serious crimes of offering to supply bogus currency and false passports. The actor was secretly videoed during an interview, in which he implicated himself as the front man in a major racket. Learning that he'd been caught, Sachak tried desperately to save himself by offering to tip the paper off about other stories if it dropped the exposé. The offer was declined and he was later jailed for four years. The trial judge praised the *News of the World* for its investigation and legitimate use of surveillance techniques.

*   *   *

In May of 1988, the affable television personality Frank Bough, known to the nation as the BBC's 'Mr Clean', was the subject of a scandal when the paper revealed he had attended parties at which he had free-based cocaine – smoking the drug mixed with chemicals – and watched couples having sex in front of him. The nation was stunned because of Bough's image as an avuncular, cardigan-wearing family man, a fact which the *News of the World* decided made his involvement with drugs and prostitutes of legitimate public interest.

The story was the result of a three-month investigation. The paper had had a tip-off from a polo-playing friend of Prince Charles, who had been at one of the parties and been shocked to see Bough there. Bough initially strongly denied the allegations and obtained an interim legal injunction on a Saturday to stop the story. Next day, deputy editor Paul Connew received a phone call at home from an old friend, Bernard Falk, the TV and radio broadcaster. Connew and Falk had once worked together on the *Daily Mirror* and Falk was also Frank Bough's partner in a video business. Falk was acting on Bough's behalf and asked for a compromise to be reached, whereby Bough would make a 'controlled confession' if the paper used the story in a way that left him with some dignity. Delicate negotiations took place over the next few days.

Finally, the injunction was dropped and a story drafted, largely telling in Frank Bough's own words how pressure of work and the loneliness of spending much of the week away from his wife had seduced him into a world he hadn't known about. Bough's confession was felt by the *News of the World* to be brave and candid. Subsequently, Rupert Murdoch gave him a job as a presenter on Sky Television.

Another story that made sensational headlines was that of call girl Pamella Bordes, a dusky Indian-born beauty who was a friend of a number of MPs. This was another *News of the World* exclusive with somewhat unusual origins. Features reporter Judy McGuire had been chasing a story about a TV game show hostess who was said to have supplied girls and drugs for the show's producer. The girl had as her agent the well-known show biz PR man, Max Clifford, who persuaded her that the *News of the World* would give her a sympathetic hearing. A meeting was arranged but his client was still reluctant to talk and offered a compromise.

That week in the *Evening Standard*, the Sports Minister, Colin Moynihan, had been photographed getting out of a car with Bordes – who was then unknown – and by a remarkable coincidence, the newspaper had received a tip-off about it from a contact who supplied escort girls. Moynihan had known nothing of Bordes's secret lift, but the TV girl told McGuire that Bordes was actually a high-class hooker whose client list read like a Who's Who of the rich and famous. The hostess had acted as Bordes's 'madam' several times and she offered to line the sultry beauty up with a *News of the World* reporter as a client if the paper would drop the exposé on her.

Three weeks of painstaking research followed, during which the paper discovered that Pamella Bordes had even penetrated the House of Commons with a security pass as a parliamentary researcher. Investigators also had names of her clients and friends, who might be prepared to talk. All that was required was the proof that she was acting as a hooker.

Reporter Stuart White, posing as a visiting businessman from Hong Kong, lined up a date with Bordes for an agreed fee of £500. The paper had booked two adjoining suites at the Park Lane Hilton. Before the meeting between White and the call girl, investigator Gerry Brown installed hidden microphones and tape recorders in the suite, then he and McGuire waited next door. Twenty-five minutes later, Bordes had accepted White's £500 and stripped naked to keep her side of the bargain. White managed to make his excuses – he was jet-lagged, he told her – and leave.

Next morning, McGuire went to Pamella's Belgravia home to try and confront her. Bordes screamed at her through the intercom and refused to emerge. The story was a huge front page splash the following Sunday and was followed up by newspapers all over the world. Bordes fled to the island of Bali, where McGuire was sent to chase her, along with the rest of the Fleet Street pack. She found herself door-stepping a grass-roofed hut in a paddy field where Bordes was hiding. She again refused to come out. Bordes herself said later: 'I could hear someone calling and I thought, "Oh, no, it's that bloody woman from the *News of the World* again." '

McGuire had to laugh. 'After all that, I never did get to meet her but perhaps it was just as well.'

There was a potentially embarrassing episode in the middle of the Bordes inquiry when it was discovered that also among her friends was Andrew Neill, editor of the *Sunday Times* which was in the same News International stable as the *News of the World*. Rupert Murdoch was informed; however, it was never suggested that the story should be dropped because of it.

Very shortly after the Bordes story, another sex-and-scandal tale blew up, this time involving the England soccer manager, Bobby Robson. An attractive 37-year-old divorcée with whom he'd had an affair had decided to 'spill the beans' to the *News of the World* because she feared she was pregnant by him. She had recorded phone calls from Robson in which he'd urged her to have an abortion. Robson was not only a family man, he was very high profile as England's World Cup manager.

Deputy editor Connew decided to send a fellow Geordie, reporter Mick Hamilton, to see Robson and try to get a confession. Connew reasoned that another Geordie might stand a better chance of getting an interview with him. Hamilton went to Ipswich and tentatively approached Robson's home, fearing a strong reaction. It was a Saturday morning and he found Robson in his garden, stripped to the waist. He introduced himself and told the England boss: 'I have something delicate I'd like to discuss with you.' Robson invited him into the house but Hamilton said, 'I don't think you'll want your wife to hear what I have to say to you.'

Robson realized the reporter wasn't there to talk to him about his next England team selection, He said: 'Hang on, I'll get a lead for the dog. He's blind you see and I don't want him to run into the road.' Robson, Hamilton and the blind spaniel went for a walk in the local park and the reporter gave Robson the gist of the story. Hamilton recalled his reaction: 'He turned to me and brought his hands up towards my neck. For a moment I thought he was going to attack me but he just straightened my tie, then tears welled up in his eyes and he said: "I'll have to resign over this, won't I? My mind is racing. I can't deny I know the woman. There are some fantastic women in the world, aren't there? What do you say about a woman like this?"'

Hamilton suggested to Robson he should talk to his solicitor and also to contact the *News of the World* office with a statement. 'I scribbled down the office number and handed it to him,' remembered Hamilton. 'Then we shook hands and I mumbled something about wishing we could have met under different circumstances. Bobby did ring his solicitor and contacted the office with a statement. He kindly told the editor that he appreciated how I had handled an embarrassing situation with tact and sensitivity. He was polite and courteous. It was all very civilized but I hated my job that day.'

Also in the summer of 1989, the paper bought the exclusive story of comedian Ken Dodd after he had won his historic court battle with the Inland Revenue. The paper offered to take him and his girlfriend away to anywhere in the world in order to interview him in the sunshine and the peace and quiet, away from other newspapers. 'Choose anywhere you like, Ken. How about the south of France or the Bahamas?' he was told by Manchester reporter Keith Beabey, who'd already packed the sun cream. Doddy thought for a few seconds, then said: 'Scarborough!'

'I was amazed,' said Beabey, 'but it wasn't until we strolled along the prom at Scarborough that I realized why he'd chosen it and not somewhere much more exotic. Wherever Doddy went, people slapped him on the back and showered him with congratulations. They even cheered him from hotel bedroom windows. How many would have recognized him on the front at Cannes?'

Another famous show biz star to be exposed was the comic

Tom O'Connor over his association with a young prostitute who was also a drug addict. This was not a story the *News of the World* had to itself, for once, but was also published by the *Sunday Mirror*.

Northern reporter Nick Pritchard had an amusing tale to relate about this exposé. He had a tip from a contact about the story but all the informant knew was the girl's name and the fact that she worked in a massage parlour somewhere on Merseyside. Pritchard spent four months combing the massage parlours and brothels of Merseyside, posing as a normal punter, before eventually finding the girl in Blackpool, where O'Connor was doing a summer season. Confronted, the pair admitted the bizarre affair.

Pritchard was ordered to keep the girl out of the way of the opposition papers, so took her to a five-star hotel. At dinner that night, he was highly embarrassed when the girl arrived in the posh dining room in her 'working gear' – a leather micro-skirt, black fishnet stockings, see-through blouse and outrageous make-up. Ignoring the sniggering gaze of the head waiter, Pritchard managed to get an out-of-the-way table. But then he was horrified to see being led to the adjoining table, right alongside, his next-door neighbours, a highly respectable couple. They were totally unaware that he was working on an assignment for the *News of the World* and when the wife went off to powder her nose, the amused husband gave Pritchard a cheeky wink and the thumbs-up sign.

It frequently happens when a big, sensational scandal story is brewing that more than one newspaper will be working on it and there will be intense rivalry, behind-the-scenes skullduggery and attempts to put one across on a rival. This was the case with the story of model Fiona Wright and her five-times-a-night lover, Sir Ralph Halpern. For once the *News of the World* was not ahead of the field with this exposé – but ended up so.

It began when Trevor Kempson got a call from a contact asking what the *News of the World* were doing about Halpern. Coincidentally, the paper received another call, also from a contact, asking if the name Fiona Wright meant anything. As it happened, no one there knew anything about the story which, it transpired, the *People* had been working on for two weeks. It was a Friday evening and extremely late in the day to start on such a major inquiry.

However, Halpern was contacted, told of the *People* story, and a deal was struck whereby Halpern made a confession to the *News of the World*, which was able to come out with the story before its great rival. 'We got the story because of our reputation. When someone close to Halpern heard that a newspaper was working on it, it was just assumed it would be the *News of the World*,' said a journalist.

The *News of the World* ran into a head-to-head confrontation with the then boss of its great rival group, Mirror Newspapers, when it published an investigation into serious irregularities at Derby County Football Club over the signing of two players from Czechoslovakia. The club's president was Robert Maxwell and he figured prominently in the allegations. Maxwell, as was his nature, threatened a libel writ, despite the fact that the *News of the World* had a stack of documentary evidence to support its story.

Deputy editor Paul Connew had once worked for Maxwell in America and before the story was published he received a phone call from the blustering, bouncing Czech. Said Connew: 'It was the usual Maxwell mixture of charm, bluff and bullying. I told him we had the story right and no amount of threats would stop us from running it. Maxwell then deluged Rupert Murdoch with calls, demanding the story should not be published. Murdoch ignored them and told us: "If we have it right, carry on."'

Reporter Gerry Brown, who led the Derby County investigation, also played a key role in another story about Maxwell. With his knowledge of bugging devices and surveillance techniques, the *News of the World* was able to reveal after Maxwell's death that the crooked tycoon had bugged his staff, executives, family and even his own yacht, where he regularly hosted politicians and international celebrities. The story of Maxwell spying on his own staff, and of an affair with his personal assistant, was written by Connew and published in the *News of the World* two weeks before the *Daily Mirror*, Maxwell's former newspaper, ran it.

More sex scandals, this time involving leading politicians, blew up in the early 1990s. In April 1991, reporter Chris Blythe was tipped off by a contact about a woman called Sara Dale who specialized in canings and beatings and who was renting the former home of the then Chancellor of the Exchequer, Norman Lamont. She was to become infamous to the press as Miss Whiplash. Blythe made an appointment to see her and quizzed her about her £90-an-hour services.

Blythe, normally no stranger to this sort of seedy inquiry, became nervous during their talk as he looked at the whips and manacles lying near Ms Dale's massage couch. He began to stutter and stammer. His apparent intimidation convinced her he was a domination fetishist and she offered him a 'therapy' session in which he was to be spanked while dressed as a schoolboy. In the usual fashion, he made his excuses. Sara Dale later told the *Sunday Times* that she considered the undercover reporter was 'deeply distressed' and in need of help. What she had failed to realize was that it was not his need for domination but the thought of the caning he might get if his bulging tape recorder were discovered that distressed him!

The second major sex scandal was that of the Heritage Minister, David Mellor, and his actress friend Antonia de Sanchez. To this saga, too, there was a convoluted background. It was somewhat reminiscent of the Lambton affair, two decades before, when the *News of the World* was approached by somebody who had made illicit tapes of the couple's phone calls and was hawking them around. *News of the World* editor Patsy Chapman was unhappy about the way the tapes had been made and decided not to buy them.

Then, the paper heard a rumour via the show business department that Antonia de Sanchez was boasting to friends about her relationship with Mellor. Paul Connew approached Mellor through a mutual contact, Tory public relations adviser Sir Tim Bell, and offered the minister a chance to 'come clean' with a controlled confession, rather as in the Frank Bough story. Mellor declined – foolishly, as it turned out, because the story was to emerge ten days later in circumstances that left him looking somewhat less dignified than he might have done.

After his phone call to Tim Bell, Connew received a call from journalist Paul Halloran of *Private Eye*, asking if the *News of the World* was investigating Mellor. He told Connew his information had come from someone in Bell's office. This was untrue. What, in fact, had happened was that Mellor had gone to Halloran, with whom he was friendly, asking for his advice on how to handle the situation. Right up to the Saturday before the story was published, Mellor was still refusing to admit the affair, by which time the *People* had bought the incriminating tapes. However, the *News of the World* had more than enough information to run a story of its own.

Sometimes, however skilled and persistent a journalist is, a huge slice of luck can be needed to secure a story. Such was the experience of reporter John Chapman and cameraman Brian Thomas when they were sent to India to try and track down the dour Yorkshire batting legend Geoff Boycott. Rumours had reached the *News of the World* that he was touring the subcontinent with a mystery maiden on his arm. Boycott was en route to Calcutta to commentate on England's appearance in the world series cricket final and Chapman and Thomas were dispatched to find him. No easy task, for Boycott was making his own travel and hotel arrangements and it would be like looking for the proverbial needle in a haystack. Also, the prickly Boycott was known to guard his privacy fiercely and had a love–hate relationship with the press.

The *News of the World* pair arrived in Bombay with just ten minutes to catch a connecting flight to Calcutta. Loaded with baggage and sweating profusely in the fierce heat, they rushed across the steaming tarmac. They were still regaining their breath aboard the Calcutta-bound plane when a familiar voice

suddenly asked: 'Are you 'ere for t'cricket, lad?' The bluff Yorkshire tones were unmistakable. There, in the seat right in front
of Chapman and Thomas, sat Boycott. And next to him, sharing a pack of cheese sandwiches, was his mystery woman.
'Have a sandwich,' Geoff offered. 'We make them ourselves
wherever we go, so we don't have to eat the local muck.'
Scarcely able to believe the incredible stroke of luck, Chapman
spent the six-hour flight chatting to the couple, discovering
the girl's identity. He was able to file a full story on arrival at
Calcutta – and Boycott was still blissfully unaware that he was
talking to his hated adversaries, the 'gutter press'.

Canny Geoff, ever a man to strike a shrewd deal, even
offered the *News of the World* men a quick financial transaction.
'Look,' he said, 'you've just come from London and I've been
here bloody ages. I've got more rupees than I know what to
do with. Why don't I sell them to you at a good rate of
exchange. I'll come round to your hotel tomorrow night.'
When Chapman offered to go to Boycott's hotel, he replied:
'I don't want anyone to know where it is. Those press boys
are always sniffing around.' Chapman and Thomas tailed Boycott and his lady friend to their hotel – and the couple left
town the next day when they discovered the *News of the World*
was around. A year later, Chapman had another story when
the girl gave birth to a baby girl. The headline read: BOYCOTT'S
LITTLE BOUNCER.

The *News of the World*'s reputation for getting the big sex stories
even preceded it during the Gulf War. Reporter Chris Boffey
was a 'pool' correspondent with the Royal Navy, covering the
war from a destroyer just off the coast of Kuwait, filing stories
from a small computer via satellite telephones. He was in the
wardroom of HMS *Exeter* when he learned that there was to
be no invasion from the sea and that the immense naval activity was just a bluff to outwit Saddam Hussein. 'I knew I was
in the wrong place. The naval war was over,' he recalled. 'The
captain agreed I could leave the ship and get on land to join
up with the army.' Boffey was helicoptered to the hospital

ship *Argus*, and was then to hitch his way, ship by ship, down the Gulf. but when he arrived on board the *Argus*, he found the atmosphere was extraordinarily tense. He was told to remain in the wardroom and not to speak to anybody. 'At first I thought it was because I knew details of the naval bluff,' he said, 'but then it became apparent that the real reason was sex.' The *Argus* was one of two British ships in the Gulf that had women on board and Boffey had discovered six months earlier, before the war, that an officer and a nurse had been flown home after having an affair aboard ship.

The story had been printed in the *News of the World*, much to the horror of the First Sea Lord. 'I was later told that I was trusted not to put lives at risk by spilling the beans about there being no invasion from the sea but the Navy was paranoid about me dredging up any scandal,' said Boffey. 'When I finally left the *Argus* I was told there was a collective sigh of relief.'

News of the World journalists frequently put themselves into situations of potential danger in order to expose wrongdoing. And sometimes the paper cooperates with the authorities to catch a villain. Judy McGuire found herself working in an undercover operation with the FBI, no less, in May last year. The paper was offered by an anonymous contact pictures of Madonna that were due to appear in her controversial book, *Sex*. The shots, showing the controversial singer in kinky poses, had been stolen from a film processing laboratory and were being offered to the *News of the World* for £60,000.

The paper pretended to play along with the contact, then sent McGuire to Los Angeles where she linked up with FBI agents. She was wired up with a hidden microphone and met the man offering the stolen pictures in a hotel room. The reporter pretended to haggle with him for over half an hour until the FBI watchers had the evidence they needed. Then they burst into the room, spread-eagled the man against the wall and arrested him for transporting stolen property across state lines.

Madonna was suitably gratified to get the pictures back. She told McGuire: 'I'm grateful to everyone, especially the *News of the World*.' However, it didn't cut much ice when it came to selling British serial rights in her book. For some reason little understood by the rest of Fleet Street, she chose to sell them to the upmarket paper, the *Observer*, despite receiving a much larger offer from the *News of the World*.

For sheer guts and courage, the paper's own unofficial award for undercover work went to reporter Chris Blythe for a remarkable exposé in 1990 of an illegal immigrant wedding racket. Blythe was ordered to spend two months living as a down-and-out alcholic tramp in order to smash the racket, which was being operated by a Ghanaian 'Mr Big' barrister. The scam involved fixing up women from West Africa, who were desperate to become British citizens, with marriage-of-convenience bridegrooms. The willing grooms were recruited from amongst drunken dossers, who were paid £800 for their services, while the brides were paying the barrister heading the racket up to £4,000.

Every day for weeks, Blythe changed from his smart office suit into stinking clothes, then mingled with the tramps in an East London park. He won their friendship and trust by providing a ready supply of lager, picked up from an off-licence on the way. Blythe was almost caught out once when two greedy tramps set about him for money and almost exposed his hidden tape recorder. There was another hazard to the reporter's undercover assignment – once or twice, after a long day's drinking with the dossers in the park, he was barely in any fit state to report in to the newsdesk. However, Blythe eventually established contact with a go-between and found himself inside the Ghanaian barrister's headquarters, where he secretly taped his conversations about the phoney marriages racket. Eventually, the 'Mr Big' came up with a bride for the 25-year-old reporter to marry. She was a 51-year-old hospital cleaner, who had paid £3,500 for the privilege of getting hitched to a *News of the World* investigator. Blythe's cut was to be the standard fee of £800.

Came the big day and Blythe and his bride walked up the

steps of Hackney Register Office to have official photos taken before the ceremony. Hidden all around were police and immigration officials. Even *News of the World* editor Patsy Chapman was watching through a pair of binoculars from her chauffeur-driven Jaguar parked in the distance. Moments before Blythe was due to be wed to his large, middle-aged dusky bride, the police and immigration officials swooped. The meticulous bust was romantically named Operation Gold Ring. Later, they arrested the crooked barrister and he subsequently got two years' jail after the jury had listened to Blythe's secret tape recordings. The reporter burned his filthy tramp's clothing and went back to wearing suits.

Newspaper folk are often accused by outsiders of being cynical and unfeeling but when tragedy strikes one of their own they feel the blow as grievously as anyone.

Such was the case on Saturday 24 April this year when freelance photographer Edward Henty was killed by the IRA bomb blast which devastated the City of London.

Henty, known to his colleagues as Ed, had worked on assignments for the *News of the World* for ten years and had been on his way to Wapping when he was diverted to the City, following an early tip-off about the bomb alert. Colleagues became worried when Ed, a compulsive communicator on his mobile phone, did not report in. It was not until many hours later that his death was confirmed.

A stunned atmosphere pervaded the newspaper's offices and, in a rare tribute, the paper came out the following day with a black masthead instead of the usual red one. Henty left a widow and two young children.

He had been involved in many of the paper's major stories. He got the first picture of Sarah 'Miss Whiplash' Dale and also took the photo of reporter Chris Blythe and his illegal immigrant 'bride' on the steps of Hackney Register Office. A senior colleague said: 'Edward Henty was a diligent, professional craftsman.'

*   *   *

It's appropriate to end this chapter, finally, by mentioning two historic court triumphs for the *News of the World*. In 1990, the newspaper won two major libel cases – the first such victories by a popular newspaper for many years. Until then, juries had automatically found against newspapers and often awarded enormous damages, to the despair of Fleet Street.

Midlands reporter Maureen Lawless had exposed a cosmetic surgery clinic for leaving a trail of maimed and unhappy patients. She had collected a dossier of over twenty patients whose operations, especially to remove tattoos, had gone horribly wrong and left them not only with a huge bill but with painful scars. A Chinese nurse had carried out some of the treatments, unsupervised by doctors. When the story appeared, the nurse sued the paper.

The case came up in the High Court in June 1990 and, at first, things didn't look good. The nurse was a tiny figure in the witness box and the *News of the World* lawyers were worried that the innocent-looking, demure plaintiff might sway the jury into believing she was a defenceless woman taking on the might of a national newspaper. However, she ruined her own case by over-acting, frequently bursting into tears when challenged. At one point the judge turned to her and said: 'Cry as much as you like but you will answer the question.'

After three weeks, the jury found for the *News of the World* and the plaintiff had to pay the costs of half a million pounds.

The other historic libel victory made national headlines and a lead story on all the TV and radio news bulletins. Just before Christmas 1990, the *News of the World* clashed in court with the wife of the Yorkshire Ripper, Sonia Sutcliffe. She had sued the paper over a story alleging she had had a steamy romance whilst holidaying in Greece with Barbara Jones, a *Mail on Sunday* reporter who was writing a book about the Ripper.

Jones had given the *News of the World* the story, via a freelance journalist, and she was joined by the paper in the proceedings as a third party. Sonia Sutcliffe had earned herself a reputation as an inveterate issuer of libel writs and had won a tidy income for herself as a result. She had not lost a single case and had taken an incredible £600,000 off *Private Eye*. The *News of the World*'s outside lawyers had been urging it to settle but the deputy editor, Connew, and legal manager Tom Crone, felt the paper should stick it out and it was decided to take on Mrs Sutcliffe all the way.

The decision was proved right. During a dramatic trial, Sonia Sutcliffe wrecked her own case with an extraordinary performance in the witness box in which she attempted to explain away her husband's crimes and showed no pity for his victims.

The jury found for the *News of the World* and Mrs Sutcliffe was ordered to pay the entire costs of the hearing. It was estimated by lawyers that she had lost every penny she had ever made by getting damages from newspapers. It was a disaster for her. It was a fine Christmas present for the *News of the World*.

THIRTY-TWO

A Day in the Life of . . .

It can be a hard life on the road as a *News of the World* journalist. It can be a fun one as well. This final chapter is a sort of pot pourri, a collection of anecdotes about life on the paper that don't quite fit into any of the previous chapters. The tales are taken from different eras but they all have one thing in common. They *deserve* to be told, either because they graphically illustrate how reporters sometimes gets their stories against all the odds, because they give a revealing glimpse behind the scenes of a great newspaper – or because they're just plain funny . . .

In November 1981, a surgeon and his attractive mistress came up at Teesside Crown Court, Middlesbrough, accused of murdering the surgeon's wife with an anti-cancer drug. It was a sensational case, dubbed by the press the Passion and Poison trial. The surgeon, Paul Vickers, was found guilty and jailed for a minimum of seventeen years but his mistress, Pamela Collison, was acquitted. She was a House of Commons secretary who'd worked for Michael Heseltine and the case also had kinky sex overtones. Immediately, the press pack were in full hue and cry in pursuit of Collison's exclusive story. Huge sums of money were being offered but with strings attached.

A *News of the World* team set up base in a Middlesbrough hotel where most of the other journalists were staying. Reporters from another Sunday newspaper were so confident they had bought the woman's story that they began buying 'consoling' champagne for their rivals. However, in the scrum outside the court earlier, *News of the World* reporter Fiona Macdonald Hull had had an amazing stroke of luck. She'd bumped into an old friend from her university days who just happened to be one of the lawyers on the Collison defence team. That night, while some of the *News of the World* team remained at the hotel, looking suitably glum to throw their rivals off the scent, Macdonald Hull and reporter David Leslie were having dinner with the lawyer and making a straightforward bid for Collison's story. Negotiations went on all Friday night and throughout next Saturday morning and into the afternoon.

Assistant editor Stuart Kuttner had taken over the negotiations and told Macdonald Hull and Leslie to go to a telephone box in Durham, outside the jail, and wait for a call. They still had no idea of Collison's whereabouts. It got to mid-Saturday afternoon, the front page and two pages inside the paper were blank, and not a word had yet been filed. Suddenly, the phone in the kiosk rang. It was Kuttner, telling the waiting reporters to go to a hotel opposite the jail, where the woman was hiding out. Collison's lawyer had demanded the agreed fee, £50,000, in full – and up front. Kuttner wrote a personal cheque for the amount, remembering to alert both his bank manager and the *News of the World*'s financial director!

Macdonald Hull and Leslie filed six paragraphs, which they had already written, from the telephone box to copytakers at the *News of the World* office in London. Then they raced at top speed to the hotel. Another team member, David Mertens, had also been diverted to the hotel and was waiting with an open phone line in the bedroom next to Pamela Collison's. From 3.45 p.m., for the next three hours, Leslie and Macdonald Hull interviewed the woman at length, taking it in turns to rush from her bedroom to the bedroom next door and file copy to London, reading it directly from hurriedly scribbled notes. All the time, vital minutes to the paper's production time were ticking away. B—— *News of the World* team managed to file enough material —— e a front page splash and two whole pages inside the —— anwhile, back at the hotel in Middlesbrough, rivals —— other Sunday papers were filing disconsolate stories —— nobody, after all, had got an exclusive.

*   *   *

Fiona Macdonald Hull also tells a hilarious tale of when she wrote the life story of the colourful pop singer, P.J. Proby, who became famous for splitting his pants on stage and, in later years, for the amount of Bourbon he consumed. The outrageous American turned up in the newsroom at Bouverie Street, dressed in a stetson and cowboy boots, and began loudly demanding his money. The equally colourful crime reporter, Peter Earle, had been gently dozing at his desk and was not amused at being rudely awakened. Earle, immaculate in pin-stripes, grabbed his umbrella, advanced menacingly on the unfortunate Proby and pinned him against the wall with the point at his chest like a sabre. 'What do you want me to do with it?' he demanded of a now hysterical Macdonald Hull and news editor Robert Warren, who was also nearly crying with laughter.

'Well, Peter,' said Macdonald Hull, 'we have to take him to the cashiers to get him some money.' Earle then marched Proby out of the newsroom, still at the point of his umbrella, to the cashiers' office, then down two flights of stairs and right out of the office into Bouverie Street where a car was waiting for him. Earle pushed Proby into the car and uttered his parting shot. 'Don't you ever speak to a member of the *News of the World* like that again,' he said.

Next day, P.J. Proby remarked to Fiona Macdonald Hull: 'Hell of a guy, that Peter Earle. I really liked him.'

Robert Warren once picked up a telephone on the newsdesk and found himself speaking to a lady correspondent who rejoiced in the rather splendid name of Argentina Greenland. He had little interest in the story she was offering but thanked her politely. Three years later, she phoned again and by chance spoke to Warren once more. 'Hello, my name's Mrs Greenland,' she began, hesitantly.

'Not *Argentina* Greenland, by any chance?' Warren asked.

'Good lord,' she replied. 'Fancy you remembering me after all this time!'

*   *   *

Series editor Roy Stockdill, when a general reporter in the 1970s, once had one of the more bizarre assignments any journalist could be presented with. Editor Bernard Shrimsley sent him and photographer Brian Thomas to Spain to buy a lion! The story concerned a safari park near Madrid that had gone bust and the owners, with the usual Spanish callous attitude towards animals, had tried to recoup some of their losses by flying in parties of so-called hunters from Germany to shoot the poor animals, who had been bred in captivity.

Stockdill recalled: 'Our orders were to try and save one. No one actually knew what we were going to do with the lion if we succeeded. We went to see the lady director of Madrid Zoo first, to sound her out. She thought we were a bit mad but, although they had plenty of lions of their own, she reluctantly agreed to take one if we managed to save it. When we got to the safari park, it turned out we were too late – the lions had all been shot already. But we tracked down the man who'd organized the slaughter, who only turned out to be a cousin of King Juan Carlos. He was very proud of the whole thing and he gave us a wonderful picture of a poor dead lion with its jaws wide open and a fierce-looking German lady in tweeds and a deerstalker posing with a rifle and her foot on its head.

'That night, we went into a bar with the picture carefully tucked away in Brian Thomas's bag. We chanced to be introduced to the English bullfighter, Henry Higgins, who got into a fight with some drunken Spanish yobs. All hell broke lose and we had visions of being locked up by the Spanish police and not being able to get our great exclusive story and pictures back to England, so we got out of there swiftly. The picture was used right across the front page. Great story – pity about the lions, though.'

Another great front page story and picture was captured by reporter Gerry Brown and photographer Ian Cutler. They had been tipped off that car workers at British Leyland's plant in Solihull, Birmingham, where they made the prestigious Range Rover, regularly snoozed the night shift away. Brown and

Cutler sneaked into the plant at 3.00 a.m. and, sure enough, found most of the shift cheerfully snoring away in camp beds and sleeping bags. Having obtained the pictures they needed of the sleeping workers, Cutler shouted at the top of his voice: 'Wakey, wakey!' As a dozen startled faces shot up from their beds, Cutler flashed off some more pictures, then he and the reporter ran for it out of the plant.

The *News of the World* once carried a prostitution story about a brothel in the Midlands and the headline read: BEHIND THIS DOOR LURKS A DEN OF VICE. A photographer had been sent to take a picture of the house but, unfortunately, it was in a street of near-identical terraced houses and the hapless cameraman captured the wrong door. The house pictured in the paper just happened to be the home of two totally innocent, elderly spinsters. Needless to say, that one cost a few quid in libel damages.

Reporter Ivan Waterman experienced something of a baptism of fire when he joined the *News of the World* from a local news agency. He hadn't long been with the paper when he was sent to interview a titled lady. A pleasant enough task, he though, feeling flattered to be given such a prestigious assignment. Little did he know what was in store . . .

'She was a Lady who had fallen on rather difficult times and who was working in a fairly humble job,' recalls Waterman. 'However, she was a good friend of a very well-known television personality and I was told to pander to her. She wanted to sell us her life story.

'I was about 24 and she was in her late 40s, quite attractive. At her flat she plied me with large Scotches before lunch and we had several bottles of wine with lunch. Then she suddenly started to blurt out intimate details about her affair with a leading politician.

'She virtually carried me back to her flat, where I collapsed on the sofa. She insisted on pouring still more drink down me, a tankard of beer with three large gins in it and then more

Scotches. Then Lady xxxxx suddenly charged across the room and hurled herself at me. I fled to the bathroom and threw up in her loo. She tried to throw herself at me again but I managed to escape and somehow got back to the office, with lipstick all over me and my hair and clothes awry.

'Next day, her friend, the TV personality, telephoned the newsdesk to say that Her Ladyship couldn't remember much of what had happened but was rather worried about what she might have said. He was assured by the news editor: "Tell her not to worry, our reporter can't remember any of it, either!"'

In the 1960s, the paper exposed a man who claimed to have in his garden a cork tree with magic properties. The man was mailing out pieces of cork – which he obtained from common industrial sources – to mugs who sent him money, saying they would bring good luck. The man wrote an angry letter to the editor, demanding an apology and adding, as an afterthought, that the story hadn't done him any harm because he'd had several more inquiries for his 'magic' cork. A week or two later, another letter arrived in rather less complaining vein, reporting that still more people had sought his lucky charms. The correspondence ended when the man finally wrote to the editor saying that his business had increased so much as a result of the story that he wondered if the paper could come and expose him again.

The *News of the World* was once banned reading material to soldiers in the French Foreign Legion. In the 1970s, a British man serving in the Legion in Corsica wrote to the paper asking for a girl pen pal. Feeling sorry for the lonely legionnaire, readers' letters editor David Gordois printed his appeal in the column. Romance blossomed through the post and one day the man skipped his post and fled back to England to meet up with his new love. They both wrote to the paper again to tell them of their joy and the heartwarming story was printed. However, other Brits serving in the Foreign Legion weren't so happy, because they were barred from reading the *News of the World* and had to get copies smuggled in. (Readers' letters editor Gordois has been responsible for bringing together hundreds of couples through the column, some of whom asked him to be best man at their weddings.)

Northern reporter David Leslie, a Geordie, was sent to Arnhem in Holland to investigate a 'cattle market' trade in British workers, who were being exploited by greedy agents recruiting them to work on German building sites, then ripping them off. While wandering around looking for someone to give him their story, he was approached by a group of scruffy, bedraggled young men gabbling in what he took to be a foreign language. 'I couldn't understand a word they were saying and told them to f*** off because I was busy,' said Leslie.

The disconsolate group wandered off. Minutes later, photographer Boyd Milligan, from Manchester, rushed up to Leslie and asked if he had talked to the men, as he had taken pictures of them. 'Some yobs came up babbling in a foreign tongue,' Leslie replied. 'I told them to shove off.' Milligan stared at him.

'You fool, they were Scousers!' he said.

Leslie managed to track down the group of men and, with Milligan acting as interpreter, the Geordie reporter managed to interview the Liverpool workers who told him their dismal story of being stranded and sleeping rough.

How DOES a reporter make an excuse and leave? Investigative reporter Roger Insall and photographer Steve Grayson found themselves with a rather more delicate task than usual when they were sent to Amsterdam to expose a paedophile author who had written a book on how to pick up young boys for sex. Insall contacted the man and pretended he was a fellow gay writer who wanted to interview him about his book. The paedophile booked the *News of the World* men into a notorious gay hotel in Amsterdam. Finding they had been given a room with only a double bed in it, Insall and Grayson decided they didn't intend to share the sleeping arrangements. So they staged an elaborate lover's tiff in the hotel foyer, in which one slapped the other across the face and called him a 'bitch'. Then they both pretended to sulk and demanded single rooms.

Pope John Paul II revealed to reporter Keith Beabey that he read the *News of the World* when Beabey met the Pontiff in Rome in August 1987. The paper had told the story of tragic mother Pat Dorian, aged 37, who had had nine children and was about to give birth to her tenth. She had been told she had terminal cancer, which could only be treated if she had an abortion. She chose to give birth to her child and die herself. The *News of the World* arranged for her to have a private audience with the Pope at St Peter's. Said Beabey: 'The Pope cradled the baby, blessing her and her dying mum. When I was introduced to His Holiness and explained who I was, he revealed he was one of our 15 million readers.'

Feature writer Maureen Lawless had completed a series about lady wrestlers, which had involved her travelling all over Britain. Confident she had covered every possible angle, she deposited her copy on the features editor's desk. 'I can't think of a thing to add, unless you'd like me to actually become a wrestler myself,' she said sarcastically. A wicked smile spread across the editor's face.

'What a good idea,' he said. 'Fix it up.'

Lawless protested that it would take months of training and she would get severely hurt. Her protests fell on deaf ears. Lawless went off to Stafford, where the top lady wrestler Mitzi Mueller promised to teach her some tricks of the trade. With a sinking heart, she went backstage to be kitted out in a leotard and a pair of wrestling boots three sizes too large. 'You won't really throw me, will you?' Maureen pleaded with Mueller. 'I don't know how to fall.'

'Don't worry,' the blonde, buxom wrestler assured her. 'I'll hang on to you and break your fall.'

In front of hundreds of shrieking spectators who had stayed on to watch the fun after the real bouts were over, Mueller then proceeded to pick Lawless up, lifted the hapless hackette above her head and spun her round and round before dropping her in a dizzy heap on the floor. Then she threw her all round the ring, to the delight of the *News of the World* cameraman who kept on urging: 'Just one more time, Mitzi. Try to smile, Maureen!'

Said Lawless: 'It only lasted about ten minutes but it seemed like ten years. It taught me one thing. Never, ever make a suggestion in fun to a features editor.'

Just another day in the life of a *News of the World* reporter . . .

Some Higlights in the History of The News of the World

1843 *News of the World* launched, price 3d.

1851 The paper moves to larger premises in Exeter Street.

1855 Death of founder, John Browne Bell.

1877 Death of John William Bell, founder's eldest son.

1891 Lascelles Carr heads consortium in sale of *News of the World*.

1892 Paper moves to Whitefriars Street.

1899 Paper moves to larger premises in Bouverie Street.

1902 Death of Lascelles Carr. Brother-in-law Charles Jackson succeeds as chairman.

1923 Death of Sir Charles Jackson. Lord Riddell succeeds as chairman.

1934 Death of Lord Riddell. Sir Emsley Carr succeeds as chairman.

1941 Death of Sir Emsley Carr, editor for fifty years. Percy Davies succeeds as editor and chairman.

1941 Circulation reaches 4,400,000.

1943 Percy Davies steps down as chairman, succeeded by Sir Philip Dunn.

1947 Philip Dunn ousted as chairman, succeeded by Harry Aldridge.

1952 Aldridge retires: Sir William Carr becomes chairman.

1955 Circulation reaches peak of 8,000,000.

1960 Stafford Somerfield takes over as editor.

1960 *Empire News* merged with *News of the World*.

1969 Rupert Murdoch acquires *News of the World*. Sir William Carr stands down as chairman and becomes life president.

1970 Stafford Somerfield sacked.
1977 Death of Sir William Carr.
1981 *Sunday*, colour magazine, launched.
1984 *News of the World* becomes tabloid.
1986 Move to new premises at Wapping with other News International titles.

Index of People